POLITICAL REASONING

EVERT VEDUNG

POLITICAL REASONING

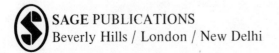
SAGE PUBLICATIONS
Beverly Hills / London / New Delhi

Translated from the Swedish by David McCune

English edition, Copyright © 1982 by Sage Publications, Inc.

Original Swedish edition, Det rationella politiska samtalet. Hur politiska budskap tolkas, ordnas och provas. Copyright © 1977 Aldus / Bonniers, Stockholm, Sweden.

For information address:

SAGE Publications, Inc.
275 South Beverly Drive
Beverly Hills, California 90212

SAGE Publications India Pvt. Ltd.
C-236 Defence Colony
New Delhi 110 024, India

SAGE Publications Ltd
28 Banner Street
London EC1Y 8QE, England

Printed in the United States of America

Library of Congress Cataloging in Publication Data

Vedung, Evert, 1938-
   Political reasoning.

   Translation of: Det rationella politiska samtalet.
   Bibliography: p.
   Includes index.
   1. Political science—Research. 2. Political science
—Methodology. I. Title.
JA86.V413   320'.72   82-5532
ISBN 0-8039-1815-1   AACR2

FIRST PRINTING

CONTENTS

Acknowledgements

For permission to reprint materials, I am indebted to the following:

Selections in Chapter 4 reprinted from pp. 101-102 of LOGIC AND CON-
TEMPORARY RHETORIC, THE USE OF REASON IN EVERYDAY
LIFE, Second Edition, by Howard Kahane. © 1976 by Wadsworth Publish-
ing Company, Inc. Reprinted by permission of Wadsworth Publishing
Company, Belmont, CA 94002.

Selections in Chapter 4 reprinted from pp. 30ff. of THE POLITICS OF
COMMUNICATION: A STUDY IN THE POLITICAL SOCIOLOGY OF
LANGUAGE, SOCIALIZATION, AND LEGITIMATION by Claus Muel-
ler. © 1973 by the Oxford University Press. Reprinted by permission of the
publisher.

Selections in Chapter 5 reprinted from THE GREAT DEBATES, CARTER
VS. FORD, 1976 edited by Sidney Kraus. © 1979 by Indiana University
Press. Reprinted by permission of the publisher.

Selections in Chapter 7 reprinted from SOCIOLOGISTS, ECONOMISTS
AND DEMOCRACY by Brian Barry by permission of The University of
Chicago Press. © 1978 by The University of Chicago.

Excerpts from "Guidelines for Concept Analysis" by Giovanni Sartori,
introductory chapter of SOCIAL SCIENCE CONCEPTS: A SYSTEMATIC
ANALYSIS, edited by Giovanni Sartori, June 1981, mimeo, reprinted by
permission of the author.

Preface to the
English-Language Edition

This English-language edition is a substantially revised version of the Swedish edition. As the book was used in courses at various universities, different sections of the presentation were subjected to considerable constructive criticism. In addition, many people have read through parts of the revised manuscript and offered new suggestions and ideas. For their opinions on the content of the book and for other support, I would like to extend a hearty thanks to the following people who have not yet been mentioned in the preface to the Swedish edition: Walter Carlsnaes, Axel Hadenius, Jörgen Hermansson, Urban Laurin, Stig Arne Nohrstedt, Lennart Nordfors, Sven Erik Svärd, and Erik Åsard in the Department of Government, Uppsala University, Nils Jareborg in the Department of Law, Uppsala University, Göran Collste in the Department of Theological Ethics at Uppsala University, and Lennart Nordenfelt in the Department of Philosophy, University of Stockholm. None of these people is responsible for my blunders.

The translation was done by David McCune in a fantastic newsroom in Rockefeller Center, New York. I am very grateful to him for recommending the book to Sage for publication, for his eminent rendering of my technical Swedish prose into understandable English, and for our stimulating and pleasant collaboration during the course of the translation.

Some of the work on the revision was carried out during a brief but intensive stay in the spring of 1980 at the Institute for Public Policy Studies, Vanderbilt University, Nashville, Tennessee. I would like to extend my hearty thanks for the excellent working conditions offered me there to the institute's director, Professor Erwin Hargrove, and to my contact in the Department of Political Science, Professor M. Donald Hancock.

I would also like to thank Elisabeth Svanbeck of the Department of Government, Uppsala University, for much practical assistance.

The revision and translation was supported financially by the Swedish Council for Research in the Humanities and Social Sciences, Uppsala

University, and the Lars Hierta Memorial Foundation. The help of these institutions is gratefully acknowledged.

Finally, I would like once again to thank my wife, Siv Vedung, for her selfless support and unabating belief in me.

— Evert Vedung

Preface to the Swedish Edition

One of the joys of bringing this investigation to an end is that it offers me an opportunity to thank all of the students, colleagues, and organizations that have helped me in one way or another in this work.

I would first like to extend my thanks to the students who participated in my courses in the analysis of political ideas at the universities of Uppsala, Lund, and Stockholm and at the university branch at Örebro for their many constructive ideas and critical objections. Warm thanks also go to all those who have taken the time to read and comment on parts of the manuscript, who repeatedly offered their views in letters or orally on problems, who made it economically possible for me to devote myself to the research, who generally encouraged and supported me, and who provided me with a roof over my head and room to work during my research travels. Special thanks go to Eric Bellquist, Stefan Björklund, Mats Bäck, Thorild Dahlquist, Nils Elvander, Sverker Gustavsson, Robert Heeger, Barry Holmström, Ove Joanson, Helle Kanger, Stig Kanger, Leif Lewin, Folke Lindahl, Lennart J. Lundquist, Anna-Karin Malmström, Knut Midgaard, Lars Nord, Claes Ryn, Gunnar Sjöblom, Bertil Strömberg, Stig Strömholm, Björn Söderfeldt and Björn Wittrock.

A portion of the work on this book was done in very stimulating surroundings during a stay of over a year at the John F. Kennedy School of Government, Harvard and the Department of Political Science, University of California at Berkeley. My work there was made possible by fellowships from the Ford Foundation and the Sweden-America Foundation. My respectful gratitude goes to these organizations.

My warm thanks also goes to my wife, Siv Vedung, for her work on the bibliography, but above all because she always believed in me.

I should add that remaining errors and shortcomings are mine alone.

— *Evert Vedung*
November 5, 1976

Uppsala, Sweden

11

Overview

One key task of political science is to criticize other political science and political conceptions in general. The present work summarizes the basic rules we must follow if we are to discuss politics and political science in a critical and rational way.

Chapter 1 presents an exposition of alternative approaches to research on political messages. Four basic questions may be posed about a political message: What does it mean? Is it really true? Why is it said? And what effect will it have? The first two questions lie within the realm of content-oriented analysis of messages. This approach focuses on the message itself. The first — with a very important qualification — the third and the fourth questions belong to function-oriented analysis. It concentrates on the context of the message. The distinction between content-oriented and function-oriented message analysis is fundamental for clear thinking about political language.

Content-oriented analysis may be a matter of merely describing the content of the messages. We may also go a step further and assess their rational soundness. This appraisal is conducted by means of a set of standards.

First of all, claims should be *supported* by reasons in the sense of grounds or evidence. Claims and reasons should also be stated in *clear* language. They must neither be tacit nor unsystematically arranged in such ways as to cause obscurity. Pronouncements issued should be *relevant,* and relevant aspects of the case should be acknowledged and presented. The messages should also be *consistent* and *true*. Together, these five standards constitute the basic rules for rational political discourse. These rules are discussed in Chapters 4 through 8.

What is described in a function-oriented analysis — this is the qualification hinted at above — is not the content of the message as such, but either the pronouncement or the espousal of the message. When we ask, "Why is it said?" we are not looking for reasons in the sense of justification, but reasons in the sense of motivation. We answer the question with reference to

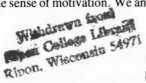

the intentions, calculations, or deliberations of the senders of the message. The purpose of such an intensionalist explanation must be to exhibit the considerations the communicators made before they uttered what they did, and in what way these considerations induced them to make the utterance.

The awakening interest in rational assessment is linked to efforts to use analytic tools to provide information for decision making on substantive issues. Rational assessment may be considered an instrument for improving the basis of knowledge for public decisions. It belongs to the broad stream of thought referred to as policy analysis. Assumptions underlying proposed or effective policy instruments could be judged from a rational assessment perspective.

Chapter 2 is devoted to the initial stage of an argumentative inquiry: constructing a language of analysis. The necessity of starting with a problem is underscored. Therefore, a section on how poorly circumscribed topics are converted into manageable research problems is included.

An important tool for creating an analytical language is concept analysis and definition. A few basic guidelines to definition are presented. The point of departure is the traditional view of meaning and the basic distinctions between words, their intensions, and their extensions. Ambiguity is characterized as a defect in the relationship between word and intension, whereas the other type of obscurity, vagueness, is pictured as a fault in the intension/extension relationship. Definition is a technique for reducing or eliminating these obscurities in the researcher's own language of analysis.

The difference between stipulative definitions—which provide rules for how words will be used—and reportative definitions—which merely describe how terms are actually used—is hammered out. A combination—the explicative definition—is given special attention. Another classification, that between specification of intension and specification of extension, is also dealt with. It is argued that a full definitional treatment should include intensionalist as well as extensionalist considerations.

There are no absolute criteria, of course, on which we can base an appraisal of the correctness of definitions. There are, however, certain guiding standards, and these are stated and discussed. Of particular interest are the criteria of fruitfulness and minimality.

A section on general principles of classification is also included. A distinction is made between formal schemes, which classify messages purely from the perspective of argumentation analysis, and substantive schemes, which take as their point of departure the substantive issue to be analyzed. The formal schemes include divisions of arguments into claims (conclusions) and reasons (premises) and the ordering of arguments into chains and clusters of reasoning. Finally, two examples of substantive schemes of analysis are given, one for claims and one for reasons.

Chapter 3 deals with how, with the aid of our language of analysis, we describe the political messages to be analyzed. A key operation is interpretation. A definition of this elusive concept is suggested. Furthermore, several types of interpretations are discerned. With respect to how well the interpretations accord with the original message, we may distinguish between correct, reasonable, and unreasonable interpretations. Correct interpretations seem impossible to attain, so for all practical purposes we have to stick to reasonable interpretations. With respect to what justificatory evidence is used for validation, we may distinguish between literal, systematic, intentionalist, and reconstructive interpretations. Attempts at establishing any of the first three interpretations undoubtedly are acceptable in argumentation analysis. The need for combining all three efforts in actual research is stressed. Endeavors aiming at advancing reconstructive interpretations are also laudable. They are, however, more rightly considered as aiming at theory construction, not interpretation.

Political language is ambiguous and vague. A message's context may help us overcome these obscurities. We emphasize the importance of putting the message in its proper context when interpreting it, as well as of applying the principle of charity during interpretation. The latter exhorts us to make the best, rather than the worst, possible interpretation of the material to be studied.

Chapter 4 deals with how pertinent messages actually are identified, how their meaning is worked out, and how they are finally portrayed and ordered in terms of our conceptual language. In conjunction with this, we can also apply our first two criteria for the rational soundness of messages. We can examine whether claims are supported by any reasons at all. And we can judge the message's clarity. We point out here that description and certain forms of assessment are not logically consecutive steps in content-oriented message analysis. We do not, for example, describe the message first and then determine that it is unclear. We must appraise its clarity at the same time we describe it.

At times, the analysts of messages find themselves in situations in which the material contains an entirely different view of what it means to interpret. Assume the investigators study how other students have interpreted a certain text. The analysts may disagree with the results of these students' interpretations and adjudge these interpretations deficient from the point of view of clarity. But the analysts may also disagree with the methods upon which the interpretations rest. Thus, the analysts may come across fundamentally divergent conceptions of the very rules that define a rational political discourse and be confronted with rules that cannot be accepted within the system of rules the analysts support.

Such second-order disagreements can arise over all five main rules for rational political discourse. In Chapter 2, the essentialist theory of meaning is used as an example containing an alternative view of meaning and interpretation. In the case of such rule conflicts, rational assessment must move to a metalevel and discuss the soundness of the very rules on which the appraisal is made. The third assessment criterion suggests that messages should be relevant. The application of this standard is discussed in Chapter 5.

We can recognize two separate standards of relevance. The one says that statements actually issued should be pertinent to the subject matter of the discussion. The other suggests that relevant aspects of the case should not be suppressed, but acknowledged and presented. The complementarity of these two criteria is established, and examples of the use of each of them in actual relevancy testing are offered.

In this context, some classical so-called fallacies of relevance are discussed, e.g., *argumentum ad hominem* and *argumentum tu quoque*. Some conflicts over the very rule of relevance are also scrutinized.

Chapter 6 expounds the standard of consistency. This rule suggests that the message should be free from contradictions. It might be split into two subrules. The one says that inferences from reasons to claims in each individual argument should be validly derived. The other subrule prescribes that claims should be consistent with other claims and reasons with other reasons. The discussion of the application of the latter rule includes sections on inconsistent propositions, inconsistent value judgments, and inconsistency between words and deeds. The chapter ends with some examples of second-order conflicts concerning the very rule of consistency.

The last major rule for rational political discourse holds that propositions should be true. Truth assessment is treated in Chapter 7.

The meaning of verification, falsification, confirmation, disconfirmation, and related concepts is explicated and the logical steps of a truth assessment are presented. Different kinds of propositions are also distinguished. A case is made for carrying out truth assessment as criticism. This means that we do not have to confirm or falsify propositions ourselves. We only have to demonstrate that what the author of the message claims is true actually is not.

Rule conflicts can also arise in the area of tenability analysis. The author whose message is under study may embrace some other view of what truth is and how it can be proved.

The argument in *Political Reasoning* takes as its point of departure the so-called correspondence theory of truth. A proposition is true if there is agreement between what the proposition asserts and the facts. Opposing theories include the coherence theory and the pragmatic theory of truth. All these different theories of truth are presented. Finally, several statements from Marxist and Nazi thought are examined; these statements contain starkly different concepts of what truth is and how tenability should be tested.

Value judgments must be assessed on the basis of the same five major standards of rationality that apply to political reasoning in general. But they are commonly regarded as having a special position. This justifies discussing them separately in Chapter 8.

Several broad approaches to appraisal of value judgments in political reasoning are identified. The so-called value-free approach draws a fundamental distinction between categoric and instrumental statements of value. The latter may be reformulated into propositions stating that certain means will lead to various ends. Such means-assertions may be judged true or false. The former, on the other hand, cannot be reformulated into propositions, implying that their truth cannot be appraised. From this it has been concluded that "political science is a science *about* politics, not a science *of* politics."

This conclusion, it is argued, is hardly tenable. It may be granted that the truth of categoric value statements cannot be established. It may also be granted that it is impossible to decide, in a fully scientific way, which ultimate value judgments are right or wrong, laudable or reprehensible, good or bad. Still, they may be appraised in a number of other ways. They may be criticized for fuzziness. The investigator may find out whether what they say can be physically realized at all or not. And if political statements include several categoric statements of value, the analyst may find out which ones deal with things that cannot be realized simultaneously.

Two other approaches to the value problem are also presented: the evaluative choice approach and the approach that attempts to avoid the whole issue by asserting that value judgments play only a very insignificant role in political language. These approaches are questioned on various grounds. The chapter and the book end by expounding some conflicts between incompatible standards for assessing value judgments.

1

APPROACHES TO
POLITICAL MESSAGES

**The historian must often distinguish two questions
about a statement: "Is it true?" and "Should it, rather
than another true statement, be made?"**
Morton White
Foundations of Historical Knowledge

Political theories . . . live on two planes or play a double role. They are
theories or logical entities belonging to the abstract world of thought, but they
are also beliefs, events in people's minds and factors in their conduct.

With these words, pronounced a year after publishing his great handbook
on the history of political philosophy, George H. Sabine clearly wanted to
draw attention to a dichotomy that is crucial to the study of political theories.
Sabine continued:

In this latter role they are influential not because they are true but because they
are believed. On this plane they operate as events, or as actual factors in
historical situations, and as such are part of the data which the historian of
politics has to deal with. But this historical reality is obviously not what
interests those persons who sincerely believe a theory to be true; such persons
are not interested in a theory because it exists but because they believe it to be a
valid explanation of something else.

From this Sabine concluded that two kinds of approaches ought to be
distinguished: "a rational criticism" and "a study of historical causes of
political theories."[1]

The two approaches to the study of political theories that Sabine hinted at
in his concluding statement are crucial for inquiries into all kinds of political

communication. At least one of them—a rational criticism—has not been developed, scrutinized, and discussed much in political science since Sabine published his article in 1939.[2] The main purpose of the present treatise is to clarify more extensively the various methodological steps involved in "rational criticism" or, as I prefer to put it, rational assessment.

1.1 Content-Oriented and Function-Oriented Message Analysis

There are other approaches to political messages—an expression that will be used throughout to cover political statements proper as well as statements about politics by, e.g., sociologists and political scientists—than the two Sabine mentioned in his article. We can regard national assessment as a variant of a broader approach that we can call content-oriented analysis, or, synonymously, argumentation analysis, argumentative analysis, or argument analysis. Similarly, Sabine's "study of historical causes" is one of a group of approaches that we can call function-oriented analysis.[3] What is the clearest way to elucidate the differences among these broad approaches to political messages?

One possibility is to utilize the simple model for communication. It tells us that communication—and so also political messages—consists of six basic elements. We have a sender, an encoding process that results in a message, a channel of transmission, a receiver of the message, and a decoding process. We should add a seventh element in our present context: a general environment or context.

On the basis of this model, we can say that content-oriented analysis focuses on the message itself, while function-oriented analysis focuses on the context of the message. The context includes everything in the model except the message. Figure 1.1 illustrates this basic idea.[4]

Content-oriented analysis of political messages, then, focuses on the message itself and on its content. The content of what is communicated and nothing else is the subject of the inquiry.

Function-oriented analysis, on the other hand, does not focus on the message. It concentrates on the remaining boxes in our extended model of communication. The context of the message, more than its content, constitutes the subject matter for function-oriented analysis.

Note at this early stage that the expressions "content-oriented" and "function-oriented" are used here in a rather technical sense. Our content-oriented approach exhibits similarities but is far from identical to content analysis. All similarities and differences cannot be elucidated here. Suffice it

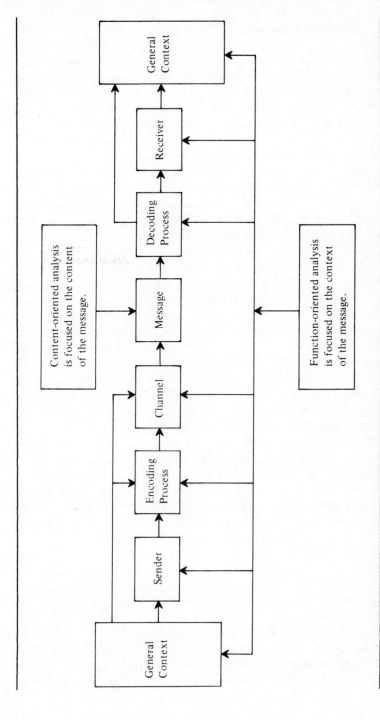

Figure 1.1 Content-Oriented and Function-Oriented Message Analysis

to say that in content-oriented analysis, the message content is always studied per se, for its own sake, not as a means to get knowledge about something else. This may, of course, also be the case in content analysis. However, the latter is also often considered a research technique for making inferences from message content to something else, e.g., characteristics of the sender or the receiver.[5] Such use of message content as an indicator is by definition excluded from our content-oriented analysis.

We must not confuse our function-oriented analysis with functionalism in social science or functionalist explanation. Function-oriented analysis is a very broad notion, encompassing much more than the notion of functionalist explanation. To be sure, so-called functionalist explanations of political messages would be classified as function-oriented analyses. Thus, a study purporting to ascertain the contribution of a set of political messages toward the maintenance of some stated characteristic or condition in a given political system to which the set is assumed to belong, would be considered function-oriented without much further ado. However, function-oriented analysis includes much more. The expression covers studies of the effects of messages as well as investigations into the causes of messages. It also covers descriptive studies concerning, e.g., which actors support the messages or who has received them.[6]

We can direct a function-oriented analysis of political messages backward toward the sender or forward toward the receiver. From the senders' perspective, it can be directed at the source, the encoding process, the channel, the general context, or a combination of these.

It may simply be a matter of finding out who the sender is. Which actor or actors stand behind the message? We may also inquire into the senders' relationship to the message. Have they merely communicated it? If so, when? Or are they also psychologically committed to the content of what they said? What is their attitude toward it? Do they like it? Do they espouse, support, endorse, or believe in the particular message they sent? And third, we can inquire into which channel was used to send the message.

Finally, the researcher can pose questions about the relationships within or between the various boxes in the model. Which senders used one channel and which used another? What motives or deliberations formed the basis for the fact that they expressed the message or that they chose a certain type of channel of transmission?

The general context of the message can come into the picture here. We can study the relationship between, say, the actors' espousal or pronouncement of the message and their general context. The researcher may, for example, try to relate the persons who espoused the message to various

sociological background factors. Do they belong to a certain class, genera-
tion, sex, nationality, profession? Are they members of some interest group?
Is the message espoused more often in some types of societies than in others?

Political background factors may also enter into the picture. What is the
relationship between the actors who pronounced or espoused the message
and phenomena such as political systems, parties, policy positions, political
processes, and political actions? Do the actors who espouse the message
belong, for example, to a certain political party, or do they advocate a
specific political ideology?

Another alternative is to search for precursors to the messages in the
history of ideas. Have the bearers of the messages been influenced by other
thinkers and their ideologies, belief systems, or philosophies? We are then
looking for genetic influences, and the purpose may be to construct genea-
logical tables for important political convictions.

One further option is to seek connections between *personality* features
and political messages. Within the framework of this psychological perspective, we may ask, for example, if certain political messages are more
closely tied to certain personality types than to others.

The groups of background factors mentioned so far—within or outside of
the general context of the message—seem to be those that occur most
frequently in modern scientific debate on political messages. But there is yet
another tack. We can investigate the influence of *geographic* factors on the
espousal of messages. Do people living in certain places or in certain regions
tend to hold, say, one political conviction more often than others?[7]

In a function-oriented analysis of messages, we can direct questions in a
corresponding way toward the three boxes on the receiver side. We can ask
about the receivers, their decoding process, their general environment, or
combinations of these three. Which people have been exposed to the messages? When and in what context did this happen? To what extent have they
grasped the meaning of the message? Have they become interested in it? Are
their attitudes positive, negative, or indifferent toward it? Which receivers
can remember anything of the message's informational content and which
cannot? To what extent have they been influenced by the message? Is the
degree of influence in any way related to various social, political, intellectual, or geographic background factors?

The relationship between studying the content of the message and studying its context or environment can, however, be more complicated than we
have assumed so far. For one reason or another, the various stages in the
sender or receiver side of the model may not be accessible for direct
observation. But messages may exist. We then have the possibility of

drawing conclusions about various factors in the sender or receiver steps based on properties in the message. The properties can be *indicators* of something else, in this case, the relationship between the sender and receiver sides. The purpose, expressed technically, is to draw *inferences* from the message box to one of the other boxes in the communication model.

To infer, it has been asserted, means to conclude from or decide based on something known or assumed; it also means to derive by reasoning. In the present case, the known is the content of the message. We can derive new information from this through a logical process. This is often done with the aid of additional information, gathered from the context or environment within which the message was sent.[8] In other words, attention is focused on the content of the message only to the extent that it is considered a valid indicator of the relationships in the other steps of the communication model. The latter, not the content as such, is the focal point of the analysis. This means that this analysis must nevertheless be considered function-oriented.

There can be several reasons for taking the detour through the content of the message instead of going straight at the sender or receiver. A direct inquiry may be theoretically impossible. Take the actors' motives as an example. They lie on an inner, psychological plane and can never be directly observed. No one can look into someone else's psyche and discover motives. We are always forced to infer motives from something else, e.g., theoretical assumptions about how people function or something that is directly observable, such as the actors' own pronouncements on what their motives are. In the last case, justifying statements are used as indicators of motives.

A direct examination may also be impracticable. The relevant material may be classified. During times of war or intense international tension, it is not possible to gather information about conditions in enemy countries from within those countries themselves. One purpose among many for postwar studies of Chinese or Soviet propaganda has been to make inferences concerning the patterns of thought and attitudes of those countries' leading politicians. Inferences concerning qualities of the sender were drawn from the content of the messages.[9]

Content is most commonly used as an indicator of qualities of the message's senders. This line of thought has become very popular within the content-analysis tradition. What motives, values, beliefs, and attitudes can be discovered in the senders through inferences drawn from their messages? What do the messages reveal about their acts? In his well-known book, *Content Analysis for the Social Sciences and Humanities,* Ole R. Holsti offers several examples from empirical literature of this type of inference.

One use of the indirect study of messages has been to secure political and military intelligence that cannot be obtained directly. During World War II, social scientists were engaged in the American Federal Communications Commission to study the propaganda of the Axis powers. A study was done of German and Italian radio broadcasts. The purpose was to determine the degree of collaboration between Italian and German propaganda agencies. Holsti summarizes:

> Because the contents of German and Italian broadcasts were consistently different, analysts concluded that there was no collaboration between the two countries. This inference was proved correct by evidence which became available after the end of the war.[10]

Based on the contents of certain messages that could be directly observed, the researchers drew an inference to something which at that particular time could not be observed directly, i.e., the existence of collaboration between German and Italian propaganda agencies.

Researchers have also studied politicians' messages in order to discover personality traits. The underlying assumption has been that there are many styles of reasoning and that one can infer other qualities of individuals from their idiosyncratic characteristics. Again following Ole R. Holsti, Nikita Khrushchev's speeches delivered at the United Nations have been analyzed this way. The inference regarding the psychological characteristics of the Soviet leader is cast as follows:

> He feels that others are prone to misunderstand his position and yet he desires acceptance and will even sacrifice other needs or ends to achieve it. He is moody and needful of approval. But with his pessimism about resolving differences, he enjoys conflict and struggle, as much for its own sake as a means to an end. . . . He trusts his own instinct, his "natural feel" for things. He is painstaking in certain areas, but in general is impatient and suspicious of detail and subtlety.[11]

Among the earliest uses of systematic documentary analysis were those designed to identify unknown authors from content characteristics. Who wrote *The Federalist Papers* Nos. 49-58, 62, and 63? Was it James Madison or Alexander Hamilton? Who was the author of the "Junius Letters," a series of political pamphlets written from 1769 to 1772?

The underlying belief is that each person's style contains certain unique characteristics such as sentence length, frequency of words, and so forth. These peculiarities are discovered through a study of works one knows were written by some person. Then the results of the analysis are compared with the results of a corresponding analysis of the work whose authorship is under dispute. On the basis of this study, the researcher draws an inference as to who did or did not write the anonymous work.[12]

The relationship between content and context of messages is complicated also from another point of view. It is very natural to use the context of the message as an instrument for eliciting the meaning of what is communicated. Does not this blur the distinction between content-oriented and function-oriented analyses? Our investigation seems to deal with both content and context at the same time. The answer is in the negative. In these cases, the focus is indubitably on the content, not the context, of the message. The context is not studied *per se;* it is only employed as a *means* to arrive at an end, which is the content. Since the latter is what we are looking for, the analysis must be regarded as content-oriented.

It is important to note that the distinction between content-oriented and function-oriented analyses of political messages refers to the *researcher's point of view*. The expressions "content-oriented" and "function-oriented," then, do not refer to properties of the messages and their contexts. It is our *study* of political messages and their contexts that can be either content-oriented or function-oriented. From a purely definitional point of view, the two approaches differ only with respect to the subject matter under study. In the one case, our inquiry focuses on one subject matter, and in the other case, it focuses on another. A content-oriented analysis focuses on the content of that which is communicated. It can, of course, deal with what a particular sender has said. But even in this case, our interest is focused primarily on the message as such, not on the actor who communicated it.

A function-oriented analysis of messages, on the other hand, focuses on the context or environment of the messages rather than on their content. It deals with questions concerning the channel of transmission, the sender and the receiver, and their relationship to the message and to the general context.

1.2   *Descriptive, Assessive, and Explanatory Analysis*

To get any further, we must introduce one more classification. This is the distinction between descriptive, assessive, and explanatory studies of political messages and their environments.

To *describe* is to make a linguistic representation of something. To describe the content of a message is to identify it, work out its meaning, and portray it. To describe something belonging to the environment of the message, e.g., an actor's pronouncement of a message, entails identifying the pronouncement, working out its meaning, and portraying it.

	Descriptive	Assessive	Explanatory
Content-Oriented	(1) Content-oriented description	(2) Content-oriented assessment	(3) —
Function-Oriented	(4) Function-oriented description	(5) Function-oriented assessment	(6) Function-oriented explanation

Figure 1.2 Six Logically Possible Types of Content-Oriented and Function-Oriented Analysis of Political Messages

An *assessive* analysis implies making an appraisal of something according to certain standards or criteria of assessment. These criteria may vary. Certain standards are used in assessing the content of messages; others are used to assess, say, pronouncements of messages.

When we *explain* the pronouncement or espousal of a message, we try to place the fact that something was said or espoused in a context of other facts in such a way as to illuminate the original fact. To explain the act of saying or espousing something is to adduce evidence to show why this act obtains rather than one of its possible alternatives. This requires that we do more than establish that the act really happened; we must show (in some sense) that it had to happen—not necessarily in the sense that it was necessary and inevitable, but that it was probable and expected. This is generally how we will use the word "explain" below.[13]

If we combine these three concepts with the basic categories "content-oriented" and "function-oriented," we will have six different and logically possible approaches to political messages. Figure 1.2 shows that a function-oriented analysis can be descriptive as well as assessive and explanatory.[14] A content-oriented analysis, on the other hand, can only be descriptive and assessive. The third position is empty, indicating that content-oriented analysis cannot be explanatory.

Why? This is because the pure content of the message cannot be explained in the sense of relating it to independent, explanatory or, more technically, explanans factors. An actors' *pronouncement* or espousal of messages can be explained; the pure message, disengaged from the actor's pronouncement or espousal of it, cannot be explained, because there is no fact to explain. The content of a message can be described. It can also be assessed, but it cannot be explained.

Below we will try to present our views on what the five different approaches to political messages mean.

1.3 Descriptive Approaches

Political messages, then, can be described in both a content-oriented and function-oriented fashion (positions 1 and 4 in Figure 1.2). The questions we pose in the course of this descriptive phase can be elucidated more closely through a slight modification of Figure 1.1 (see Figure 1.3).

Content-oriented descriptions are important because they constitute a necessary first step toward assessive analysis or, as I will say from now on, rational assessment of the message. They should not, however, be regarded as mere preliminary steps toward something else. Description may be a valuable research enterprise in itself. Describing in a qualified way the structure and content of complicated but crucial chains of political reasoning may constitute an important scholarly contribution. The attainment of good descriptions is most often no trivial task. The difficulties associated with descriptions are something egregiously underestimated by analysts of political messages.

Description includes several different phases. All analysis of political messages must be preceded by some intellectual effort, which, if we may wax solemn for a moment, we could call theoretical work. Selecting a topic is, of course, absolutely indispensable. At a minimum, in scientific contexts, scholars must formulate a research problem about that topic as well as develop some concepts or even schemes of classification to help them answer the research question. The various steps in this preparatory work include topic selection, problem formulation, and concept formation. These theoretical preliminaries must, as we said earlier, precede every qualified description—both content-oriented and function-oriented. Otherwise, in the content-oriented analysis, the description risks being an uninteresting repetition of what has already been said.

In a strictly logical sense, the actual description of the message is done

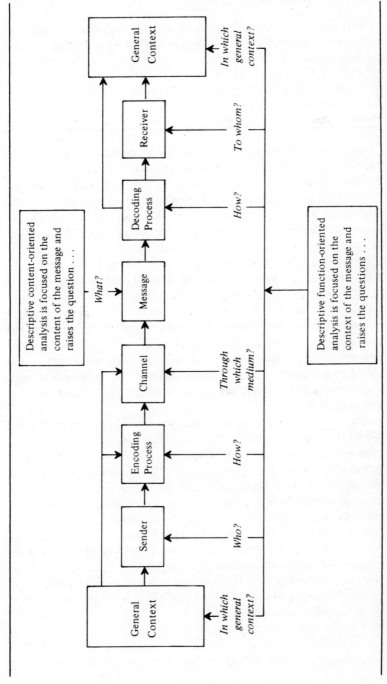

Figure 1.3 Content-Oriented and Function-Oriented Description

only once the theoretical work has been completed. Content-oriented description of arguments and chains of argumentation can be divided into the following three steps:

(1) identifying claims and reasons;
(2) working out the meaning of them; and
(3) portraying and organizing them.

The process of identification must begin with the collection of material to answer the content-oriented research question. This work can, of course, be both extensive and time-consuming. Depending on the question, we might have to collect material from books, newspapers, magazines and journals, parliamentary records, or publications from the cabinet or public agencies. Then we must skim through the material in order to find roughly the pertinent passages.

The next step entails penetrating deeper into the material in order to work out the meaning of what is communicated. It may not be clear what the statements mean. Political language abounds in ambiguous words and vague expressions. Some steps in the argument may be tacit and, so, unclear. Comprehension may also be difficult if different parts of the argument are presented in various places.

We may utilize several different methods of interpretation to work out the meaning of our material. If the interpretations are to be more than pure paraphrases or unrefined collections of material, then they must be executed in the light of certain concepts.

In the third step, finally, we must portray and arrange the arguments. We write out the messages in terms of our own analytic language, differentiate positions and reasons, and order the whole case according to some systematic principle.

Recall that by definition, function-oriented analysis never focuses primarily on the content, but rather, on the context of the message. This means, as Figure 1.3 indicates, that function-oriented descriptions can refer to various types of relationships that may exist between agents and messages. Descriptions may, as we see in Figure 1.3, refer to the pronouncement, comprehension, or espousal of messages.

We can say approximately the same things about these descriptions as we did about the content-oriented sort. They both have an inherent value and a value as one part of an explanation or assessment. As pointed out previously, they must, of course, be preceded by theoretical considerations. The description itself is constructed by identifying agents' relationships to messages, working out what they mean, and portraying the relationships.

1.4   Assessment Approaches

Both content-oriented and function-oriented description can constitute a preparatory phase of appraisal. Recall that positions 2 and 5 in Figure 1.2 above are not empty.

Making an appraisal means that the messages or their contexts are compared to a set of standards or ideals. We ask whether the messages' contents are valid. We ask whether the agents' relations to the messages are correct. If we add this to our running model of the communication process, it looks like Figure 1.4.

1.4.1   Rational Assessment of Messages

Let us begin with content-oriented analysis. An assessment of the content of the message—a "rational criticism," to refer back to our opening quotation from Sabine—entails investigating whether claims and associated reasons meet certain standards for good reasoning or not. This means taking a close look at claims (also called "conclusions" or "positions") put forward in political discussions and reasons (also called "justifying statements," "grounds," or "premises") offered to sustain or weaken these claims. Then, claims and reasons are compared with a set of rules for rational discourse. These standards of rational reasoning are applied in order to discriminate good reasons for or against a claim from bad ones.

Thus, in this context at least, the expression "rational assessment" is used to describe a scholarly activity. It implies the comparison of claims and reasons with a set of standards for good reasoning. The immediate purpose of this scholarly activity is to shed some light on the issue of whether what is communicated is correct or incorrect, sound or unsound, valid or invalid.

The logical starting point for a rational assessment is the phrasing of the fundamental question: Is the message valid? This question may be broken down, however, into five assessment-pertinent subquestions:

(1) Are claims supported by reasons in the message?
(2) Is the message clear?
(3) Is the message relevant?
(4) Is the message consistent?
(5) Is the message true?

Each of these five assessment-pertinent questions presupposes a standard by means of which one aspect of the intellectual quality of claims and reasons can be appraised. These standards of assessment can be framed as rules

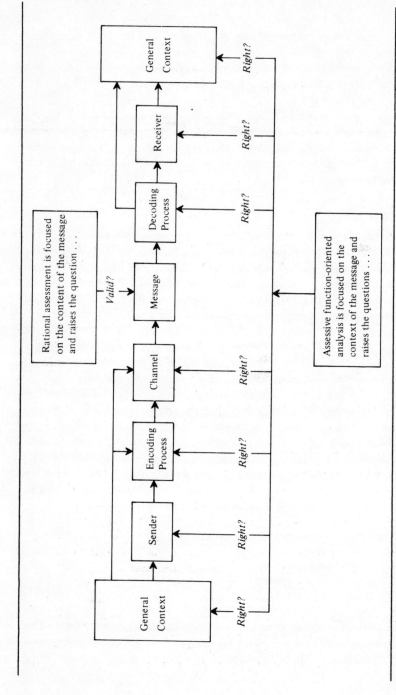

Figure 1.4 Content-Oriented and Function-Oriented Assessment

constituting a rational political discourse. In order to acceptably participate in such a rational political discourse, participants must follow these rules. We may present the five major rules as follows:

(1) Claims should be supported by reasons in the message.
(2) The message should be clear.
(3) The message should be relevant.
(4) The message should be consistent.
(5) The message should be true.

The five fundamental rules for a rational political discourse can be called the rule of support, the rule of clarity, the rule of relevance, the rule of consistency, and the rule of truth, respectively.[15] The further implications of these rules will be developed in Chapters 4 through 8. Only brief elucidations will be proffered here.

The *rule of support* says that claims (conclusions, positions) should be accompanied by reasons. Coming along with flat claims would hardly impress anyone who agrees with the rules for a rational discourse of messages. If claims are not supported by reasons, then there would normally not be any need to consider the message further. It does not matter if it is repeated several times or not. To be taken seriously, a message must normally contain at least one reason.

The *rule of clarity* holds that a message must be clear. Obscurity cannot be tolerated in rational political discourse. But terms like "lucidity," "clarity," "clearness," and their opposites are not very clear themselves. In the present context we consider three main sources of obscurity. It may exist because some things are left out or tacit, because words are unclear, or because the presentation has been unsystematic and confused. Based on this short typology of obscurity, we can formulate the following three subrules to the rule of clarity:

(1) claims and reasons must not be tacit and so give rise to obscurity;
(2) words must not be used unclearly; and
(3) the presentation should be systematically arranged so that it does not give rise to unclarity.

Note that we are not prescribing perfection. The message does not need to be perfectly or absolutely clear in order to pass the clarity test. The rule of clarity suggests something less ambitious. It suffices for a message to be stated and arranged as clearly and unequivocally as necessary under the circumstances.

The *rule of relevance* can also be broken down into two subrules. The one states that pronouncements actually offered should be relevant to the subject matter under discussion. The other holds that relevant aspects of the case should be acknowledged and presented. The first subrule allows us to dismiss expressly presented arguments as beside the point; idle chatter that does not deal with the subject is not accepted. The second subrule permits us to show that relevant considerations have not been presented; biased selection of facts does not belong in a rational debate.

The fourth rule, the *rule of consistency,* says that the message should be consistent and free of contradictions. To claim one thing at one moment and then its contradiction at a later moment is not acceptable in rational discourse. The rule of consistency can be divided into two subrules. The first has to do with the relationship between claims and their reasons. It holds that inferences from claims to reasons should be derived in a logically valid fashion. The second auxiliary rule has to do with the relationship among claims themselves and among reasons themselves. It says that claims should be consistent with other claims, and reasons with other reasons.

The *rule of truth,* finally, says that messages should be empirically true. This rule has no subrules.

If we count up the main rules and subrules, we have a total of nine rules for a rational assessment of political messages. These major and minor rules for rational political discourse may be summarized as follows:

(1) The Rule of Support: Claims should be supported by reasons in the message.
(2) The Rule of Clarity: The message should be clear.
    (2.1) Claims and reasons must not be tacit in such a way as to cause obscurity.
    (2.2) Words must not be used unclearly.
    (2.3) The presentation should be systematically arranged so as not to cause obscurity.
(3) The Rule of Relevance: The message should be relevant.
    (3.1) Pronouncements should be relevant.
    (3.2) Relevant aspects of the case should be acknowledged and presented.
(4) The Rule of Consistency: The message should be consistent.
    (4.1) Inferences from reasons to claims should be derived in a logically valid way.
    (4.2) Claims should be consistent with other claims, reasons with other reasons.
(5) The Rule of Truth: The message should be true.

If a message conforms to all these rules, it is considered sound. Note that *sound, soundness,* and *rational soundness* are used here as comprehensive expressions, indicating that the message consists of a claim supported by at least one reason and that the message is clear, relevant, consistent, and true.

How do the nine rules relate to each other? Are some of them more important than others? It is not easy to give a general answer to these questions. In some situations, though, violations of some rules must be considered more serious than violations of others.

Take, for instance, the first rule, which says that claims should be supported by reasons. Suppose that we are faced with a very questionable normative claim, and that it is stated again, and again, and again, but that it is not justified by any reasons at all. The senders may well believe that they strengthen their case by repeating their thesis. They may also believe, in fact, that they have presented reasons, although all they have done is repeatedly lay down a claim.[16] This is a serious violation of the rule of support. Entirely unsupported claims about controversial matters cannot be taken seriously at all. The error of sustaining claims by repetition rather than by reasoned evidence is called the *fallacy of argument ad nauseam*.[17] It provides an excellent ground for dismissing the whole argument.

Assume on the other hand that we are faced with a claim that takes the form of a statement of fact. It is not followed by any reasons. The argument then does not fulfill the demands stated in the rule of support. This is a serious flaw and must be criticized. But there still may be a reason not to dismiss the entire argument at this early stage in the assessment. It seems that in some situations it is meaningful to let the rejection be dependent on a truth assessment instead. The message can only be rejected if it turns out to be false.

Also consider Rule 1.1 that claims and reasons may not be left tacit in such a way as to cause obscurity. Presume that a claim is supported by reasons, though the latter are based in part on unstated assumptions. Sometimes assumptions are left out because they seem obvious. To state them explicitly would seem superfluous in the eyes of the communicator. However, they may also be left out because they are controversial, e.g., contested value premises.[18] Attention should be called to violations of this rule. But they should not always lead us to write off the whole argument. Instead, investigators ought to act according to the so-called principle of charity. In the interest of a rational assessment, they should avoid discarding arguments on too shaky grounds. They should make their critical task a bit more difficult for themselves by struggling to build up positions really worth attacking. To that end, they ought to give arguments a charitable treatment, which means, among other things, uncovering unstated assumptions. This enables them to raise the intellectual level of their appraisal by executing it with the help of other, more advanced, more interesting, and more crucial standards of assessment.

Now consider the rule of clarity again, but this time look at the second subrule, which suggests that claims and reasons be stated clearly. When claims and reasons are obfuscated by fuzzy words and sentences, understanding and intelligibility are impeded.

In extreme cases, claims and reasons may be formulated in such an obscure way that they are entirely incomprehensible to the reader. Not even the most persistent and charitable reader may make any sense out of them. In such cases, the reasoning must be dismissed. Excessive fuzziness is a ground for completely discarding claims and reasons in a debate.

In most cases, unclear wording does not make a message entirely incomprehensible. It only makes understanding more difficult. Messages may, for example, contain vague and ambiguous words that allow different reasonable interpretations. In one interpretation, a sentence may express a statement of fact, in another, a statement of value. It may also be interpreted as a proposition about an activity or a proposition about the body performing that activity. In a way, these cases constitute violations of the rule of clarity. The strategy recommended in these cases, however, is to call attention to fuzziness while trying to restate the claims and reasons in clearer language in order to give the argument the benefit of a fair trial against more important standards.

Systematic arrangement is the third subrule to the general rule of clarity. It pertains to the case as a whole rather than its component parts. It is actually not easy to specify this criterion sharply enough so as to make it possible to determine in each and every case whether a message violates it or not. We may have to be satisfied with a few general formulations. We can say, a bit indefinitely perhaps, that ideas must be marshaled into a cohesive design so they can be followed by those who receive them. An overall systematic organization of reasons and claims makes the case as a whole as well as singular arguments more accessible. Orderliness facilitates contact and enhances comprehension. An arrangement that appears to be random makes arguments more difficult to grasp. Messy, disorganized compositions may invalidate what is communicated if they make the message impenetrable. On the other hand, a presentation can be unsystematic without necessarily being incomprehensible. In these cases, the flaw should be pointed out and condemned, but again, the investigators should act in accordance with the principle of charity. They should try to rearrange reasons and claims in their own, more systematic (one hopes) fashion.

As a final example, consider the rule of relevance. The phrase "being relevant" is roughly synonymous with "belonging to," "being pertinent to," or "being important for" the matter under consideration. Relevance implies close substantive belongingness to the subject matter. Assume that in a public discussion a debater provides some reasons for a claim, and another participant attempts to refute the claim by showing that the former's grounds clearly have nothing at all to do with the subject. Assume that the latter is right. The former's reasons are irrelevant in relation to the claim. Such a violation of the rule of relevance must be considered serious. Irrelevant reasons must not be considered in any further assessment.

Consider also the situation in which the opponent in the debate is able to show that the first debater overlooked the strongest counterreasons. The latter's reasoning, in other words, is seriously plagued by bias. This must also be considered a rather serious breach of the rules for rational political discourse.

To sum up, in some situations the rule of support seems to indicate some sort of minimum level of quality that a message must reach in order not to be completely discarded in the first round of assessment. The rule of relevance is also an important rule. Its first subrule, however, does not dismiss the entire argumentation, but only the irrelevant parts of it. The second subrule weakens the overall strength of the case, but if relevant reasons are presented, they must still be considered.

Finally, violations of the three subrules of the rule of clarity—that tacit portions of the reasoning, words, or the presentation's general arrangement may not give rise to obscurity—may be overlooked entirely on certain occasions in order to give the reasoning the benefit of an appraisal against other, more fundamental yardsticks such as relevance, consistency, and truth.

The nine rules of assessment have been placed in some sort of weak logical order. The underlying idea is that, from a logical point of view, these rules must be applied roughly in the same order as they are enumerated. The rule that claims should be supported by reasons must logically be applied before the rule that the message should be clear; and this rule should, in turn, be applied before the rule of relevance and the rule of consistency, and so forth.

But this order is weak and far from indisputable. For instance, it is debatable whether the rule of relevance must be applied only after the third subrule of the rule of clarity, i.e., the rule that in general, the presentation should be arranged so systematically that it does not give rise to obscurity.

The fact that the rules are logically ordered does not mean, of course, that they also must be applied in exactly this order in practical research. One might, for example, clear away all irrelevant reasons before beginning to interpret and refine those that remain.

It must be underscored that it may not be necessary to apply *all* nine rules in order to perform a fully satisfactory rational assessment. The use of, say, one, or five may be quite sufficient.

Take, for instance, the first rule, that claims must be supported by reasons. If a normative claim has been proposed and repeated time after another without any reason being produced in its favor, then on at least some occasions the reasoning can be refuted on account of the first rule alone. Obviously, there is no point in going on and applying, for example, the rules of consistency and relevance if there is absolutely no reason at all to which these rules might be applied.

Similarly, an argument may be refuted by applying only two rules. A given reason may fulfill the first rule but not the third. This is the case when an agent states some sort of support for his claim but words it in such a messy way that it cannot be given any reasonable interpretation by any outside examiner. Then it might be discarded according to the second subrule of the rule of clarity. When the obscurity and unclearness of the reason have been established there is no sense in trying to apply the subrule of systematic arrangement, or the rules of relevance, consistency, and truth.

Third, take the case of one or several actors asserting that they have actually offered a few reasons for a given claim. It turns out that it is quite possible to interpret what these reasons mean and ascertain that they also contain all necessary premises. Now if they are all irrelevant as reasons for or against the claim, it is perfectly acceptable to rebut them with reference to the rule of relevance. But there is no point in applying, say, the rules of consistency and truth since that would be unnecessary overkill.

Before we can *apply* any of the rules for a rational assessment at all, we must answer one of the most fundamental of all questions in content-oriented analysis. Does the senders' message belong to the subject matter at all?

We can use several criteria to answer the question. One conceivable criterion is that a message must contain at least one relevant claim and one pronouncement advanced as a reason in order to be paid any attention to in the first place. But this criterion is too strong. It would preclude an interesting error in debate: claiming something without presenting a single reason pro or con.

Because of this, we will use a weaker criterion. In order that a message shall be considered as belonging to the subject matter, it is enough that it contains at least one claim that deals with the subject. A reason does not have to be presented. If this minimum criterion is not satisfied, then the five standards of assessment cannot be applied to the message at all. We can call this criterion *the fundamental principle of participation*.

One might conceive, however, of a third and even weaker criterion. According to this, it would suffice if the actors claimed that they were participating in the discourse in question. They do not need to present even *one* relevant claim to qualify as participants. They may have spoken entirely beside the point. They may have been silent on the issue. The main thing is that they have stated that they want to be considered participants. But this criterion is too weak to be useful in this context.

Let me conclude this section on the rules of rational assessment of political messages by giving a few concrete examples of such appraisals.

A good case on point is T. D. Weldon's well-known work, *The Vocabulary of Politics*, published in the 1950s. Weldon discourses on the content of Plato's, Aristotle's, Hegel's, and Marx's beliefs on state, authority, freedom, and political rights. His study is an assessment because it seeks to answer questions about the lucidity, organization, consistency, and truth of classical political ideologies.

Another instance of rational assessment of political reasoning is Robert Nozick's famous study, *Anarchy, State and Utopia*. Nozick contributes to the continuing discourse on the so-called Manchester-liberal watchman state. The state is justified only to the extent that it limits itself to guarding citizens against violence, theft, and fraud as well as to enforcing contracts. If it goes beyond this minimum, Nozick claims, it will infringe on the rights of the individual. This means, among other things, that the state is not allowed to use its power to force the more advantaged to help others who are less well off. Nozick's work may be considered an important contribution to an ongoing exchange on the merits and demerits of the minimal state.[19]

1.4.2 Function-Oriented Appraisal

Even function-oriented studies of messages can contain appraisals. Here we decide on the correctness of *expressing* certain messages, *entertaining* them, and *using* a certain channel to transmit them, and so forth. We can ask whether these actions are justified at all or if they are justified in certain given situations.

A function-oriented assessment is made based on standards of assessment different from those used to make a content-oriented rational assessment.

The latter is, as we saw, based on such intellectual ideals as clarity, relevance, consistency and truth. It is the rationality of the message per se that is appraised. In assessing the act of pronouncing or entertaining messages, we may also appraise the rationality of the message being pronounced or entertained. This is, however, only the starting point. Actions must be appraised by other criteria as well. In this context we will only hint at what these criteria are. It may be a matter of assessing the moral quality of the action based on norms for what one should or should not do in various situations. And so it may be a question of assessing the usefulness or efficacy of an action for the attainment of ultimate political goals. Thus, we judge the action's efficacy as a means toward an end. We usually say that we judge an action's means/end rationality.

We may illustrate the method with a fictive, though not unrealistic example. An influential member of the government makes some statement on prime-time television about unemployment. He deals only with unemployment and states emphatically that it has soared dramatically from three to ten percent during the time his party has been in office. Everyone knows that he has told the truth. But this truth creates a sensation in the media and among politicians and the public. His political opponents are jubilant. His political comrades are irate. Was it necessary that he make his statement in precisely this situation, even if it happened to be true? It may weaken the party's position in public opinion and may weaken the spirit of unity within the party. Ultimately, he is jeopardizing the existence of the government. Did he really act correctly? This is the question that can be the starting point for a function-oriented assessment of the action.

Assume instead that the minister expressed himself very vaguely on the issue of unemployment figures, that he continually dealt with the decreasing rate of inflation when reporters asked him about unemployment, and that he presented doctored unemployment figures. Neither the media nor politicians would have reacted very strongly, and the public would have noted the good news about the decreasing rate of inflation. Did the minister act correctly? Even this question falls within the framework of what we call function-oriented assessment.

The examples show two crucial things. In a rational assessment, it is the rationality of the content of the messages that is appraised; in a function-oriented assessment, it is *acts* that are assessed. And the criteria on the basis of which the appraisals are done differ in the two cases. The content of the message is audited against criteria of message rationality or validity. Actions are judged on the basis of moral criteria or criteria of means/ends rationality.[20]

1.5 Explanatory Approaches

Function-oriented analyses can be explanatory. But as we have seen, content-oriented analyses cannot. This can be drawn into our communication model as is illustrated in Figure 1.5.

Most social scientists seem to agree that explanations consist of three essential components:

(1) something that is to be explained;
(2) some explanatory factors; and
(3) a relationship between what is to be explained and the explanatory factors.

What is to be explained may also be called the *explanandum* or the *object of explanation*. That which explains or constitutes the explanatory factors may also be referred to as the *explanans* or the basis of *explanation*.[21] Figure 1.6 is an attempt at visualizing the three main features of an explanation.

The same political message can enter into an explanatory context in two ways. It can be regarded both as cause and as effect. Figure 1.7 shows the role of the message in the context of explanation.[22]

The message M can be included in the explanandum, i.e., considered an effect of something else. This situation is recreated in Figure 1.7A. It is convenient to say that the "message" is an effect of something. As we are well aware of by now, however, it is not the message itself that is explained but some human action related to the message, e.g., some actor's pronouncing it, embracing it, or sending it through a certain channel. Why was the message pronounced by the actor? Why was this particular channel chosen for sending the message? Why does just this actor embrace the message?

When searching for causal factors in these cases, we must naturally look to phenomena that lie chronologically before the message box in Figure 1.5. We are oriented toward the sender side in the communication model. The message is caused by, for example, a series of considerations or attitudes or social background variables. These causes are indicated by $C_1, C_2, C_3, \ldots C_n$ in Figure 1.7A.

But the message M, caused by other events, has been communicated, possibly with effects on others. The latter situation is shown in Figure 1.7B. In this case, the message is part of the explanans and treated as a cause. Now, we will become interested in the receiver side of the communication process. Has the message gotten the receiver to show interest in the content? Has it changed the receiver's attitudes? Has it led to any action? The variables affected by the message M are indicated by $E_1, E_2, E_3, \ldots E_n$ in Figure 1.7B.

Figure 1.7C shows the complete cause and effect analysis of message M.

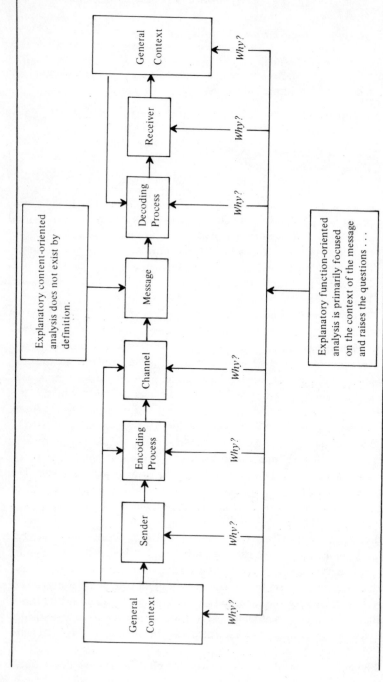

Figure 1.5 Explanatory Function-Oriented Analysis

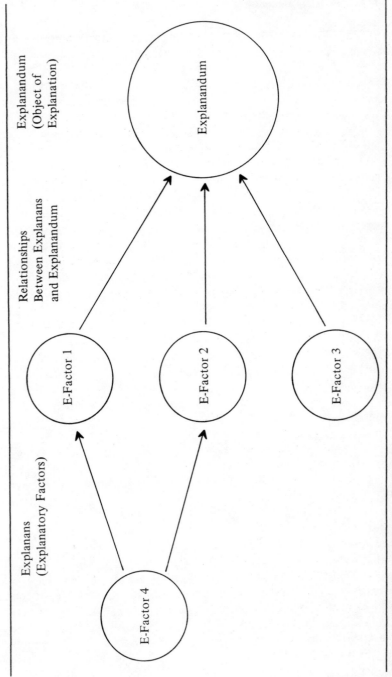

Explanandum
(Object of
Explanation)

Explanandum

Relationships
Between Explanans
and Explanandum

E-Factor 1

E-Factor 2

E-Factor 3

Explanans
(Explanatory Factors)

E-Factor 4

Figure 1.6 Three Components of an Explanation

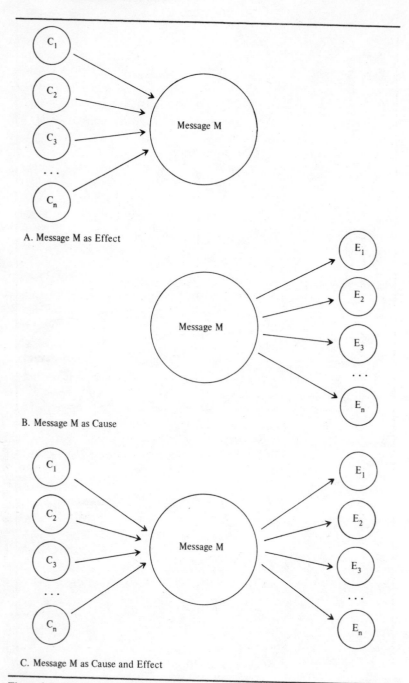

A. Message M as Effect

B. Message M as Cause

C. Message M as Cause and Effect

Figure 1.7 Message M as Cause and Effect

1.5.1   Intentionalist Explanation

In Section 1.1 of this chapter, we reviewed the various explanatory contexts to which messages may be related. None of this need be repeated here. Instead, we shall describe in detail a special type of explanation, which we can call "intentionalist." The reason for this concentration on intentionalist explanation is that it can be confused with rational assessment. By separating out and effectively describing intentionalist explanation, I hope to shed more light on what rational assessment is and is not.

The defining characteristic of intentionalist explanations is that they are based on a specific type of explanatory factors. These may be labeled "motives," "intentions," "goals," "reasons," "reflections," "calculations," or "deliberations" of the actor or the acting party. Common to them all is that the actor is conscious of them and considers them. An intentionalist explanation is aimed at explaining something with reference to the operative motives of an actor.

Perhaps it would not be far-fetched to say that an investigator who tries to carry out an intentionalist explanation looks *inside,* but not *outside,* the actor for explanatory cues. This is only partially correct. One must, for example, differentiate between physiologically and psychologically internal factors. Both take place inside the actor. Explaining an act with reference to physiological factors in the brain—e.g., in the hypothalamus—does not constitute an intentionalist explanation. An intentionalist explanation contains references to psychological factors but not to physiological ones. All explanations that refer to inside factors, thus, are *not* intentionalist. A researcher who tries to make an intentionalist explanation, then, intends to use the actors' conscious deliberations as explanans factors. This does not mean, of course, that every intentionalist explanation must contain references only to conscious calculations.

Researchers can, of course, cite the absence of motives but still claim on very good grounds that they are doing an intentionalist explanation. Assume that our researchers formulate some bold conjectures about operative motives behind a crucial action. When they persistently submit their (we hope) highly informative guesses to severe critical tests, it turns out that the actor was unconscious of these motives. They were not a part of his decisional calculus. Now perhaps the researchers can show hypothetically that if the actor had been conscious of these particular factors, he would probably have chosen another option. The actor chose to act as he did in part because he was *not* conscious of certain circumstances. The explanation of the actor's action will then consist in part of references to missing motives.

It seems natural to characterize this as an attempt to do an intentionalist explanation. The crucial criterion of such an explanation cannot be that positive empirical proof of existing motives must exist. The important thing must be which type of explanans the researchers *intend* to use. Perhaps the following key formulation can serve as a criterion for delimitation: In intentionalist explanation, the intent is to test explanatory hypotheses about operative motives of actors. It is not necessary that one succeed in one's intent of *empirically* proving the *existence* of such operative deliberations in order to be able to speak about intentionalist explanation. The absence of deliberations can be a fact that is included in such explanations. One can also prove the existence of calculations with theoretical arguments and still speak of intentionalist explanations.

A variety of other labels have been used to denote intentionalist explanations. They are, for instance, quite often referred to as "reason explanations." They have also been called "motive," "motivational," or "finalistic" explanations. Georg Henrik von Wright, in his later contributions to the theory of action explanation, declared himself in favor of the term "intentionalist explanations."[23]

Explanation by motivating reasons is sometimes also referred to as "rational" or "rationalistic." The use of "rational explanation" is justified, according to William Dray, because such an explanation "displays the *rationale* of what was done" by offering "a reconstruction of the agent's *calculation* of means to be adopted toward his chosen end in the light of the circumstances in which he found himself. To explain an action we need to know what considerations convinced him that he should act as he did."[24] One obvious drawback with the term "rationalistic" is that it may give the impression that the actions explained are rational in some sense of the word.

In this volume, the phrase "intentionalist explanation" will be used throughout. The term "rationalistic explanation" will be avoided.

We sometimes speak of "causal explanations" in conscious juxtaposition to "reason explanations" or "intentionalist explanations."[25] However, the causal/intentionalist dichotomy is not very satisfactory for two reasons. First, such a classification gives the reader the impression that two principles of division have been used, when, according to baby logic of classification, only one should be employed. Obviously, defining one type of explanation as "intentionalist" implies using a trait in the explanans as a limiting characteristic. An explanation deemed "intentionalist" must refer to the presence or absence of certain kinds of explanatory factors such as motives or intentions. The term "causal," however, cannot refer to any feature in the explanans at all. More often than not it directs us to think of some characteristic trait in the *relationship* between explanans and explanandum. It does not seem unnatural to believe that a "causal" explanation is an explanation demonstrating that there is a relationship of a certain kind between what is to be explained and the factors used in explaining it.

Thus, the term "causal explanation" seems to delimit explanations characterized by a certain relationship between explanans and explanandum, whereas the term "intentionalist" seems to refer to a set of explanations using certain types of factors in the explanans.

Second, juxtaposing causal with intentionalist explanations seems simply to imply that the latter, by definition, cannot be causal. However, this is one of the most hotly debated issues in the philosophy of intentionalist explanations. Some scholars would definitely argue that in intentionalist explanations, there is also a causal—at least a quasi-causal—link between the intentions of the actor and the action to be explained.[26] Others contend that there is no such causal relationship.[27] The former opinion is sometimes called the causalist view, the latter the logical connection argument. It seems reasonable to avoid taking a stand on this complicated issue by not juxtaposing intentionalist explanations with causal ones at all. In this context, I will not deal at all with types of explanation other than intentionalist.

1.5.2 Models of Intentionalist Explanation

What exactly do we want to know when we look for an intentionalist explanation of a speech act? To say that the purpose of such an enterprise is to elicit the agent's intentions—motives, reasons, and so on—when he said what he did is only a beginning. Let us try to develop a little more what could possibly be meant by phrases such as "intentions" and "motives."

A useful point of departure can be found in Donald Davidson's general account of what he calls "rationalizations" in his famous essay, *Actions, Reasons and Causes*. According to Davidson, an intentionalist explanation explains an action only if it leads us to see something the agent saw, or thought he saw, in his action—some feature, consequence, or aspect of the action the agent wanted, desired, thought dutiful, beneficial, obligatory, or agreeable. However, notions like reasons, motives, or intentions are equivocal, Davidson says. They fail to discriminate attitudes from beliefs or aims from perceptions. Realizing this, Davidson attempts to take it into account in his outline of a reason-explanation. Whenever someone does something for a reason, Davidson says, he can be characterized as (a) having an attitude in favor of actions of a certain kind, and (b) believing (or knowing, perceiving, remembering) that his action is of that kind.

related belief. In a fully reconstructed reason-explanation, however, both these phenomena ought to be explicitly stated. They constitute an explanatory factor for the action. Davidson calls this pair of phenomena the primary reason why the agent performed the action.[28]

The idea that a reason or a motive in intentionalist explanation consists of two discernible parts, one evaluative and one cognitive, is a common denominator in most expositions of intentionalist explanations. This is evident, too, from what another authority in the field, Georg Henrik von Wright, has written on the subject. Von Wright, however, has suggested that intentionalist explanations may be cast in a more formal and elaborate framework. It is possible to construe them in the form of practical syllogisms. Consider the following, slightly revised, example:

- From time t_1 to t_2, actor A intended to bring about the goal g at time t_3.
- From time t_1 to t_2, A considered that he could not bring about g at time t_3 unless he performed the action a no later than at time t_2.
- Therefore, no later than the time he thought t_2 had arrived, A did a.

The starting point of an intentionalist explanation, von Wright says, is that someone does or has done something. We ask "why?" The answer is simply to bring about the goal g. It is then taken for granted that the agent considers the action that we are trying to explain causally relevant to the bringing about of g and that the bringing about of g is what he is intending with his action. Maybe the agent is mistaken in thinking the action to be causally related to the end in view. His being mistaken, however, does not invalidate the suggested explanation. What the agent thinks is the only relevant question here.[29]

We may view the actor's intention and deliberation as his reason or motive for his action.

Even in von Wright's account, a reason or a motive entails both an evaluative and a cognitive component. An intention to realize a goal is not in itself sufficient to explain why the actor performed an action of a certain kind. Something more is required. It must be shown that the agent believes that reaching the objective of his intention requires some specific kind of action.[30]

Neither Davidson nor von Wright has had as his primary aim the presentation of suitable models for structuring intentionalist explanations. Above all, they wanted to discuss the type of relation that exists between the explanans and the explanandum in such explanations. Davidson has been a forceful proponent of the causalist view, while von Wright has advocated the logical connection argument just as strongly. The work of both scholars has attracted much attention and discussion.

But their writings can, of course, also be read from the perspective of how one might suitably construct a model for intentionalist explanations. That their work then seems incomplete is not to criticize their contributions. One drawback in Davidson's and von Wright's approaches to simple intentionalist explanations is that it does not shed much light on the fact that political decisions can be consequences of choosing among *many* alternatives for action. Their models seem to provide for only one possible course of action. Another possible weakness in their schemes is that they only differentiate between a cognitive and an evaluative component among the explanans-factors. It may be fruitful to clearly distinguish within the cognitive component between an impact and the possibility of that impact. And within the evaluative component it may be fruitful to distinguish between goals and meta-goals such as those labeled decision rules. These distinctions are made in those models of rational choice that have been developed in the mathematical theory of decision making.

There are, however, many problems with using these so-called *decision-theoretical schemes* as models for intentionalist explanations. One is that explanatory models for obvious reasons ought to be descriptive, whereas rational choice models are prescriptive or normative. Their prescriptive character is obvious from the fact that it is claimed that rational choice models may help decision makers make their decisions more rationally. The models are useful, it is argued, when it comes to structuring the situation before a decision is made. Most of all, however, they may offer some practical guidance as to which course of action is most rational to pursue considering the information available. Thus, in these models the decision is not yet made, and the fundamental question is: Which option is the optimal one to choose? Such a decision theory says how people ought to act, not how they do act.

It might be argued, however, that choice models could be used also to describe how people actually make their decisions. In this case, the issue is not to find out which option is the optimal one to choose. On the contrary, a choice has already been made and the task is to reconstruct those considerations that led the actor to choose as he did.[31]

Let us first consider the theory of *decision under risk*. The distinguishing characteristic of this model is that each course of action is supposed to lead to one set of possible specific consequences and each consequence is assumed

In ordinary discourse, Davidson continues, giving the reason why an agent did something is often a matter of naming either the pro attitude or the to occur with a known probability.[32] An explanation molded according to this theory might be structured according to the following schema. Note that the explanandum is presented first and that all remaining questions deal with the explanans and the relationship between the explanans and the explanandum:

(1) Which option, i.e., course of action, did the actor really choose?

(2) Which set of goals were considered important by the actor and how were these goals ranked according to their importance, i.e., arranged into a preference order?

(3) Which set of alternative options were actually canvassed by the actor before he made his choice?

(4) Which impacts—consequences—were associated with each of the alternative courses of action? How likely were the possible impacts considered to be?

(5) How were the impacts evaluated according to the preference order of the actor, i.e., which were the payoffs?

(6) Given the evaluation of the impacts of each alternative, according to which decision rule or criterion did he finally balance and order all alternatives in order to choose among them?[33]

To simplify the schema a little, stages 2-6 may be collapsed into two main questions: Which alternative options were actually canvassed? Which were his motives for acting as he did? From this we see that motives contain considerations about goals, impacts and probabilities, evaluations of impacts in terms of goals, and evaluation of alternatives in terms of decision rules.

The same choice situation may also be illustrated by drawing a decision tree. But this means that stage 1 above is placed last and that the model begins instead with stage 2. Otherwise, the order of the questions is the same. The decision tree shown in Figure 1.8 depicts a very simple choice situation.[34]

In our simplified case of decision making under risk, the actor considered only three *goals:* maximizing the percentage of votes in the next general election (G_1), maximizing internal support in the party (G_2), and realizing as much as possible of the party program in the energy field (G_3).

The basic *options* he faced were: Should the party remain a member of the coalition cabinet or should the party resign? Remain or resign, this was the choice of options our actor actually canvassed. To the left in the figure, a square, or decision node, is drawn to indicate that at this point a decision was deliberated. The two lines labeled ''remain'' and ''resign'' branching out from the decision node indicate the possible options actually considered by the actor.

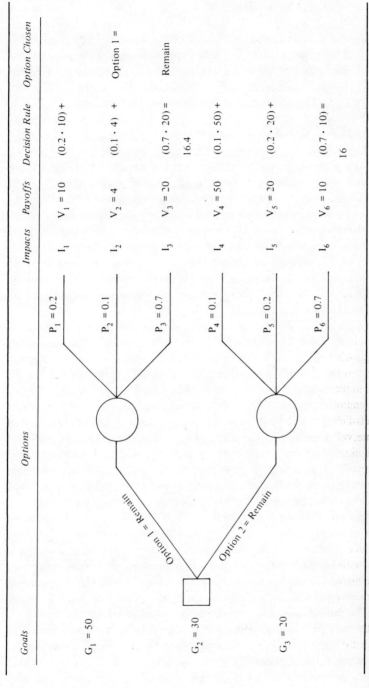

Figure 1.8 Intentionalist Explanation According to the Decision Theory Under Risk

Next we ask, according to the actor, what would actually happen if he followed the upper branch, i.e., if he chose to remain? In this explanatory model, the finding is that he was not quite sure. It all depended on chance. Hence, at the end of the "remain" branch we have drawn a circle, or a chance node, to indicate that at this point there was uncertainty about the possible consequences. The actor calculated three possible *impacts:* a tiny increase in the percentage of votes (I_1); sustained internal party support (I_2); and full realization of the energy program (I_3). Three branches are drawn in Figure 1.8 for these possible results and they are labeled accordingly.

However, some of these consequences were considered more likely to occur than others. In Figure 1.8 we can see that the actual probabilities, P_1, P_2 . . . P_n, were exactly known to our surprisingly well-informed actor. He calculated with 20, 10, and 70 percent probability of each impact. These numbers are recorded along the appropriate branches in the figure. Furthermore, we also see that if all probabilities of all impacts associated with each option are added, the sum is one. This is an assumption in the prescriptive model of decision under risk, which our extraordinarily rational actor actually fulfilled in our example.

Now it is also necessary to bring the utility of the different impacts into the picture. The utility or *payoff* of an impact is its value to the acting agent. The payoff value is an overall measure of the happiness or usefulness of that impact to the actor.[35] In calculating the utility values, the actor relates his goals to the impacts. But the goals, as they have been portrayed so far, are only enumerated. No order is established among them. Our prescriptive model of choice under risk, however, presupposes that goals are arranged on an interval scale so that the utility of each impact can be expressed by a cardinal number. In an explanatory context this means that we have to find out how the actor related his goals to each other into a system of preferences in order to attach cardinal values to the impacts. Let us assume that we found that he assigned the values 50, 30, and 20, respectively, to the goals. Let us also assume that, in relating this preference system to the impacts, he actually assigned the payoffs 10, 4, and 20 to the latter. The payoffs are indicated at the tips of the chance branches.

As to the second option—resign—the actor calculated the following three consequences: a strong increase in the percentage of votes (I_4); strengthened internal support (I_5); and partial enactment only of the party's energy policy (I_6). The probabilities and payoffs are indicated in the figure.

The problem now is to reconstruct how the actor used all this information to reach his decision. First, let us take a look at the payoffs. Interestingly, they seem to be considerably greater for the option "resign." For that option, the greatest payoff is 50, the smallest 10. This compares very favorably with option "remain," which has only 20 as the biggest payoff and 4 as the smallest. To resign, then, seemed to entail larger chances of profit than to remain if one looks only at goal achievement.

If we now direct our attention at the probabilities, we can make an additional interesting observation. Our actor's calculus shows that the chance of attaining the highest payoff values for the option "resign" was very small. On the other hand, the chance of attaining the highest payoff values for the option "remain" was very large. This seems to indicate that he should perhaps have chosen "remain" instead of "resign."

So now our actor stood there with facts pointing in two entirely different directions. He could not get any further with the help of his original goals; they had already served their purpose by pointing out the payoff values. He could not get any further with probability calculations; he was certain that they were correctly calculated. Now he needed something else, a *decision rule,* a criterion or a standard with which to rank options even though the payoffs and probabilities, taken separately, pointed to different solutions. A decision rule, then, is a sort of meta-preference, a meta-goal that the actor uses to order the options that he earlier analyzed as well as he could in terms of impacts, probabilities, and payoffs.

In prescriptive decision theory under risk, one decision rule has gained wide acceptance. It is that of maximizing expected utility. The expected value associated with each option is computed by multiplying for each possible impact of the option its probability with its payoff and adding the products. A rational actor is assumed to select that option whose expected value is maximal in the sense of not being exceeded by the utility of any other option.

The formula for calculating expected value looks like this:[34]

Expected value of 0_1 $P_1 \times V_1 + P_2 \times V_2 + P_3 \times V_3$

Expected value of 0_2 $P_4 \times V_4 + P_5 \times V_5 + P_6 \times V_6$

In our example, the model is not used prescriptively but rather, in order to explain. Let us assume that our empirical investigation of the motives shows that our fantastically conscious actor made his computations exactly according to the formula presented. The actual expected value he arrived at was 16, 4 for option 1 and 16 for option 2. He chose option 1, then—to remain in office.

It seems obvious that this model generates interesting yet difficult problems when used in an explanatory context. We are usually far from having the empirical data required by the scheme. It is not very easy to conceive of political situations where the actors have such certain knowledge that they can predict the probabilities of future impacts of a proposed action. Furthermore, it assumes that impacts are ordered by the actor on an interval scale. It is not sufficient, then, to establish that the actor actually rank-ordered the impacts, that he arranged them on an ordinal scale showing that impact I_1 was preferred to I_2, I_2 to I_3, I_3 to I_4 and so on. We must exhibit exactly how much he preferred I_1 to I_2, I_2 to I_3, I_3 to I_4, and so on. The exact distance between the impacts on this value scale must be established, not just the rank order between them. This means that the numerical values the actor assigned to each impact must be shown. In most political situations, this seems unrealistic.

More realistic are those assumptions underlying a second decision model, the model of *decision under uncertainty*. Here, the assumptions are similar to those of the model just presented, with one exception. This model does not assume that the actor knows the probabilities of the impacts. This lack of knowledge gives rise to problems concerning the choice of decision rule. Contrary to decisions under risk, there is in the prescriptive theory of decisions under uncertainty no unanimity as to which decision rule is the most appropriate one. Several quite different criteria have recently been set forth in decision theory.

The best known of them is the famous *maximin rule*. It directs us to choose the option that maximizes the minimum payoff. Each option is thus appraised by looking at the worst impact associated with that option. The optimal choice is the option whose worst possible impact is better than, or at least as good as, the worst possible impact by any alternative. The optimal choice is the one with the best worst state.[37]

The maximin rule obviously represents a policy of extreme caution. Taking the maximin principle seriously means, as pointed out by Harsanyi, that you could never cross a street (after all, you might be hit by a car); you could never drive over a bridge (after all, it might collapse); you could never get married (after all, the marriage might end in disaster). Concludes Harsanyi: "If anybody really acted in this way he would soon end up in a mental institution." The examples show the basic trouble with the maximin principle. It makes the decision maker extremely dependent on highly unlikely unfavorable contingencies, regardless of how little probability is assigned to them.[38]

Of the two decision-theoretical schemes described here, the model of decision under uncertainty seems to be most useful in empirical contexts. This is primarily because we have abandoned the prerequisite of knowing the probabilities of the impacts. But even this model contains prerequisites that political decision makers seldom fulfill, e.g., the demand that every impact must be assigned a utility value. Political goals are hardly ever ordered in interval scales. This leads to problems, of course, when the aim is explanatory.

If we do not find empirical evidence for utility values, then we can assume, of course, that such values have existed. We can also add other assumptions of the same type to the model. We then arrive at an explanation of the type: Given this and this assumption about rationality, the action A is explained by the motives M_1 and M_2. The assumptions such an explanation is founded on are, of course, open to empirical criticism.

Both the model of decision under risk as well as the model of decision under uncertainty contain features that are undoubtedly very useful in an explanatory context. They direct us to look for those alternative options that were actually considered. They draw our attention, in other words, to the fact that the actors may have calculated with different alternative actions. This is important since it is desirable to have certain variance in that which is to be explained. Further, the models help us to search for the actors' calculations of the consequences of the various alternatives and for their preference orders and preference systems. They also lead us to look for the decision rules considered and actually used by the actors. In all of these cases, these models give us tools to reconstruct, after the fact, what an actor's decision calculus could have looked like and so explain why he made the decision he did. In all of these respects, the model of decision under uncertainty seems superior to the simple primary reason model that was used—though for an entirely different purpose—by Donald Davidson.

1.5.3   A Mortal Sin: Confusing Rational Assessment and Intentionalist Explanation

Finally, now let us indicate the most important differences between a rational assessment and an intentionalist explanation of political messages.

Logically, we are dealing with two fundamentally different activities. In practice, though, they exhibit many similarities. Both deal with actors and their speech acts. Both direct attention to positions and reasons, decisions and grounds. The vocabularies are to a large extent identical. This means that the two approaches are easily confused. In political contexts, it is sometimes advantageous to confuse the two in order to score cheap but valuable points.

Let us observe the following, admittedly naive, example which can nevertheless serve the purpose of illustrating the risks for confusion. Presume you attend a workshop meeting by the European Consortium for Political Research. In a lobby you meet a famous policy analyst who starts a discussion on government overload and suddenly exclaims: "In 1960, the scope of the public sector averaged 15 percent of GDP in Western countries whereas by 1975, it had increased to 70 percent." This flat assertion puzzles you a little, so a bit surprised you ask, "Why?"

One possible aim of this surprised question may be more adequately conveyed if we frame it as follows: "What good reasons are there for saying that the scope of the public sector has increased that much?" In asking that question we make it evident that we are interested in the intellectual content of the utterance. We wish to know the reasons for maintaining or accepting what is asserted. The information that we wish to elicit will be used for the purpose of assessing the validity of the content of the message. Interpreted in this way, our surprised question is assessment-oriented.

The question, "Why is this so?" may also be open to an explanatory-oriented interpretation. Startled, we may ask ourselves, "Why on earth does this knowledgeable man assert that the scope of the public economy has increased that much when he should know better?" Or, more simply, "What are his reasons for saying this?" The wording of this tacit version of the question is similar to the formulation of the assessment-oriented question just presented. We see, for instance, that the terms "reasons" and "saying" are used on both occasions. This should not deceive us because in the explanatory case we are looking for something different. Now we wish to know why the asserter *pronounced* what he did. The focus is not on what is said, but on the *saying* itself and the *motives* for saying it. The question pertains to the fact that something was communicated and the motivating forces behind this.

There is also another explanatory-oriented interpretation of our basic question. In this version, the question, "Why is this so?" may be rephrased as, "Why on earth does he believe this?" or "What are his reasons for believing this?" What is at stake now is neither the content of what is said nor the fact that the asserter is saying something. Our attention is focused on another fact, the fact that the asserter believes in what he says. Why does he entertain this particular message? And what are his motives for doing so?

Even though there are other explanatory-oriented interpretations of our basic question, the two already cited will have to suffice as examples. With them we have illustrated that assessment-oriented and explanatory-oriented questions may be deceptively similar. But we have also shown two decisive differences between the two approaches.

In a rational assessment of political messages, we are interested first of all in what is communicated; in an intentionalist explanation, we are interested in the fact that something is communicated or entertained. In a rational assessment, we are interested second of all in reasons as evidence, verification, or support for what is said. In an intentionalist explanation, on the other hand, we look for reasons in the sense of operative motives behind the fact that something is said or entertained. We may need to develop the latter difference in more detail.

Grounds for a claim can be expressed and accessible for direct observation. Motives, on the other hand, are inner psychological entities that are never directly ascertainable. No one has ever directly observed a motive and no one ever will. Then how are we to establish the existence of motives? This is completely necessary if we decide to undertake an intentionalist explanation.

The answer, of course, is that it must be done indirectly. The existence of a motive must be inferred from something else. In intentionalist explanation, we must always wrestle with an inference problem, one that can be avoided entirely when we are involved in rational assessment.

One possibility is to refer to the actor's own statements about what his motives were.[39] This is illustrated in Figure 1.9.

We can look for pronouncements that are immediately tied to the action we are trying to explain. These statements may be pronounced after, at the same time as, or before the action was made. In all of these cases, the pronouncements are used as indicators of underlying motives. Methodologically, we are making an inference from the pronouncements to motives.

Making inferences is an especially problematical activity. Statements justifying the action can, of course, be identical with the actor's motives. But we can never be certain. In political contexts, the expressed purpose of a measure can be entirely different from the real motive. The pronouncement can be made with the conscious intent of deception. One might want to conceal motives that for one reason or another cannot stand the public light. There is something to Voltaire's dictum: "[M]en use . . . words only to conceal their thoughts." One might also want to present one's motives in a more advantageous light than is actually true. If the pronouncements are made after the fact, e.g., when the researcher interviews the actor, the actor may have forgotten what the original motives were.

Justifying statements, then, cannot simply be equated with motives. This is important to keep in mind when comparing rational assessment and intentionalist explanation.

A third interesting difference between rational assessment and intentionalist explanation concerns the overall purpose of the effort. The ultimate rationale for a rational assessment is to appraise the validity of the whole reasoning. The intellectual quality of the messages is measured against a set of standards for valid or rational discourse. The purpose of an intentionalist explanation, however, is to exhibit which deliberations an actor made before he said or believed in something, and which way they induced him to act in

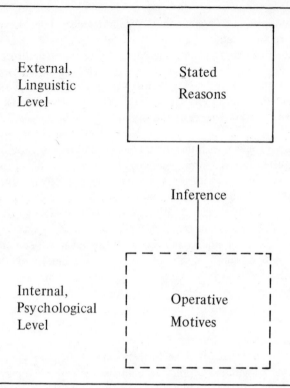

Figure 1.9   Inferences from Stated Reasons to Operative Motives

the way he did. Whether his considerations, or motives, were obscure, irrelevant, inconsistent, or false is not of primary interest in this explanatory context. The main purpose is not to assess, appraise, or judge his intentions. The ultimate point is to show that they really have been entertained by the actor and that they have propelled him to say what he did or believe what he said.

We have now concluded our attempt to provide a review of various approaches to political messages. An important purpose of the review has been to delimit content-oriented analysis from other perspectives. In the coming chapters we will try to describe the different steps in a content-oriented analysis of political messages. We will deal with both the descriptive and the assessive parts, but we will emphasize the latter—the rules for a rational political discourse.

2

TOPIC SELECTION, PROBLEM FORMULATION, AND CONCEPT FORMATION

The belief that we can start with pure observations alone, without anything in the nature of a theory, is absurd. . . . Observation is always selective. It needs a chosen object, a definite task, an interest, a point of view, a problem. And its description presupposes a descriptive language, with property words; it presupposes similarity and classification, which in its turn presupposes interests, points of view and problems.

Karl R. Popper
Conjectures and Refutations

To catch a dependent variable is the first rule of academic survival.

Richard Rose, in a lecture at the First International Summer School for Comparative Research, Cologne,
1972

It has been asserted that students of political communication manage quite well without their own tools of analysis. After all, all claims and chains of reasoning are expressed in the material. All the researchers need do is open their eyes and observe, paraphrase, and quote the pronouncements of the participants in the controversy.

This entirely untheoretical outlook is fundamentally wrong. We cannot be satisfied to portray the lines of reasoning in a message with the sole aid of the message's own words and expressions. On the contrary, every qualified description of a text must be in terms of analytical language. The researchers must decide what they want to investigate, they must develop their own terminology, and then use it consistently to describe the content of the message. In order to describe the object language of the message we must develop and use our own analytical language.

2.1   Object Language and Analytical Language

The term "object language" is used here to refer to the language in the message being analyzed. It may be the language used in a study by a government commission, in a decision by a parliamentary committee, in a book by a political philosopher, or in a newspaper editorial. By "analytical language," we mean in this case a language system that also contains, over and above the pronouncements of the object language, concepts and pronouncements that refer to the object language. It is the language that we use to talk about the object language. Our analytical language is a metalanguage in the sense that it is a language by means of which we make statements *about* another language.

It is also a special language, a technical language. It is developed to satisfy the need for precision in communication of political knowledge. It should not be confused with ordinary language, in which the need for elimination of obscurity is less.

Analytical language can also be compared to a kind of basic equipment. Just as farmers need tools to cultivate their land, researchers need tools to analyze a text.

Research consists of finding, stating, wrestling with, and solving problems. "Science starts from problems, not from observation," Karl R. Popper wrote in his *Conjectures and Refutations*. Nothing can be more correct. A researcher must first of all establish a problem, an interesting, difficult, fertile problem, a problem of some depth, one worth investigating. We cannot overemphasize that this may be the single most important moment in all research. A clearly stated problem will help the investigator make wise decisions in every remaining stage of the research process. The problem formulation is a crucial tenet in the analytical language of the researcher. Problems are the fountain of scientific research.[1]

Various schemes of analysis are other central elements in the analytical language. Such schemes consist of sets of concepts that may be used to classify the answers given in the message to our research problem. With the aid of such schemes we can join sundry attempts at discourse into a more comprehensive whole. The schemes also help us clear away that which is not essential to answering the research problem. They help us to order and classify claims and reasons into more comprehensive patterns and to compare them and confront them with each other.

How do we *discover* problems and schemes of analysis? There is no methodology for that in the same sense that there is a methodology for solving problems and classifying solutions to problems once problems and schemes are invented. Methodology belongs in the context of justification, not in the context of discovery.

There are, however, certain rules of thumb we may follow. We may look for shortcomings in theoretical and empirical work of others and state problems to overcome these flaws. We may borrow problems from neighboring academic disciplines. We may also read newspapers, reason with friends, participate in informal bull sessions, brainstorm with colleagues, listen to contributions at conferences, or gain inspiration from political debate. Another important source of ideas is reading the material that we have decided to work with.

It is a truism that, from a logical point of view, schemes must be invented before they can be applied. This simple insight is commonly misunderstood. It is often believed that researchers must have hit upon and worked through a scheme of analysis before they can begin their study of the material at all. But we can study the same object language both for the purpose of generating the scheme and for applying it, once it is generated.

Researchers may begin by examining a given set of messages from the perspective of some vaguely worded question. And then they may come upon a more precise delimitation of the problem. They then continue their study of the material and discover after a while that the formulation of the problem must be honed further. There may be many rounds of study of the object language and sharpening of the problem on the level of the analytical language before the final problem has been chiseled out.

Once the problem and the scheme of analysis have been given their final formulations, we must return once more to the material. Our purpose now is to classify solutions to the problem. For the first time, we find ourselves in the context of justification.

In the context of discovering and inventing problems, rule-governed and standardized procedures are set aside in favor of the creative, unconventional, and innovative. "The mere selection of a problem, i.e., of a question for worthwhile inquiry, is as a rule no mechanical act but an act of the creative mind, and in the most important cases, one of genius," Arnold Brecht declares in his seminal *Political Theory*. "There is no rule of procedure to describe how the creative mind hit on such a question, except that it must be guided by curiosity, inquisitiveness, and independent creative imagination."[2]

2.2   The Six-Step Approach to Problem Refinement and Argument Description

Framing a problem is the key to the whole investigation. This is, however, more easily said than done. In practice, inquiries seldom start with an accurately elaborated problem. The point of departure is usually an extensive, indeterminate notion of a *topic* that must be successively refined in order to pass as an acceptable problem formulation.

The stage of problem refinement in argumentation analysis may be arranged on three different levels. The next phase in the research process—describing actual claims and reasons—may also be divided into three steps. The following arrangement, inspired by Michael Scriven in his book *Reasoning,* [3] will be called the Six-Step Approach to Problem Refinement and Argument Description:

(1) Select a topic.
(2) Frame a research problem about the topic.
(3) Form concepts and construct schemes for classification of conceivable solutions to the research problem.
(4) Identify pertinent lines of reasoning in the materials.
(5) Work out their meaning by careful reading of the argumentative materials.
(6) Portray in one's own conceptual language the lines of reasoning found in the materials.

The first three theoretical steps will be discussed in this chapter, while the last three empirical steps will be left to the next.

2.3   Converting Topics into Problems

The framing of a research problem is usually an iterative enterprise. Its successive character is most easily brought out by an example.

Suppose an unexperienced researcher has come up with the admittedly very comprehensive idea of assessing "the controversy over nuclear energy." For a one-person study, however, this is an impossible subject. It is too vast. It must necessarily be narrowed down into something much more manageable. I agree entirely with Mario Bunge's recommendation: "Begin by asking clear-cut and restricted questions: adopt the piecemeal approach to problems instead of starting with sweeping questions." [4]

The most important way of limiting the topic is to pick out some particular, substantive aspect of it. In this case, an obvious first step would be to distinguish between peaceful and military uses of nuclear energy. The two aspects cover enormous ground. A political scientist would probably quail before the thought of simultaneously assessing both of them in any competent way. Let us suppose, therefore, that our researcher leaves out the military side altogether and concentrates his efforts on the peaceful use of nuclear energy. Let us assume that the subject, consequently, is rephrased as "the controversy over nuclear power."

But still, our student seems to have bitten off far too big a chunk. Again, a more refined framing can be achieved by means of analysis of the key concepts in the wording of the topic, i.e., nuclear power and controversy.

In the seventies, there was wild dissension in many Western countries surrounding the issue of nuclear power. But what was disputed? Numerous problems seem to have been involved; four of them are outlined below:

(1) Should nuclear power be maintained or abolished?
(2) If it is to continue, which security regulations should be adopted?
(3) Which ancillary industrial operations should be performed within national borders? Uranium mining and milling? Uranium enrichment? Fabrication of fuel rods? Reprocessing of spent fuel? Storage of spent fuel and radioactive wastes?
(4) Which of these facilities ought to be owned and managed by national governments?

Now, let us suppose that our researcher chooses to investigate whether nuclear power should be maintained or abolished. Still, the concept of nuclear power refers to many different things. Naturally, light-water reactors are included. These are fueled by enriched uranium. But heavy-water reactors are also included. Because very few countries have chosen heavy-water technology, which is based on natural, nonenriched uranium, let us assume that our investigator decides to exclude the debate on those from further considerations.

Now our researcher has begun to penetrate the real issue. The more involved he gets, however, the more he understands that the subject demands further delimitation. At the same time, the justification for each delimitation becomes more difficult to understand without expert knowledge of the substantive issue.

In the next step, he begins to think about whether the subject should also be limited with respect to the stages of the light-water reactor fuel cycle. The four main technological options are summarized in Figure 2.1.

The first cycle implies a once-through use of nuclear fuel. No raw energy material from spent fuel is recovered. The second type entails recovery of uranium through reprocessing of spent fuel and recycling of it in ordinary

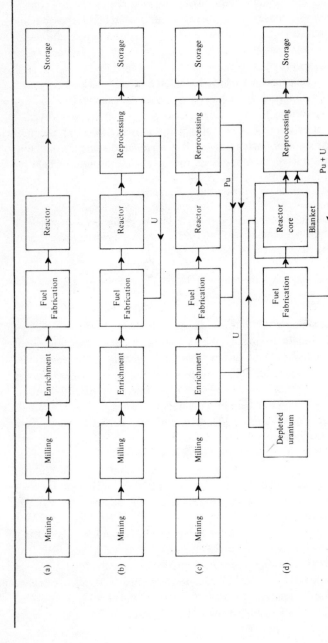

(a) once-through.
(b) uranium recycle.
(c) uranium plus plutonium recycle.
(d) uranium plus plutonium recycle in fast breeder reactors.

Figure 2.1 Nuclear Fuel Cycles

light-water reactors. All plutonium is stored with wastes. The third cycle implies separate recovery of uranium and plutonium and recycling of both in ordinary light-water reactors. The fourth possibility, finally, is that of recycling uranium and plutonium in so-called fast breeder reactors.[5]

Our author realizes, of course, that it may be reasonable to omit some of these options in order to scrutinize the debate on the others even more carefully. He also knows, naturally, that the main controversy has concerned light-water reactors. As a consequence, let us assume that he decides to ignore entirely the dispute over fast breeder reactors and concentrate all his efforts on the heated altercation over light-water reactors whether they are used as in cycle 1, 2, or 3.

So far, our systematic student has considered in the second part of his initial topic formulation "the controversy over nuclear energy" only the concept of nuclear energy. Let us now see how he treats the concept of controversy in order to narrow down and clarify his research problem.

First, he may consider a geographic limit. Light-water technology has been hotly debated in most Western countries. Living in Sweden and studying at the venerable Uppsala University, it may come naturally to our researcher to concentrate on the Swedish controversy.

Indubitably, there is also a need for a time limit. In the Swedish case, it may be convenient to concentrate the study on, say, the period since 1973. It was in the spring of that year that the nuclear power debate flared up, leading to the fall of two governments and to a national referendum on nuclear power.

Furthermore, the drawn-out battle over Swedish nuclear power has taken place in different arenas: state commissions, parliamentary sessions, committee meetings, regulatory agencies, newspaper editorials and columns, professional journals, radio and television programs, and so forth. A selection has to be made according to some defensible principle. Suppose that our researcher opts for studying positions taken by political parties.

Having subjected himself to stringent limits of aspect, time, geography, and forum—eight different delimitations in all—our exemplary researcher now has a research problem that may be stated as a purpose-description in the following dull though complete manner: The purpose of the study is to assess discourse by Swedish political parties since 1973 on the future of nuclear power—in the sense of light-water technology.

What has been said so far shows how a broad subject may be boiled down into a specific research problem. The transition is effected by analysis of the main concepts of the successive topic formulations. This illustrates another crucial point. Whenever we engage in the study of political communication, we must invariably deal first with questions of definition. If we do not know the precise meaning of the terms in our research question, we cannot know exactly what we are asking, and consequently, what answers we should look for.

2.4   The Tripartite Structure of Research Problems

Although problem formulations in political message analysis exhibit an enormous range of substantive and stylistic variations, there is a common structure to them. Three types of concepts are always involved. Again, let us consider our exemplary research problem; now, though, we shall frame it as a question: What are the merits and drawbacks of the arguments by Swedish political parties since 1973 on the future of nuclear power?

The expression "Swedish political parties since 1973 on the future of nuclear power" indicates the subject matter of the study. "Discourse" hints as to what we are looking for about the subject matter. It is also obvious that we wish to portray the lines of discourse actually advanced by the participants in the controversy. Thus, we have expressions indicating:

(1) the subject matter of the study;
(2) discourse on the subject matter; and
(3) actually advanced lines of discourse on the subject matter.

In his *Theory and Method of Social Research,* Johan Galtung observed that research problems in many social science traditions exhibit the same tripartite structure. He never touched upon argumentative analysis in his book.[6] I would argue, however, that it too may be subordinated under his general thesis. In all traditions the terms used to indicate the various parts of the problem differ considerably. Undoubtedly, these differences in verbal outlook have impeded argument analysts and, for example, survey researchers from realizing common methodological problems.

In general social science methodology, the notions of units of analysis, dimensions, and values are regarded as indispensable tools for structuring research problems. In combination, they also constitute the so-called data matrix.

Units of analysis refer to the objects of investigation, i.e., those empirical phenomena about which information will be collected. They are the constants of the inquiry. *Dimensions* are concepts indicating those characteristics of the unit that will be explored. They refer to the variables of the inquiry. Finally, there are the *values* of the units on the dimensions to be

General Terms	Units	Dimensions	Values
Variable Language	Units of Analysis	Variables Studied	Values on Variables
Stimulus-Response Language	Units of Analysis	Conditions, Stimuli	Outcomes, Responses
Survey Language	Subjects, Respondents	Psychological Objects	Responses
Intentionalist Explanation Language	Actors, Agents	Actions and Motives	Actual Actions, Actual Motives
Content-Oriented Analysis Language	Topic, Subject Matter	Lines of Reasoning	Actually Advanced Lines of Reasoning

Figure 2.2 The Tripartite Structure of Research Problems Expressed in Different Social Science Languages

studied. These are the empirical characteristics the units actually have on each dimension.

The different expressions used for units, dimensions, and values in various social science traditions are summarized in Figure 2.2 (adapted from Johan Galtung's pioneering analysis of the data matrix).[7] The terms used in the languages of content-oriented message analysis and intentionalist explanation are added here to the three types of language displayed in Galtung's original table.

The data matrix may be used as a convenient way of arranging all social science materials according to units, dimensions, and values, with units in the rows, dimensions in the columns, and values where rows and columns meet. This device makes the tripartite structure of research problems particularly visible (see Figure 2.3).[8]

If we replace the expression "units" with "topics," "dimensions" with "lines of reasoning," and "values" with "actually advanced lines of reasoning," then we have the basic structure of the research problem in argumentation analysis. In our example on nuclear power, each of the Swedish political parties may be considered a unit of analysis. The designations U_1 to U_5 can be assigned to the Left Party Communists, the Social Democrats, the People's Party, the Center Party and the Moderate Unity Party, respectively.[9]

Discourse on nuclear power is treated as a dimension. If we focus in our investigation on four types of claims, we can label them D_1 to D_4. Similarly, reasons for or against claims can be numbered D_5 to D_n. The actual claims advanced and reasons offered are entered into the various boxes of the matrix and given designations from V_{11} to V_{mn}.

	Dimensions				
	D_1	D_2	D_3	D_4 $\cdots$ D_n	
U_1	V_{11}	V_{12}	V_{13}	V_{14}	V_{1n}
U_2	V_{21}	V_{22}	V_{23}	V_{24}	V_{2n}
Units U_3	V_{31}	V_{32}	V_{33}	V_{34}	V_{3n}
U_4	V_{41}	V_{42}	V_{43}	V_{44}	V_{4n}
$\vdots$ U_m	V_{m1}	V_{m2}	V_{m3}	V_{m4}	V_{mn}

$U_1 \cdots U_m$ = units of analysis.
$D_1 \cdots D_n$ = dimensions.
$V_{11} \cdots V_{mn}$ = values.

Figure 2.3   The Data Matrix

2.5   *The Traditional View of Meaning*

In the introductory section of this chapter, we stressed the need for an analytical language. Problem formulation is an important part of such a special language, as are schemes of analysis. Both are created by analysis and formation of concepts. In this section we will examine the issue of how concepts are formed.

The most important tool for concept formation is definition. Definition is specification of meaning. What do we refer to when we speak of the meaning of a word or an expression? To find an answer, we must briefly ponder a celebrated problem: What is the meaning of meaning?

According to a conception that may well be called traditional, it accords with common sense to distinguish two dimensions or aspects of meaning for

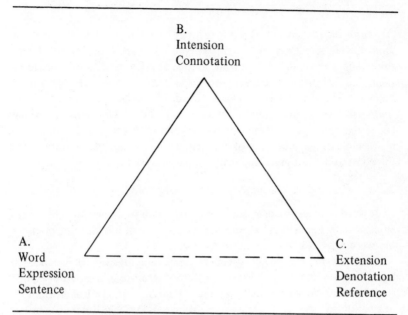

B.
Intension
Connotation

A.
Word
Expression
Sentence

C.
Extension
Denotation
Reference

Figure 2.4   The Ogden-Richards Triangle

a word or an expression: the *intension* or *connotation* of a word or an expression and the *extension, denotation,* or *reference* of a word or expression. When we speak about specifying the meaning of a word, then, we can be talking about three things: (1) specification of the intension of the word, when the word has an intension; (2) specification of the extension of the word, when it has an extension; or (3) both. Ordinarily, perhaps, we indicate the intension of a word when we specify its meaning. However, this is far from always the case. All three different meanings of the expression "specification of meaning" are prevalent.

The two English linguists, Charles K. Ogden and I. A. Richards, presented this triadic relation between word, intension, and extension in the form of a triangle.[10] Figure 2.4 is a somewhat revised version of the Ogden-Richards triangle.

In the original version, the three lines of the semantic triangle were all solid. But it has since been discovered that the relationship between word (A) and extension (C) is indirect; in moving from word to extension one always passes intension (B). We indicate that the word-extension relation is rarely direct by drawing a dotted line between A and C.[11]

2.5.1   *Intension and Connotation*

Words have intension. But it is difficult to clearly explicate what intension is. One might say that intension consists of those attributes which a thing must have in order for a word to truly apply to it. A word's intension then, consists of a collection of attributes that determine whether a thing belongs to the class referred to by the word.[12] In his *Guidelines for Concept Analysis* — certain to become a standard in its field — Giovanni Sartori has suggested that "the intension or connotation of a term consists of *all* the characteristics and properties of that term, that is, assignable to a term under the constraints of a given linguistic-semantic system."[13]

2.5.2   *Extension, Denotation, and Reference*

A word's intension must not be confused with its extension. The extension is what we are talking about when we use a word. It is the thing or things the word refers to or is the name for.

The extension may be a relatively common thing. It may, for instance, be a person (as in the words "President Ronald Reagan"), a group of people ("all former U.S. presidents"), a book ("*Who Governs,* by Robert Dahl"), or a building ("the White House in Washington, D.C."). But the extension may also be abstract: "the Grand Old Party" refers to the Republican party of the United States.

Obviously, intension is different from words and their extensions. Words have intension; they also have extension. Intension, however, is identical with neither the words nor their references. This distinction is easier to maintain if we note that:

(1) words can have intension but no extension;
(2) words can have extension but no intension;
(3) different words can have the same intension and the same extension;
(4) different words can have different intensions but the same extension; and
(5) different words cannot have identical intensions and different extensions.

Words can have intension but no extension. Words can still have intension, even if extension is missing entirely. We may call such words *empty terms.* Examples are "the current president of Canada," "the ongoing war between Belgium and Holland," and "the second political party in the Soviet Union's Supreme Soviet." The phrase "the current president of Canada" is not without meaning, even though Canada's formal head of state is a monarch.[14]

Words can have extension but no intension. Some words can have reference without intension. One view of the matter is that many proper names are words with extension without intension. The name "Helmut Schmidt" certainly has extension: it refers to a specific person who in 1982 happens to be a leading Social Democrat in the Federal Republic of Germany. But does the name carry any meaning? More than a few philosophers would argue that it certainly does not. Proper names, while they have extension, are devoid of intension. This is why we have drawn a dotted line between A and C in the semantic triangle.

Different words can have the same intension and the same extension. According to its constitution, Switzerland is governed by what is called the *"Bundesrat,"* the *"conseil fédéral,"* or the *"consiglio federale."* Spelling and pronounciation indicate that these are three different terms—in German, French and Italian. Interestingly, the intension seems identical in all three cases: they all signify the Swiss cabinet. The extension is also identical in all three cases, i.e., all past, present, and future Swiss cabinets.

Different words can have different intensions but the same extension. "General Charles de Gaulle" and "President Charles de Gaulle" refer to the same famous Frenchman. "General Charles de Gaulle" says that the extension is a general called Charles de Gaulle, while "President Charles de Gaulle" says that the extension is a president called Charles de Gaulle. We know that these two persons are identical, but since "general" is not synonymous with "president," the two expressions carry different intensions. We must conclude, then, that two expressions can have identical extension but different intensions.

Different words cannot have identical intensions and different extensions. Strictly stated, extension is a function of intension; as intensions are established, unique extensions are also determined.[15]

To sum up, it is easier to know what meaning is not than to specify what it is. If we are to avoid undue complication, the most we can say in positive terms is that meaning is what is expressed by the expression. In negative terms, meaning is neither the expression itself nor its extension. However, we might also say that meaning is clarified by specification of both intension and extension. To specify meaning in a comprehensive way is not to indicate either intension or extension. It is to specify both.

At this point, it may also be convenient to introduce the notion of a *concept*. A concept is related to all three corners of the semantic triangle. A concept has intension, it is expressed by a word, and it may refer to an extension. To analyze concepts means to study the relationships between words and their meanings in the sense of their intensions and extensions.

We have consistently used so-called singular terms to illustrate the differences between intension and extension. Proper names like "Charles de

Gaulle'' constitute a special type of singular term. Other linguistic expressions are also included. We do not usually call them proper names, but they are used that way in the sense that they pretend to refer to one and only one thing or person. ''The current president of Canada'' may lack extension, but it is just as much a singular term as ''General Charles de Gaulle.'' The decisive factor is the pretension of extension, the fact that both expressions do the same job as proper names.

Notice, however, that the traditional theory of meaning is also applicable to other linguistic entities, such as general terms. The latter do not stand for one but for many different objects. ''President'' is a general term. Such a term is said to denote those objects for which it stands; and those objects are called the denotation of the term. We also speak of the extension of reference of general terms. ''President,'' then, denotes all the presidents in the world; they are, collectively, the denotation or extension of the term. The meaning of a general term is called its connotation or intension.[16]

The traditional theory of meaning also applies to complete sentences. A sentence is a string of words that can have intension and extension. A full descriptive sentence such as ''General Charles de Gaulle was elected president of France in 1958'' certainly has intension. ''General Charles de Gaulle was chosen president of France in 1958'' is not the same as the first sentence, though it expresses the same intension. Clearly, two different sentences can express the same intension.

A descriptive sentence is commonly said to express a ''proposition.'' When we grasp the meaning of a descriptive sentence, we understand the proposition it expresses. A descriptive sentence, or a proposition, may be either true or false. Two true sentences (or propositions) have the same truth value: the value of being true. Two false sentences (or propositions) also have the same truth value: the value of being false.[17]

2.5.3   Ambiguity

Words can carry several different meanings in the sense of different intensions. When there is uncertainty about in which of these meanings a word is actually used, the term is employed ambiguously. For example, we all know that the term ''democrat'' can have different meanings. A democrat is an advocate of a form of government in which the *demos*, the people, rule. But a person practicing social equality may also be called a ''democrat.'' The word is equivocal. The property of being equivocal—one word having many meanings—is illustrated in Figure 2.5a.

A synonym for equivocity is homonymy; a homonymous word is one that has at least two meanings.

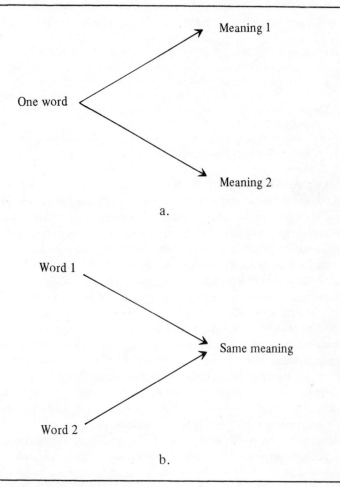

Figure 2.5 Homonymy and Synonymy

The opposite of homonymy is synonymy. One word is synonymous with another if both have the same meaning. Synonymy—one word having many meanings—is illustrated in Figure 2.5b.[18]

Equivocity is an extremely common characteristic of modern language, as well as of political language. In his *Guidelines for Concept Analysis,* Giovanni Sartori argues "that in a natural language almost no word is univocal, i.e., endowed with only one meaning."[19] We can easily convince ourselves of this by looking up in dictionaries of Western languages a few of the most common daily expressions, words like the English "and," "or," "be," "some," or "all."

Consider, for instance, the word "state." Webster's *New Collegiate Dictionary* lists eight different meanings; the most common are:

(1) a mode or condition of living, i.e., a state of readiness;
(2) a body of persons constituting a special class in a society (estate);
(3) a politically organized body of people, usually occupying a definite territory, especially one that is sovereign (e.g., the states of Western Europe);
(4) the political organization of such a body of people (e.g., the Swedish state machinery);
(5) one of the constituent units of a nation having a federal government (e.g., the United States of America).

One equivocity that has been very important in the history of political philosophy is associated with the German expression *Aufhebung* in Hegelian and Marxist dialectics. The verb *aufheben* can assume at least two different meanings: (1) abolish and (2) raise to a higher *niveau* (level) and preserve while surpassing. When Marx speaks of the *Aufhebung* of the state, is he using the first or second of these meanings or is he vacillating between the two? Marx is probably equivocal in this regard.[20]

Although almost every word has a variety of meanings according to the time and circumstances, we are usually able to understand what a specific word means in a given context. An equivocal expression is used unambiguously when it is clear which meaning it really carries in a particular situation. An equivocal word is used ambiguously only when we are unable to determine which of two or more alternative, plausible meanings to adopt in a particular situation. Following Max Black quite closely, I would suggest that a linguistic expression is ambiguous in a certain usage when in that occurrence the interpreter is unable to to choose between two or more alternative meanings of the word, any of which would seem to fit the context.[21]

Thus, ambiguity is defined relative to context and interpreter. A word may be ambiguous in one usage and unambiguous in another. A sentence may be ambiguous for one listener and unambiguous for another.

Once we have noted the difference between equivocity and ambiguity, equivocity poses no problem in and of itself. If an expression is equivocal, but is used in a completely clear way, then we have no problem using it to communicate with others. The only time we have trouble with multiplicity of meaning is when it is unclear which meaning is intended.[22]

Concepts such as ambiguity, equivocity, and homonymy are undoubtedly tied to the relationship between word and intension. Ambiguity is a defect in the word-to-intension relation. Giovanni Sartori has shown this in a pedagogically very illuminating way by making a few simple additions to the basic Ogden-Richards semantic triangle (see Figure 2.6).[23]

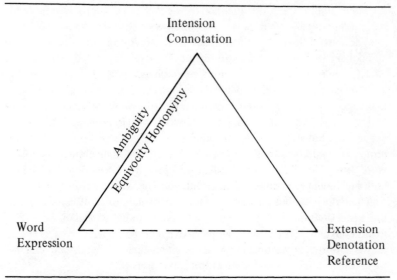

Figure 2.6   Ambiguity, Equivocity, and Homonymy

Ambiguities may be easier to discern if we classify them and give them names. The following typology of ambiguity is fairly standard in the literature. It is based upon what the ambiguity confuses:

(1) word and reference;
(2) process and product; or
(3) lexical and contextual meaning.

A peculiar characteristic of language is that it can be used to refer to itself. A word, for instance, may refer to itself. In this particular context, *confusion between expressions and their references* may arise. Consider the following simple example:

> Democracy is a form of government in which citizens may elect their leaders and in which civil rights are widespread. One precondition for a stable democracy is social and economic equality among the citizens.

The term "democracy" may be used equivocally in this example. In the first case, the term is probably used to point to a symbol, the word "democracy" itself. It says that the word "democracy" carries a certain meaning. In the second case, "democracy" is used to refer to the set of all past, present, and future democracies in the world.

Our example directs our attention to one of the most pervasive features of natural languages—their capacity to refer to or describe themselves. Language can be reflexive, or turned back on itself. A property of almost every symbol seems to be that we can refer to it merely by mentioning it.

The terms "mention" and "use" are often recommended in the literature as a means to differentiate between the reflexive and nonreflexive use of language. A symbol is "used" when it refers to something outside itself; it is "mentioned" when it is used to refer to itself. Following John Lyons' suggestion, however, I will make no further use of these words as technical terms. It would be almost impossible to avoid the nontechnical use of the word "use," and it could be confusing to allow such a common word to have both a technical and nontechnical meaning in a book on argument analysis.[24]

There is a better way to eliminate this sort of ambiguity. When we refer to the expressions themselves, we will put them in quotation marks. According to this convention, then, our example above must be changed from "Democracy is a form of government in which adult citizens may elect their leaders" to " 'Democracy' signifies a form of government."

Ambiguity is quite easy to discern in our example. But in many other cases it can be extremely difficult to detect. This mix-up gives rise to a paradox, which we will discuss in the next chapter in connection with Mannheim's thesis on the relativity of knowledge, that has given and still gives social theorists a headache. One can even say that hardly any ambiguity has spawned so much muddled thinking as this one. From Plato through Hegel and Marx and even up to contemporary philosophers of the so-called classical western tradition, it has been believed that insights into the nature of things could be achieved through the study of what words really mean. Philosophers believed that the connection between symbols and objects was natural and not the result of human convention. They assumed, therefore, that properties of the symbol indicated properties of the object. They believed they could penetrate into the essence of the state, politics, capitalism, or national interest by studying what the words meant.[25]

A common characteristic of many words is that they may fluctuate between emphasis on a *process* and the *ensuing result of that process*. The term "policy analysis," to take a handy example, exhibits this characteristic shift of meaning. It can mean the business of studying policy options and policy instruments as well as the end result of this activity in the form of written reports. "Policy analysis produces policy analyses," E. S. Quade pointed out on the subject of this ambiguity in his well-known book, *Analysis for Public Decisions*.[26]

A whole batch of terms used in scholarly language exhibit a similar shift between process and product, e.g., "science," "philosophy," "thinking," "investigation," and "study."

Max Black has suggested that this shift between process and product is particularly characteristic of words ending in "-tion." "Regulation" may refer to what is done while something is being regulated or to the result of such an activity. "Administration" may mean administering or the body performing the administering. But any word that refers to an activity is subject to this kind of shift and may generate a corresponding type of ambiguity.[27]

Many words seem to have a general or standard meaning. But each speaker or writer usually gives the words a more specific meaning to fit each individual context. There is a risk, then, that the interpreter will confuse the *general meaning* with the *specific contextual meaning*.

Some people use the word "conservative" to signify people who are opposed to changes in the status quo. But those with some basic knowledge of the history of political ideologies know that the term may signify something quite different. A political conservative may advocate fundamental reforms and changes in the existing state of affairs in order to attain conservative goals. Was Italian fascism "conservative"?

The use of the term "liberal" is another example. A liberal in modern American usage advocates government regulation of free enterprise as well as government intervention in the market economy in order to secure basic social security for all citizens. The term "liberal" also retains its original meaning—a liberal political view emphasizes individual freedom from government restraint, free competition, the self-regulating market, and private ownership of the means of production. This is a considerable shift in meaning; if not taken note of, any discussion of whether a certain party's policy is "liberal" or not may be confusing indeed.

All kinds of shifts in meaning treated here can be summarized in a general formula. The cases above dealt with words or expressions that sometimes refer to A and sometimes to B. And the referents A and B relate to each other in some fashion. According to our typology of ambiguity, in the first case, A was a word and B its reference; in the second, A was a process and B the product of this process; and in the third, A was the dictionary meaning and B its contextual meaning. This illustrates what Max Black calls the principle of the spread of meaning. Whenever two things are related to each other, there is a tendency in every living language for the name of one to also be applied to the other.[28] Knowledge of this general tendency enhances our chances of

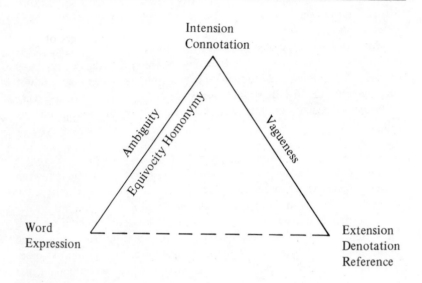

Figure 2.7 Ambiguity and Vagueness

discovering and criticizing ambiguities and faulty reasoning caused by ambiguous words.

2.5.4 Vagueness

Vagueness is a semantic property quite different from ambiguity. A term is vague if it does not delineate clearly cases where it is or is not applicable. The outer border delimiting the extension of a vague word is so fuzzy that it is impossible to know what is included in the extension and what is not. A vague term may, for instance, demarcate a field where it may undoubtedly be applied and another where it clearly cannot be applied. In addition, though, there is a diffuse borderline area where it is truly unclear whether the word can be used or not.[29]

We recall that ambiguity is always a matter of flaws in the relationship between term and intension. Vagueness, on the other hand, reflects flaws in the relationship between intension and extension. Following Sartori, we have already demonstrated how ambiguity can be represented on the semantic triangle. If we add vagueness, the triangle looks like the one in Figure 2.7.[30]

Returning to our discussion of the word "democrat," suppose that it is used to refer to an advocate of a form of government, in which the *demos,* the people, rule. Now, we might argue that an advocate of the U.S. system of government is a "democrat." This individual is an adherent of a system in which the body of citizens comprises a *majority* of the members of the community. And it may seem reasonable to assert that a vindicator of a political system in which those who take part in political decision making constitute the majority of the people is a "democrat."

However, some people would certainly argue that this is a crazy interpretation of the word "democrat." In the United States, the state is inevitably an instrument by which the bourgeoisie maintains its exploitation of the masses, its dehumanization of men, and its distortion and impoverishment of human capacities. Only supporters of socialist states are democrats because they favor states in which the final aim is human equality. The majority may not take part in political decision making in these countries, but the state is ruled in the *interests* of the *many*, and that is a necessary property of a democracy.

What belongs to the extension of the term "democrat" is obviously contested in our example. It seems that—taken at its face value—our original phrase—advocate of a form of government in which the *demos*, the people, rule—is vague, in that it *may* entail both interpretations. It is not clear who is considered a democrat or not under the expression.

This uncertainty surrounding what belongs to the extension of a term is not due to a lack of empirical information. No matter how much knowledge we get about adherents of the U.S. system of government or supporters of the idea of people's democracy, we will still be unable to tell whether they really are democrats in the sense of vindicators of a form of government in which the *demos*, the people, rule. Indeterminacy is linked to the relationship between the intension of the expression and its extension and is not dependent on our current knowledge. We are faced, in other words, with a genuinely semantic problem.[31]

The language of politics and political science abounds with vague expressions like "policies of peace," "détente," "revolution," "neutrality," "totalitarian states," "power," "political representation," "socialism," and "progressive forces." There are also words that do not seem vague. "Attorney General" is one such word, since there are precisely defined rules for who is Attorney General. "Republic" is another such word; a country is either a republic or it is not, and there does not seem to be any fuzzy border area. Other nonvague words are "voting participation," "roll call," "parliamentary decision," "factor analysis," and "binomial distribution."

Vagueness is generally more difficult to master than ambiguity. Our goal, therefore, should not be to eliminate all vagueness from scientific terminology. We should satisfy ourselves with making our words as precise as our inquiry demands. We should strive to clear away any vagueness that, in our special context, might give rise to misunderstanding and unanswered questions.[32]

2.6   Definition

After these preliminaries, it is time to return to the problem of constructing an analytical language. To repeat, the most important tool for concept formation is definition. How shall we proceed when we form concepts through definition?

2.6.1   Stipulative, Reportative, and Explicative Definitions

One answer has been proffered by Felix E. Oppenheim in his article on the language of political inquiry in *Handbook of Political Science*. He differentiates between stipulative, reportative, and explicative definitions. All types can be used, he seems to mean. Most commendable, however, is explicative definition, which constitutes a combination of the other two.

Stipulative definitions regulate language. They give rules for how terms will be used or in what sense words will be employed. It is self-evident that they are enormously useful in content-oriented analysis and other types of research. In order to express himself clearly, the researcher must stipulate how he will use key terms in his analytical language.

Some authors, for example, Irving Copi, link the expression "stipulative definition" to the very first introduction of a brand new term. Others use the expression in a wider sense. According to them, one can either stipulate a meaning with a newly coined term or give a technical meaning of an already well-known one. In the following we will hold to the latter, broader usage.[33]

The following stipulative definition is drawn from an article by Fred W. Riggs which has attracted attention in the field of comparative politics:

(1) A *bureaucracy* is defined here as a hierarchy of non-hereditary positions subject to the authority of the executive.

The definition should, of course, be read in such a way that the expression to be defined—the *definiendum*, bureaucracy—is synonymous with the defining expressing—the *definiens,* a hierarchy of nonhereditary positions subject to the authority of the executive. Instead of the latter, lengthy expressions, Riggs declares that he will use the first, much catchier one.[34]

A stipulative definition is, in the words of Carl G. Hempel, "a convention which merely introduces an alternative—and usually abbreviatory—

notation for a given linguistic expression."[35] Giving a stipulative definition of the expression E entails that we adopt a rule of synonymy saying that E will be used in the same sense as conveyed by another, usually longer and supposedly more familiar expression.

Stipulative definitions express rules or regulations and have prescriptive content. They do not express factual assertions. In a formal sense—as in our example 4 below—they may remind us of propositional sentences. However, they do not tell us anything about the state of the world. This means, of course, that they cannot be true or false.[36]

An interesting question is, of course, *what* is defined in stipulative definition. Most of us would probably answer as Hempel: It is *words* or *expressions* that are defined. We may also assert, however, that we define *concepts,* i.e., nonlinguistic entities, for which expressions are names, but we cannot ascertain that we define things or states of nature.[37]

Typographically, we can write stipulative definitions in several ways. In our example 1 above, Riggs chose to distinguish between definiens and definiendum by italicizing the latter. Another possibility, mentioned by Hempel, is to put definiendum and definiens within quotation marks. Then the whole expression takes the following form:

(2) Let the term "bureaucracy" be synonymous with "a hierarchy of nonhereditary positions subject to the authority of the executive."

A third alternative dispenses with italics and quotation marks. It introduces instead the notation "= Df," which may be read as "equal by definition." In this form, our example appears like this:

(3) Bureaucracy = Df if a hierarchy of nonhereditary positions subject to the authority of the executive.

All of the ways of writing out stipulative definitions presented so far are useful. One has only to choose a method and hold to it consistently through the presentation.[38]

In many situations it can seem overly pedantic and annoying to mark stipulative definitions in special ways. We can choose to write it out as an ordinary, simple be-sentence. Then, our definition would look like this:

(4) Bureaucracy is a hierarchy of nonhereditary positions subject to the authority of the executive.

Reportative definitions describe the way actors define their concepts and actually use their expressions. These reports consist of propositions indicating the sense in which words or expressions are used. Naturally, they may be true or false. This is the decisive difference between reportative and stipulative definitions.[39]

Reportative definitions also have a given place in a scientific enterprise. In order to criticize the concepts of others, of course, we must describe them first. On the other hand, reportative definitions can obviously not be used directly to stipulate concepts for an analytical language, but they can be a starting point for such usage regulations. So we have arrived at Oppenheim's third and most important category, explicative definition.

Explicative definitions are something between reportative and stipulative definitions. Like stipulations, they regulate the meaning of an expression. They also report about how the expression is commonly used; a characteristic of good explicative definitions is that they conform as nearly as possible with established usage.

The originator of an explicative definition begins by portraying the customary usage of the term to be explicated. He attempts to show the dimensions with reference to which the word is usually defined. Then he may name the various dimensions, establish their limits more precisely, and deepen their content. Once he has done all this, it may turn out that the word is used in several different senses and that in some respects, it is not sufficiently precise for scientific communication. Then he may throw in his own stipulation in order to attain the necessary clarity.

The definition he has arrived at differs from ordinary language; this is what is attained through the stipulation. In this regard, it is entirely correct to speak of a reconstructed concept. However, the departure from ordinary usage is not too great; this is what the description of various customary meanings should guarantee.[40]

This method of definition is particularly useful in the social sciences. In their analytical language, social scientists must to a great extent employ the terms of ordinary discourse, though in sharpened and clarified form. Surprisingly, though, the method has been used very little. We agree gladly with George J. Graham, Jr.: "The process of explication has not been employed in political science as often as perhaps warranted."[41]

An instructive example of how one can proceed with an explicative definition may be drawn from Robert Heeger's *Ideology and Power: An Analysis of Antonio Gramsci's Quaderni.* Heeger's first task in this incisive and original work is to portray Antonio Gramsci's definitions of the concept of ideology. The purpose is to portray the intellectual content that Gramsci brought to the concept of ideology.

It is worth pointing out that Heeger is concerned with Gramsci's *concept* of ideology, and not with his definition or use of the Italian counterpart to the *word* "ideology." He has not limited his analysis to Gramsci's definitions of the *word* "ideology." He also describes the intellectual content of a group of *synonymous* expressions. Gramsci's concept of ideology could, of course, have been indicated with the Italian counterpart to the word "ideology." As I interpret Heeger, it can also be expressed with the help of other words.

Heeger obviously needs an analytical language in order to execute this description; he forms one based on his own explication of the concept of ideology.[42]

Heeger's explication can be divided up into four steps. They are common to all work with explicative definitions. They can be summarized as follows:

(A) perusal of the relevant literature to see which dimensions the concept (of ideology) usually consists of; an ordering of these dimensions into a useful overview;
(B) characterization of each dimension with the aid of suitable terms;
(C) clarification of the limits and content of the dimensions; and
(D) discussion of and decisions on what should be included in the final stipulative definition of the concept (or ideology).

After a review of the literature, Heeger arrives at six requirements that must be fulfilled in order that a phenomenon can be labeled "ideology." It must be

(1) a set of convictions that
(2) is prevalent,
(3) demonstrates coherence, and
(4) fulfills specific psychological, social, or political functions; or
(5) has a social or political content; or
(6) is invalid.

With this grouping of the dimensions that are usually included in the concept of ideology, Heeger has passed step A of the process of making explications. He has collected and ordered the dimensions from the most to the least comprehensive.[43]

All proposed definitions in the literature contain a common feature, which Heeger labels "convictions" (step B in the explication process). The expression "ideology," then, is usually defined as some sort of *set of convictions*. Now many authors avoid this term, writing instead about "ideas," "statements of fact," "values," "theories," "conceptions," "programs," or "strategies." But all of these expressions refer to statements of value (step C). The term "convictions" is a common label for both these types of notions. Should all of this be included in a stipulative definition of ideology? Heeger thinks so. It is unwise, he argues, to decide already in the definition whether ideologies consist primarily of cognitive or emotive elements, and so the definition is analytically neutral in relation to Gramsci's texts (step D).

Then, asks Heeger, what kind of set of convictions is an ideology? Many authors think that ideologies are sets of convictions that are *prevalent*. Prevalence is, of course, a vague expression. Heeger distinguishes between a strong and a weak requirement. The weak one says that at least two people must embrace the conviction for it to be prevalent. The strong requirement, on the other hand, holds that parts of large social groups or a majority of the members of a society must embrace the conviction for it to be an ideology.

Should the prevalence demand be included in an explicative definition of a fruitful conception of ideology? Heeger thinks it should, but he does not want to include any more detailed clarification of the expression in the actual definition. The size of the groups that embrace the conviction in question can vary greatly from hypothesis to hypothesis. The question of a closer determination of the prevalence of the set of convictions should, in other words, be an empirical issue.[44]

Heeger goes through the demands of coherence, psychological, social, or political functions, a specific content, and invalidity in a similar way. He assumes a critical position on whether they should be included in the concept of ideology.[45] He then sums up, adding the stipulative element to his explication:

(5) Ideology = Df (i) a set of convictions that are held by (ii) a large social group and that (iii) contain values and factual conceptions that covary and that (iv) fill political functions and that (v) contain elements of action-oriented political thought.[46]

With the aid of this explication, Heeger then tries to uncover what Gramsci adds to the concept of ideology. Thanks to the conceptual scheme, he can pose relevant questions, see what Gramsci's concept contains and does not contain, and classify the content so that an overview is created. We can ignore how all of this was done here.[47] We should only add that Heeger—using the words of Oppenheim—has made an explicative definition of the concept of ideology that then has been used for achieving a reportative definition of Gramsci's concept of ideology.

In sum, it is evident that stipulative definition is a useful, nay, indispensable tool for constructing an analytical language. This is especially the case with those stipulations that constitute the final result of processes of explication.

2.6.2   *Intensionalist and Extensionalist Definitions*

There are other ways of looking at definitions than the three just mentioned. We can, for instance, talk about intensionalist and extensionalist

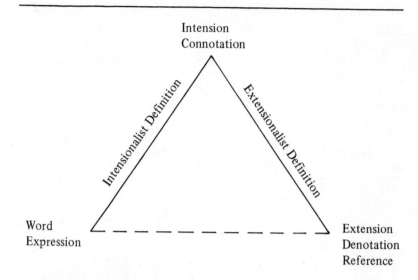

Figure 2.8 Intensionalist and Extensionalist Definition

definitions. An *intensionalist definition* says something about the relation between words and their intension (meaning, connotation) whereas an extensionalist definition is associated with the relationship between intension and extension (denotation, reference). This can be elucidated in the version of the Ogden-Richards triangle illustrated in Figure 2.8.[48]

It seems that both intensionalist and extensionalist definitions can be referred to as stipulative as well as reportative. They are obviously neutral as far as the division into regulative and descriptive definitions goes. In this context, however, we will assume that they are always stipulative. As stipulations, in what way can they contribute to formation of concepts for an analytical language in argumentative analysis? This can be brought out by means of an example.

"Policy evaluation" has become a fashionable term in applied social science. But it is far from clear-cut. Presume that we stipulate the following definition:

(6) x is a policy evaluation = Df x is a report containing systematic reasoning on the question of whether the goals that should guide a policy have been fulfilled and if, in that case, the recommended policy instruments contributed to goal achievement.[49]

"Policy evaluation," then, refers to analyses of actually existing policies, i.e., *after* they have been decided upon. The word may also refer to

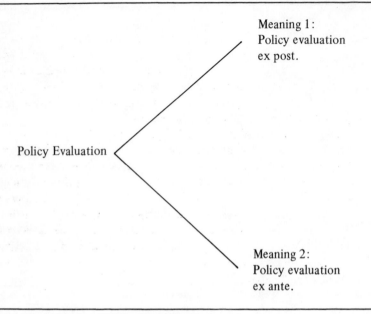

Figure 2.9 Ambiguity of "Policy Evaluation"

analyses of policy options *before* they are decided upon and implemented. The word evidently has two different meanings that can be difficult to keep separate. The relations between the word and its intension is not satisfactory. We can illuminate this ambiguity as illustrated in Figure 2.9.

If we return to our definition 6, we see that it clearly precludes meaning 1 in Figure 2.9. Since the definition cleared away a potential ambiguity, i.e., since it clarified the relationship between the term and its intension, it is an intensionalist definition.

Assume now that we undertake an empirical study of policy evaluations. Our intensionalist definition proves to be too vague to provide sure guidance. We are genuinely unsure as to whether certain reports are really to be labeled policy evaluations or not. These borderline cases must naturally be eliminated. This is done through specification of the extension or through *extensionalist definition*.

The following is a brief rendering of positions that could conceivably be part of an extensionalist definition of "policy evaluations":

(1) only written reports that consist of at least one standard typed page of text are coded as policy evaluations;

(2) different methods of data collection yield different policy evaluations; if in the same report there is one measurement made through interviews and another by means of an examination of application blanks, then it is coded as two different policy evaluations; and

(3) varying samples of investigated objects yield varying policy evaluations, even if the same policy instrument is being investigated and the methods are the same; in other words, if we ask two entirely different groups the same questions about the same policy instrument, then the resulting analyses are coded as two policy evaluations.

Our example shows how ambiguity and vagueness are eliminated by intensionalist and extensionalist definition. It also shows another thing. A comprehensive analysis of concepts to be used in empirical investigations has to do with more than just intension. The extension or reference must come into the picture as well. A proper conceptual analysis should include specification of intension as well as of extension. Why? If we devote ourselves only to specification of extension, we get operationalized concepts without theoretical import. If we engage only in specification of intension, then we get theoretical concepts without empirical import. In empirical investigations we must combine the theoretical aspect with the empirical. That is why the two forms of concept formation must be combined. This thesis was argued by Hempel in his *Fundamentals* and has been developed more recently by Giovanni Sartori in his *Guidelines for Concept Analysis*.[50]

There is one additional way of looking at concept formation; it contrasts very sharply with the basic view that has pervaded our entire presentation of the subject. This is the doctrine of *real definitions*. According to this view, definition is not primarily a matter of terms or concepts but has more to do with things and states of affairs.[51] This view is completely wrong. It should be dismissed from argumentation analysis and social science in general. It will be dealt with in more detail in the next chapter.

2.6.3   Criteria for Adequate Definitions

We have repeatedly stated that stipulative and explicative definitions cannot be judged true or false. They must be appraised by other standards. These criteria suggest that definitions should be

(1) relevant to the research problem, e.g., analytically neutral;
(2) lucid;
(3) not too broad;
(4) not too narrow;
(5) not circular; and
(6) fruitful.

Definitions should be relevant to the research problem. This is a fundamental standard. If concepts are not formed according to the demands of the research problem, the research question cannot be answered properly.

Definitions should be analytically neutral. By this we mean that they should make it impossible to do a nonpartisan analysis of the positions to be investigated in the object language.

According to Robert Heeger, Gramsci defined ideology as a set of convictions including both statements of fact and statements of value. Heeger's research problem was to ascertain whether the Italian philosopher included, among other things, both cognitive and evaluative components in his conception of ideology. It would have been wrong for Heeger in his own definition of ideology to establish that the concept includes only the one component, e.g., cognitive elements. Then his concept would not have been analytically neutral in relation to the problem in the object language that it was to elucidate. The concept would not have been really useful for finding an answer to the stated research problem.[52]

Definitions must be lucid. The defining statement should be clearer and more readily understood than the expression being defined.

Definitions should be neither too broad nor too narrow. They must be framed so as to exclude all items that in ordinary language do not properly fall under the term being defined, and encompass all characteristics that properly fall under the expression being defined.

By definition, the properties of broadness and narrowness are associated with the comprehensiveness of a term's extension, not with the size of its intension. The extension of a broad concept is too large. Adversely, the reference of a narrow concept is too small. In creating an analytical language, a balance must be struck between these two extremes.

There is, however, a kind of inverse logical relationship between the size of the intension and the comprehensiveness of the extension. The smaller the extension, the bigger the intension; the smaller the intension, the bigger the extension.[53]

Again, "ideology" may be used as an illuminating case. To deserve the signification "ideology," we remember, a phenomenon must be (1) a set of convictions that (2) is prevalent, (3) demonstrates coherence, and (4) fulfills specific psychological, social, or political functions; or (5) has a social or political content; or (6) is invalid.

Assume we define ideology with respect to the first dimension only:

(7) Ideology = Df a set of convictions of some type.

This concept seems outrageously broad. It cannot discriminate ideologies from a large array of other sets of convictions that are not commonly given that label, such as scientific theories, conceptions of gardening, or notions about what constitutes a good novel.

The problem with social science concepts, however, is usually not that they are too broad. The difficulty is sooner that researchers keep on including too many characteristics in the intension of their concepts, making their fields of application too tiny.

Assume we fashion the following definition of ideology:

(8) Ideology = Df a set of convictions embraced by at least one-third of the population, rather systematically expounded, giving directives for political action, having a political content, offering a biased view of states of affairs, and consisting mainly of false propositions.

This definition contains elements from all six dimensions in Heeger's explicative scheme. This makes the concept exceptionally narrow. It is obviously too narrow.

Narrow definitions suffer from two weaknesses. First, they hamper empirical research: They make it impossible to empirically test a number of hypotheses about such phenomena to which the expression to be defined customarily refers.

There is a connection between what is included in a definition and what can be tested empirically. In order that we should be able to empirically test a proposition about a phenomenon, that characteristic, which this proposition is a proposition *about,* may not be an element of the definition of the phenomenon in question. That which is included in the definition as a characteristic of a phenomenon, then, cannot be made into an object of an empirical proposition about this phenomenon. It follows from this that the more characteristics that are included in the definition of a phenomenon, the fewer that will be left over for empirical hypothesis formation about the phenomenon.

Take, for instance, the question of to what extent ideologies contain biased selections of facts and false propositions. We might want to find out whether some ideologies offer a view of society that is more biased and less true to reality than do others. If we work with the concept of ideology (8) above, this is not possible. Bias and falsity are included there among the definitional criteria. In order to be labeled "ideology," the pronouncements in question must be biased and false. The question of whether ideologies contain biased selections and false propositions is decided by definition. This means that it cannot be made an object of empirical testing.

Second, narrow definitions are impractical to handle because their proper application presupposes an enormous empirical labor. This objection is, as we shall see, a reflection of the former one.

Before we can test propositions *about* ideologies, we obviously must identify the phenomena in the real world that we label *as* ideologies. In order to establish what are ideologies according to definition 8 above, we must carry out comprehensive empirical investigations. From among all political convictions in our society, we must distinguish that set of convictions that is embraced by at least one-third of the population. This means that we must undertake an enormous empirical survey investigation. And once we have arrived at such a set of convictions, we must separate out that set that gives directives for political action, that gives a biased view of reality, and that primarily consists of false propositions. Clearly, this too would require an immense amount of empirical research. The impractical part is that these enormous labors must be done in order that certain sets of convictions can be delimited *as* ideologies, and not in order to test empirical propositions *about* ideologies. In spite of our Herculean labor, we have succeeded only in establishing the object of the study, but we have not expressed a single empirical statement *about* that object.

Apparently, excessive narrowness and broadness should be avoided in concept formation. Neither of these criteria, however, offers accurate guidance in concrete situations. Their meaning is too opaque.

The rule that we should avoid narrow definitions might be formulated in a more positive and forceful way: Strive for *minimal definitions*. Even though this criterion is very important, none of its proponents have yet succeeded in giving it any exact meaning.[54] It is probably not possible to find a general formulation of a minimal rule that would provide unequivocal directives in each and every single situation. Let us attempt the following formulation: A definition of W is minimal if in the defining expression only those characteristics of a phenomenon are included that are absolutely indispensable to discerning the phenomenon in question, provided that we want the defining expression to conform with W's meaning in ordinary language.

This means that as few properties as possible are used to portray the meaning of the word to be defined. Sartori has argued that we should at least get a clear idea of what should *not* be regarded as the phenomenon we are focusing on.[55] It is easy to agree with this. On the other hand, this contribution gives us little in the way of concrete guidance. Perhaps we can rely on nothing but sound judgment here.

A minimal definition of ideology might be framed like this:

(9) Ideology = Df a coherent set of convictions having a societal or political content and containing elements of action-oriented political thought.

This is a considerably broader definition than Robert Heeger's definition 5 above. This is an asset, however, because in my opinion, the latter violates the minimal criterion. Nothing associated with prevalance or political functions should be included in a definition of ideology.

Definition 9, on the other hand, is not as broad as definition 7. This is a strength since the latter is so broad that it tends to lose its substantive content.

Definitions should not be circular. The whole of the term to be defined should not appear in the defining expression.[56]

Definitions should be fruitful. This criterion is, by far, the most important one. It is also the most difficult one to elucidate. It will be presented in the next section.

2.7 Classification

The standards for adequate concept formation dealt with so far are general. They are applicable when, to return to the language of the data matrix, we delimit our unit of analysis. If we wish to study ideologies or positions on nuclear power, we must define what we mean by these expressions. Concept formation, however, must be carried further. Ideologies or positions on nuclear power must be divided into various types. In other words, we must classify. This is a special kind of concept analysis that should be treated in a separate section.

A few criteria of adequacy are common for definition in general and for classification. Among them is the requirement of conformity with the basic research question. Other standards are applicable only to classification. The most crucial of them are:

(1) the classes should be distinguished according to one and only one basis of division (*fundamentum divisionis*);
(2) the classes should be jointly exhaustive; and
(3) the classes should be mutually exclusive.

The *single basis rule* is a guard against confusion. Assume nuclear options are divided into three classes: that nuclear power must be phased out, that it should be expanded, and that there should be a concentration exclusively on heavy-water reactors. Whether this categorization conforms with the single basis rule is contingent upon what is meant by nuclear power. If we follow our earlier definition, then we are referring to light-water but not heavy-water reactors. In that case, our classification violates the rule. Evidently, there are two distinct principles of division involved: whether we should concentrate on the light- or heavy-water technique, and whether the light-water technique should be expanded. Given this, we can draw up the diagram illustrated in Figure 2.10.

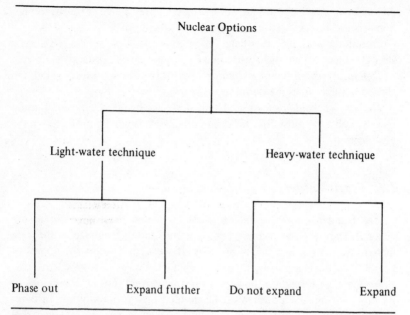

Figure 2.10   Nuclear Options: Illustration of Single-Basis Rule of Classification

We see that the categories are ordered on various levels, or ranks, from the most general to the most specific. The expressions "light-water technique" and "heavy-water technique" distinguish two classes that are coordinate. This means that they belong on the same rank. The phrases "phase out" and "expand further" distinguish two classes that are subordinated under the class of light-water technique. They reside on different levels.

Classes should be *jointly exhaustive*. This implies that they must take account of the whole domain or universe of discourse. We should be able to place all elements of the domain of discourse in some category of the classification scheme. No element may be left outside.

Assume we distinguish between two nuclear options: that nuclear power must be phased out and that it should be expanded further. Assume moreover that in reality we find a group of politicians demanding that nuclear power must be maintained at the present level. In which of the two classes do we place this last group? The politicians do not want to phase out nuclear power and so do not belong in the first class. But neither do they want to expand it further, and so they do not belong in the second class. We clearly lack a pigeonhole in which to put this option. The classification is not exhaustive. There is an element in the domain of discourse, circumscribed by the concept of nuclear option, that does not fall into either of the two classes. To become

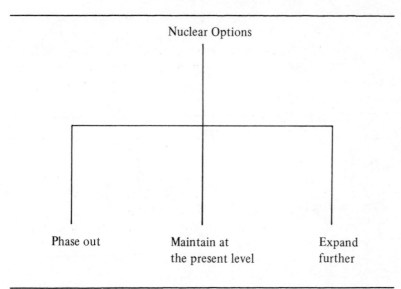

Figure 2.11 Nuclear Options: Illustration of the Exhaustiveness Rule of Classification

exhaustive, a third class must be included in the classification scheme: Nuclear power should be maintained at its present level. This new scheme of classification is illustrated in Figure 2.11.

The rule of *mutual exclusiveness* holds that we must be able to unambiguously order every element in the universe of discourse into one and only one category. We must not be able to place any element with certainty into two or more classes simultaneously. There must not be the slightest doubt as to which class is the proper one for a certain element.

Again, assume that nuclear options are divided into two classes: that nuclear power should be phased out and that it should be expanded further. When we apply this scheme to the Swedish case, we find that there actually exists a political group that advocates a far more complex alternative. In the future, these people argue, nuclear power must be phased out; before then, however, it must be expanded. We ask ourselves how we can fit this alternative into our scheme. Since the alternative advocates phasing out nuclear power, it belongs partially in the first category; but it also belongs partially in the second since it advocates expansion. Actually, it does not belong unequivocally to either of the two categories. It cannot be fit into one and only one pigeonhole; the classes are not mutually exclusive.

But even this flaw can be corrected. We can order the classes on two levels according to Figure 2.12. The unforeseen position ends up under "expand now" and "phase out in the future."

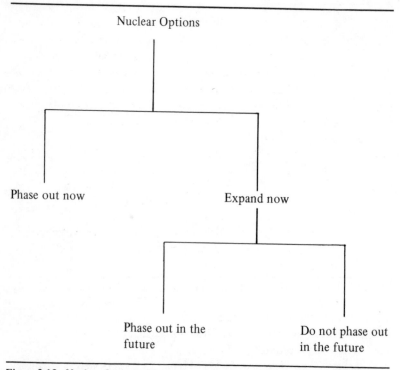

Figure 2.12   Nuclear Options: Illustration of the Exclusiveness Rule of Classification

The requirement of *fruitfulness* concerns, as we have seen, not only classification, but formation of single concepts as well.

There are almost innumerable ways to create a property space that conforms with the single basis rule and the rules of exhaustiveness and exclusiveness. It is important, therefore, to create schemes that yield the most interesting possible class divisions. We can draw up some basic principles.

If the scheme is constructed such that there are no empirical cases in any of the pigeonholes, then the classification is empirically sterile. If all empirical elements bunch up in a small number of pigeonholes, then this is a sign that the scheme is not very fruitful. It discriminates too little. The solution may be to merge some empty classes and further divide those that are well filled. That way we attain a more equal distribution of empirical cases in different pigeonholes. The scheme is most interesting, perhaps, when empirical cases end up in every pigeonhole. We can, however, also conceive of situations where one or a couple of empty classes in an otherwise well-filled scheme might be interesting.

Another criterion of fruitfulness is that those criteria that end up in the same class should have something more in common than the mere fact that they occupy the same class. These common features over and above the classification properties should also distinguish them from cases that occupy other classes. We should be able, for example, to create interesting empirical hypotheses for each class. A classification of viewpoints can also be fruitful in that it shows that the viewpoints have been supported by different types of arguments.

2.8 Formal Schemes of Classification

In content-oriented analysis, it may be necessary to use certain formal schemes of classification. The basis for these schemes is purely technical. They have no ties whatsoever to the substantive issue to be analyzed. It is absolutely necessary to be able to talk about claims, reasons and arguments.

Consider the phrase, "Because Sweden has not joined any military defense alliance, it is a neutral country." The first part — "because Sweden has not joined any military defense alliance" — is offered as support for the second part — "Sweden is a neutral country." It is argued that the latter part is true *because* the former is held to be true. This is a paradigm case of an argument. By definition, an *argument* is a statement or a set of statements offered as support for another statement. The statement offered as support is called the *premise,* the *ground,* the *reason,* or the *justifying statement* of the argument. The statement for which the support is given is called the *claim,* the *conclusion,* or the *thesis* of the argument.[57]

It may also be useful to distinguish between chains and clusters of reasoning.

When different arguments are successively linked to each other, we get *chains of reasoning.* Such chains have structures such as those illustrated in Figure 2.13. The conclusion in one argument serves as premise in the next. Conclusion 1 in the first argument also serves as premise 3 in the second argument; conclusion 2 in the second serves as premise 5 in the third. In this fashion, arguments can chain together into long series.[58]

Often, a claim advanced by an asserter is supported not by one reason or chain of reasoning, but by a whole bunch of independent reasons. We may call this a *cluster of reasoning.*[59] Such clusters exhibit structures as illustrated in Figure 2.14.

Thus far, we have only discussed schemes for classifying reasons in favor of claims. Sometimes it may be fruitful, however, to examine both reasons for and against a claim in a common context. There are several models to follow. One possibility is that we first present all reasons supporting a claim

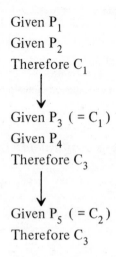

Given P_1
Given P_2
Therefore C_1

Given P_3 ($= C_1$)
Given P_4
Therefore C_3

Given P_5 ($= C_2$)
Therefore C_3

Figure 2.13 The Structure of a Chain of Reasoning

and then all reasons that weaken it. Another possibility is to directly confront reasons for the claim with corresponding reasons against it. First we look at reason 1, which is grounded in some area of fact, and then we look at a counterreason that deals with the same area of fact.

A third possibility is to present the reasons for and against group by group. First we present all reasons advanced by group G, then all reasons presented by group H, and so on. Within each group, then, we can either directly confront reasons for and against with each other, or first present all reasons for, and then, one after another, all reasons against.

There are reasons speaking for both methods of arrangement; we would be going into too much detail if we were to explore this here.[60]

2.9 Substantive Schemes of Classification

Formal schemes of classification are necessary but not sufficient tools in argument analysis. Schemes based upon the substantive issue under scrutiny are evidently also needed. Two such schemes would seem entirely necessary, one for claims and one for reasons.

In our general discussion of classification we used a few simple schemes to classify various nuclear options. These alternatives can be regarded as claims in our example. The division "phase out," "maintain present level," and "expand further" was such a classification. A careful phrasing

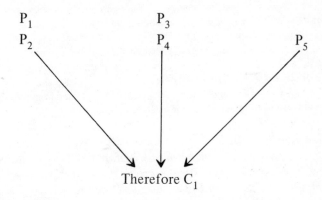

Figure 2.14 The Structure of a Cluster of Reasoning

and ordering of statements expressing different substantive claims of the controversy is a necessary prerequisite of a deep-probing argument analysis.

Reasons in favor of the claim "expand further" could be classified as follows:

(1) The profitability reason: Nuclear power is economically profitable in comparison to other ways of producing energy.
(2) The environmental reason: Nuclear power is especially favorable to the environment during normal use.
(3) The inexhaustibility reason: Nuclear power is a large and boundless source of energy.

There are other reasons that are tied more specifically to Swedish conditions:

(4) The independence reason: Nuclear power can make Sweden independent of imported energy.
(5) The balance of trade reason: Nuclear power improves the country's balance of trade.
(6) The employment reason: Nuclear power creates jobs as it is being built up.

Reasons for the claim "phase out" might be classified as follows:

(1) The nuclear accident reason: Nuclear power can lead to severe nuclear reactor accidents.
(2) The plutonium danger reason: Handling of plutonium is very dangerous.

(3) The waste reason: There is no secure method of storing highly radioactive wastes.
(4) The terrorism reason: Nuclear power plants are very vulnerable to terrorist attack, which could lead to a radiation catastrophe.
(5) The nuclear blackmail reason: The use of nuclear power entails a risk that weapons-grade nuclear materials will be diverted and used for blackmail.
(6) The police state reason: Nuclear power plants require such stringent guarding that there is a risk for society developing into a police state.
(7) The nuclear proliferation reason: The plutonium obtained from reprocessing can be used to produce nuclear weapons.

Our substantive schemes are not exhaustive. That would require too much space. Another obvious weakness is their low level of theoretical ambition. The important point to make is that some substantive classification of claims and reasons must be found to enable us to master the materials.

3

INTERPRETATION AND
ITS PROBLEMS

We can describe political messages only if we interpret them. But what do we mean by "interpret" or "interpretation"?

3.1 Interpretation Defined

When a person interprets a message, he extracts its meaning. He presents this extracted meaning as a reformulation—in one way or another—of the original message. If his understanding of the new formulation agrees with his understanding of the original message—if he believes both express the same meaning—then he has interpreted the message. We can use the term "interpretation," then, to denote a reformulation of this type, i.e., one that for a given person in a given situation has the same meaning as the original formulation.[1]

Primarily following the Norwegian philosopher Arne Naess, we might define "interpretation" as follows:

> Expression A is an interpretation of a different expression B if there exists at least one person P and one situation S such that A expresses the same assertion as B for that person P in that situation S.[2]

Less formally, this means that A is an interpretation of B if it is conceivable that A conveys the same information as B to at least one person in at least one situation.

Obviously, Naess's definition of "interpretation" is both minimal and very reasonable. An expression is an interpretation of another expression as long as the possibility exists that one person in one situation believes that the expressions express the same assertion. This does not mean that the person must actually hold such a belief; it is sufficient that we can conceive of a situation in which he would.

Naess's definition also deserves praise because it makes no mention of the quality of interpretation. Whether an interpretation is good or bad, exact or inexact, reasonable or unreasonable—that question can be discussed separately from the question of definition. We have attempted to offer a minimal definition of the term "interpretation."

We will have to modify Naess's concept of interpretation somewhat if it is to be of use in our present context. First, it is associated mainly with the interpretation of expressions. However, content-oriented analysis can, in principle, also be applied to discrete terms and concepts, as well as to nonverbal communication. We can cover these eventualities by replacing the word "expression" in our definition with "message."

Further, Naess's concept refers most often to the cognitive or informative use of language.[3] Since this use of language is also central to argumentative analysis, the concept would seem particularly useful here. However, argument analysis, one might object, must also enable the researcher to interpret and assess noncognitive messages. A somewhat broader notion of interpretation seems necessary; we achieve it by replacing "same statement" with "same meaning" in our original formulation of the definition.

My modified definition of interpretation—in the sense "result of interpretation"—is as follows:

> An expression E is an interpretation of a message M if there exists at least one person P and one situation S such that E can have the same *meaning* as M for person P in situation S.

This, I hope, is a working and comprehensible definition of interpretation.

We must add a final note on interpretation. In our definition, an interpretation is a formulation, i.e., something on the linguistic level. The term is, however, equivocal. It is a process-product concept. It may also refer to the act of producing interpretations, or both to the act and to the result of the act. We may say that interpretations produce interpretations. We will accept this ambiguity and use the word in all three senses. We hope the reader will be able to derive from context when we are using the term to mean interpreting, or result of interpreting, or both.

3.2   Kinds of Interpretation

One seemingly fruitful way of classifying interpretations is according to what justificatory evidence is used for validating them, i.e., showing that they are "correct." Then we get four types of interpretations:

(1) *literal interpretations,* which are validated by reference to the meaning extracted solely from the letter of the text;

(2) *systematic interpretations,* which are justified by reference to the meaning messages have when they are viewed in their larger contextual situations;

(3) *intentionalist interpretations,* which are justified by reference to the meaning intended by the sender of the message; and

(4) *reconstructive interpretations.* How these should be justified must be left open because it is doubtful whether they actually represent any other message at all. They need not agree with the letter of the text, nor with the intended meaning of the sender. They contain constructive elements and seem to transcend the meaning of the original message.

One might also typify interpretations with respect to their degree of validity, i.e., how well they accord with the original message. Roughly, we can distinguish between:

(1) correct interpretations;
(2) reasonable interpretations; and
(3) unreasonable interpretations.

A correct interpretation is so well supported that we can contend with absolute certainty that it is an accurate representation of the message. A reasonable interpretation has only enough support that we can insist that it probably—though not certainly—accords with the original message. An unreasonable interpretation, finally, is one that exhibits strong reasons for being discounted.

We can combine both ways of classifying interpretations into a property space with three entries on one side and four on the other. Since reasonable interpretations are of greatest practical significance, we can ignore correct and unreasonable interpretations for the moment. Our typology of interpretations is represented in Figure 3.1.

Let it suffice here to note that only three kinds of interpretations can be judged by their degree of validity. It is doubtful whether reconstructive interpretations can be appraised in this way because they do not seem to represent any original message.

We will now discuss interpretive methods, i.e., how we proceed for attaining literal, systematic, intentionalist, and reconstructive interpretations. Later, we will consider the distinctions between correct, reasonable, and unreasonable interpretations.

3.3 Literal Interpretation

Interpretation is literal when it purports to represent a message's meaning by describing the message's wording or formulation. There are several ways to determine the literal meaning. One is to study the grammar and logic of the message itself. Analysts must form their own opinion about what it means;

Kind of Justification	Degree of Validity		
	Correct	Reasonable	Unreasonable
Literal	–	Reasonable literal interpretation	–
Systematic	–	Reasonable systematic interpretation	–
Intentionalist	–	Reasonable intentionalist interpretation	–
Reconstructive	?	?	?

Figure 3.1   A Typology of Interpretations

they may have a general feeling for the language, or they may acquire it by studying dictionaries and encyclopedias. All of this may help them construe the literal meaning of a message. It would be difficult to entirely ignore the context within which the message was enunciated, though the point of a literal interpretation is that the text is the focus of study.[4]

It is, as far as I can see, quite in order for an analyst of political ideas to use the literal method. It can often yield fully satisfactory results, but such an interpretation is uncomplicated, rather like producing an unsophisticated paraphrase or rewrite of a text. Clearly, then, the literal method is sometimes entirely inappropriate, e.g., in ferreting out the meaning of more complicated documents. At best, it can only help us to illuminate certain possible meanings or possible reasonable interpretations. Within this framework, it often cannot help us decide which we are to favor. However, the latter may be a truth in need of modification. When the interpreter makes use of lexical aids, a certain contextual connection arises that may be decisive in determining which interpretation is most reasonable.

The literal method suffers from another serious shortcoming. Since by definition it must focus entirely on the actual text, it cannot be used to uncover tacit premises or conclusions. Another drawback is that the method focuses primarily on the manifest content or the surface meaning of the message. Thus it cannot penetrate what Ole R. Holsti has called ''the deeper layers of meaning embedded in the document.'' It cannot, in other words, capture the latent meaning of the message.[5]

These deficiencies should not, however, lead us to reject the literal method as entirely useless. It would be appropriate to use literal interpretation during the introductory phase of a study. However, when the limits of what it can accomplish have been reached, the analyst should choose another method to complement literal interpretation.

3.4 Systematic Interpretation

An obvious complement to the literal approach is the method of systematic interpretation. Its basic idea is simple: The meaning of a message can be disentangled if it is placed into the larger context or system to which it belongs. To present all possible contextual factors surrounding a message would be a Sisyphean task. There seems to be no end to the context of a text. The context may be a greater theoretical construct. Sometimes, it is possible to elicit the full meaning of individual messages only after we have determined their theoretical context. The context may also be cultural. Words and expressions may have overtones and embedded meanings within one culture that they totally lack in some other culture. The systematic method of interpretation allows us to get at latent meanings of a much more comprehensive and complex kind than we can get at with the literal method of interpretation.

We can distinguish two kinds of systematic methods. In the one case, the sole purpose is to bring out the meaning of the message. In the second case, the purpose is also to uncover a basis for eliminating inconsistencies in the message. The first variant will be called pure, the second, ameliorative systematic interpretation.

An example may illustrate how we proceed in *pure systematic interpretation*. It is taken from a study of the dissemination of news on the civil war in Nigeria. The investigation focuses on news reports in a number of prestigious news magazines, e.g., *Time, Newsweek, U.S. News & World Report, Jeune Afrique, L'Express,* and *Der Spiegel*.[6]

Time reported a massacre in northern Nigeria. The event was stigmatized as an ''orgy in mass savagery.'' What was meant by ''savagery'' in this context? What meanings could this short, apparently insignificant expression convey?

The author places the expression ''savagery'' in its cultural context and claims that the term can have two main historical meanings. In the one case, "savage" and its derivatives are used in accordance with the notion of "the noble savage." This notion was popular in Europe in the eighteenth century. The idea had an almost mythical meaning. The savages of Africa and America lived in a pastoral, earthly paradise. Their way of life was more natural and original, their behavior more unadulterated, generous, and innocent. What is good in man was more alive and less repressed in these people than in the degenerate Europeans. The prototype of the noble savage was the American Indian.

In the second case, the idea is used in accordance with a diametrically opposite notion that evolved in the nineteenth century. According to this perspective, the savages were uncivilized barbarians. Their cultural level could not measure up to that of the Europeans. Their customs were raw, brutal, and primitive. Their way of life included cannibalism, fornication, and paganism. These barbarians lacked all of the good that Western civilization had produced.

Which of these meanings shall we give to *Time*'s "orgy of mass savagery"? The latter, of course. This conclusion is reinforced above all by the fact that the event referred to was a massacre of people.

We might object that the example is unrealistic since savagery in the sense of noble savage seems precluded right from the start. That part of the investigation of meaning seems to be redundant. On the other hand, the author manages in his examination of the notion of the savage as the bestial barbarian to add an extra dimension to the expression "savagery" that transcends a narrowly applied literal interpretation.

Pure systematic interpretation is extraordinarily useful in describing political messages, regardless of whether they will later be included in, say, a content analysis or a rational assessment. The first step, for example, may be to use the literal method to elicit a certain number of possible and reasonable interpretations. The pure systematic method can then be used in a second step in order to arrive at more and deeper possible and reasonable interpretations and in order to indicate the most reasonable interpretation.

The systematic method of interpretation is also used in jurisprudence, but there it is not seen as a method of merely producing meaning. It is also used to dispel certain inconsistencies. It is this variant that we might call ameliorative.

Ameliorative systematic interpretation implies that contradictions between rules of a higher and a lower order within a legal system, however conceived, should be eliminated through reformulation of the lower rules so that they become consistent with the higher ones. Systematic interpretation suggests that legal rules are related to each other and to general principles in the legal system under discussion. Considerations concerning the system as a whole or concerning a large part of it become reasons for interpreting single rules in certain ways. Once it is demonstrated that a legal rule of lower order contradicts one of higher order, this type of systematic interpretation suggests a reformulation of the lower rule to eliminate the inconsistency. A principal point of departure for the ameliorative method is that the legal system must be coherent and free from contradiction.[7]

A similar systematic approach to textual exegesis is also used by social scientists. In *The Open Society and Its Enemies,* Karl Popper advocates this technique. An interpretation, he writes,

> must take the form of a rational reconstruction, and must be systematic; it must try to reconstruct the philosopher's thought as a consistent edifice. . . . We ought to start with the assumption that a great philosopher is not likely to be always contradicting himself, and consequently, wherever there are two interpretations, one of which will make [him] consistent and the other inconsistent, prefer the former to the latter, if reasonably possible.[8]

Popper, then, recommends a rational construal of the text so as to make it, as far as possible, internally consistent. He is not advocating the literal method of determining the common or technical meaning of the text. He wants something more. His principal point of departure is that a great thinker's philosophy ought to be considered free of elementary contradiction. And this assumption of consistency becomes a justification for dispelling, wherever possible, contradictions between different parts of the message.

The ameliorative systematic method seems to imply that we should never take textual contradictions at their face value. We should consider instead whether their context might not offer a clue as to consistency. If possible, we should favor an interpretation that makes the message consistent over one that makes it inconsistent.

We can discern another feature of Popper's interpretational method. In order to make the doctrine he is about to criticize as intellectually compelling as possible, Popper does not hesitate to invent new reasons in its favor. He writes about this in the introduction to *The Poverty of Historicism:*

> I have tried to make a case in favour of historicism in order to give point to my subsequent criticism. I have tried to present historicism as a well-considered and close-knit philosophy. And I have not hesitated to construct arguments in its support which have never, to my knowledge, been brought forward by historicists themselves. I hope that, in this way, I have succeeded in building up a position really worth attacking.[9]

In summary, the thrust of Popper's systematic method of interpretation is (a) to eliminate contradictions in the text to be analyzed and (b) to add reasons not even offered by its author so as to state a position really worth attacking, i.e., in order to establish a foundation for a really strong critique that gets at the heart of the matter.

The ameliorative systematic method of interpretation is very similar to the "principle of charity." This is an important guideline for argument analysis, requiring that we try to make the best, rather than the worst, possible interpretation of the material under study. Michael Scriven describes it as follows:

> [E]ven if as a matter of strict grammar, we could shoot the writer down for having said something that doesn't follow or isn't strictly true, it may be more charitable to reinterpret the passage slightly in order to make more "sense" out of it, that is to make it mean something that a sensible person would be more likely to have really meant. . . . What the Principle of Charity does mean is that "taking cheap shots" is something we shouldn't waste much time doing. Other words that come in from ordinary language about this point are "nit-picking" and "attacking (or setting up) a straw man." These terms all refer to poor argument analysis, either to making irrelevant criticisms or to making criticisms that are not relevant to the main thrust of the argument or that are unfair in some other way.[10]

The principle of charity is an ethical rule requiring criticisms to be generous, fair, or just. We should not take advantage of a mere slip of the tongue or make a big thing out of some irrelevant point that was not put quite right. Indeed, adherence to this rule of conduct is also sound practical advice since it makes us less vulnerable to counterattack. We should choose that interpretation of an argument that makes it most sensible and forceful; otherwise, a slight reformulation of the argument will nullify our objections. It may be possible to get away with setting up some straw men and winning some easy victories in the short run, but for the long term, this is a poor strategy since our criticisms may be refuted by modest changes in the argument being criticized.

These two reasons for using the charity principle were formulated by Michael Scriven.[11] His reasoning seems compelling. It might seem that this principle should be put to general use in order to create the strongest possible foundation for a forceful rational assessment. That conclusion, however, is hardly well considered.

The usefulness of a method of interpretation must always be appraised with respect to the aim of the investigation. A rational assessment always aims to test the validity of a message. Within the framework of this goal, we can discern, roughly, three levels of ambition. It is my opinion that the ameliorative systematic method and the principle of charity should be permitted a significant role in only one of these three cases.

In the first case, our aim is to test the validity of a position assumed by some specific actor. We might, for example, want to effect more rational decision making in a situation where the participants already support certain alternatives and have locked themselves into certain reasons for supporting their positions. The declarations may even be fixed as national policy goals and as notions about how government should act to attain them. In these cases it may be justified to try to determine exactly how the participants have reasoned. Their opinions are of such social and political import that it is legitimate to ignore the principle of charity entirely and to discover exactly how they think or thought. The ameliorative systematic method and the charity principle are less useful here. Instead, the literal method combined with the intentionalist method can lay the foundation for a validity test. The intentionalist method will be presented in the next section.

Our aim in the second case is also to appraise the validity of a certain actor's position. In this case, we are more interested in the position per se than in the agent's concrete formulation of it. Nothing prevents us from testing various alternative renderings of the position and reasons in order to determine which of them best stands up to our appraisal. We can be consistently benevolent and interpret the arguments according to the principle of charity. We might, in accordance with the ameliorative systematic method, add our own reasons for or against in order to further test whether the position is really valid. However, the criterion of whether an interpretation is reasonable is still whether the participant whose viewpoint is being assessed could accept the interpretation if he were given the chance to familiarize himself with it and think it through.

The reason that we apply the principle of charity in this situation is not—as Scriven argues—because it is a good ethical principle for how we should behave in a debate, nor is it due to fear of leaving ourselves open to justified counterattacks. The reason is more positive: We are genuinely interested in the thing we are dealing with and so want to obtain the best possible formulation of what the participant has said. It is precisely this aim for which the ameliorative systematic method and the principle of charity are useful.

In the third and final case, we are concerned exclusively with appraising the validity of a position, regardless of which participant formulated it. We may, of course, take as our point of departure a specific participant's formulations of the arguments and the position. We can assess alternative interpretations of this participant's position and see which one best meets the test. We can add reasons not presented by the participant. The difference between this and the second case is that we do not have to concern ourselves at all with whether the author of the text we are working with would agree with our interpretation or not. We do not claim to present a precise rendering of a specific participant's formulation of the subject. We are interested in the position as such, regardless of who presented it. Our interpretation, or rather our presentation, should not be made on the basis of who happened to say something, but on the basis of what we judge to be relevant to an appraisal of a position's validity. All relevant formulations of positions and reasons — regardless of who conceived them — are admissible in the analysis. This is the most general form of rational assessment.

Even in this third case, the literal method, the systematic method or the intentionalist method can, of course, be useful, but a fourth method — the reconstructive method of interpretation — becomes even more important. It will be presented in the section following the discussion of the intentionalist method.[12]

3.5 Intentionalist Interpretation

This interpretive method is aimed at discovering what an author intends to say with his text. It is the intended meaning of the author's message we are trying to get at.

In intentionalist interpretation, the letter of the text is of secondary importance compared with the author's intent. The author's intent may coincide with the literal content of a document, of course, but it may also differ entirely from what a normal reader, or one who is familiar with the technical language, finds the most reasonable interpretation, or the document may be so old that the meanings of the words have changed. In that case, a modern literal interpretation would yield a very different result than a representation of the author's intended meaning.

Among the data used in an interpretation based on an author's intent, we should note, besides the actual text, preparatory studies, drafts, memoranda, and other material that can shed light on the writer's thoughts during composition of the document. This method of interpretation is characterized by a combination of intensive study of the actual text with assiduous use of any preparatory works.

Let us take as an example the interpretation of the Swedish law for municipal energy planning. The original law of 1977 and amendments added in 1980 and 1981 are divided into seven short sections that together cover no more than one page in *The Swedish Code of Statutes*.[13]

The introductory section of the law prescribes that municipalities, in their planning, shall "promote energy conservation." As we can see, the decree is formulated in extremely general terms. What does the prescription that a municipality shall "promote energy conservation" really mean? What is the national government enjoining the municipalities to do?

The law itself does not offer any clues. It does not contain a single word that could aid in a deeper understanding of the phrase just quoted. If one were to stick to depicting the law's literal meaning, then, one would get no further than the statement that municipalities should "promote energy conservation." But this would be unsatisfactory. One natural way to penetrate deeper into the meaning of the law would be to expand the basic data of our interpretation to also include memos, sketches, and drafts that preceded the law. This would take us from literal to intentionalist interpretation. In fact, such a study of preparatory work underlying the law does suggest certain ways to make our specific decree more concrete. Municipalities should "give special consideration to energy issues," says the report of the Parliamentary Committee on Civil Affairs. "This responsibility means . . . that the municipalities . . . should strive for solutions which promote conservation of energy—solutions aimed at achieving more effective energy use at reasonable cost without impinging on essential or desirable needs." The key formulation is "more effective energy use at reasonable cost without impinging on essential or desirable needs." This attempt by the committee to clarify the term "energy conservation" refers back to the special statement of reason in the bill that the government sent to the parliament. Nearly the same phrase is repeated there, but this time with a clarifying addition: "Such measures are, for example, the use of more efficient [energy production] plants and better insulation of buildings."

Similar formulations are also found in the general statement of reason in the government bill. In one sense the latter is a bit more detailed than both the special statement of reason and the committee report. Thanks to this, it is clear that the expression "energy conservation" in the law refers to measures to be taken both in the use and production of energy. This is a clarification since it would otherwise be easy to let the term "energy conservation" refer to measures taken only in the way energy is used. The Minister of Energy writes:

> The obligation to promote energy conservation entails that municipalities in their planning will take advantage of any ways possible to limit their energy needs without encroaching on other pressing needs. This entails further that energy-efficient means of producing the energy necessary to meet these needs will be sought.

A similar distinction between conservation in consumption and production of energy is contained in the report of a state commission, which was the basis of the government bill. The report says:

> *Energy conservation* refers to such measures aimed at a more efficient use of energy which can be taken without ignoring those needs which people feel are essential or desirable. Examples of such measures are, as regards energy production, the use of more efficient plants and, as regards consumption, better insulation of buildings or a reduction of indoor temperature such that comfort is not affected.

Thus, even if we consider preparatory texts, the prescription on energy conservation in the law on municipal energy planning is rather void of meaning. Municipalities should strive for solutions aimed at more efficient energy use. Conservation refers to measures taken in the areas of both production and consumption. An example of conservation in the area of production is the use of more efficient energy production plants. With respect to consumption, building insulation might be improved.

The point of this intentionalist interpretation of the law on municipal energy planning could be to lay a foundation for a rational assessment of the goal contained in the decree. Our example evidently lends further support to a critical view that continually crops up in the literature on policy analysis, policy implementation, and policy evaluation: The goals of public policies are often terribly diluted, vague, and difficult to get a grip on. We will not deal further here with ways to criticize the goal; we are more interested instead in the method of eliciting the meaning of the decree.

During the course of our reconstruction of the intent of a decree in the Swedish law on municipal energy planning we made use, in order, of the following preparatory texts:

(1) the report of a parliamentary committee;
(2) the special statement of reason in the government bill;
(3) the general statement of reason in the government bill; and
(4) a report of a state commission, including a proposed text of the law as well as statements of reason.

The point has been to establish the intent of the government decree. The order in which we consult the preparatory texts is, therefore, significant. Reports by parliamentary committees are often the result of compromises between parties and are generally passed by the parliament without any changes. They offer a more reliable picture of the parliament's collective intent than, say, a government bill, since the latter is formally an expression of only the government's view, not the parliament's. The government bill is also useful in interpreting the parliament's intention because, in this case, the government's proposal was passed intact.

The bill contained a so-called special statement of reason that expressly clarifies statements in the law. This, in turn, must be considered more important than the bill's general statement of reason, which, of course, also contained some clarifications. A report by a government commission— made up of both experts and politicians—was the basis of the government's proposal. In Sweden's political system, important compromises are reached even while a commission is still studying a problem. This happened in this case, but the government's bill diverged on a few points from the commission's report. Thus, a comparison between the two can shed some light on the intent of the bill and so also on the intent of the parliament's decision.

Several other preparatory texts could be used in the course of an intentionalist interpretation of a Swedish law. They are, in no special order:

(5) the government's final proposal, along with statements of reason that may have been rewritten as a result of remarks by the so-called Law Council;

(6) remarks by the Law Council;

(7) the text of the government's original proposal, including statements of reason;

(8) motions forwarded by the parties and individual members of parliament consequent to the government's bill;

(9) contributions to the parliamentary debate;

(10) remarks on the commission's report solicited from various authorities and organizations;

(11) executive directives issued by the minister to the government commission that has been appointed to develop data so that a decision can be reached.

One might also shed light on the import of the decree by comparing it with other relevant decrees. The conservation target in the law on municipal energy planning could be compared with conservation targets for the whole country as established by the parliament in connection with energy decisions on the broad national level. One could then distinguish differences that would allow us to characterize the prescription in the law on municipal energy planning in terms of what it does *not* contain.

Reconstructing the intent underlying the formulation of a law can be a difficult enterprise. It is commonly asserted that an intentionalist interpretation will be acceptable only if three prerequisites are fulfilled. The message being interpreted must be:

(1) attributable;

(2) datable; and
(3) testable.

Certain writers have argued that, at a bare minimum, the actor whose intent is being discussed should be identifiable. If the author is unknown, they argue, then it is impossible to establish his intentions with any degree of certainty. This seems exaggerated; we may be able to find and use many preparatory texts, enabling us to reconstruct an intended meaning even if the author is anonymous.

We may face a real problem, however, in ferreting out the intended meaning of collective documents. We may come across several different intentions. This is often the case with respect to international treaties and even to domestic legislation. Our previous example concerning the meaning of a particular prescription in the Swedish law of municipal energy planning shows how we may proceed in ascertaining intentions behind statements issued by collectivities.

Once the originator of a message has been designated, the researcher must also determine when the particular intention existed. This may require some consideration. The originator may have had varying intentions at different points in time. A government may have had one intention when the law was first discussed, and another when it was written. In our example above, obviously, it is the intention at the time the bill was passed that is important.

Finally, the researcher must show how the hypothetical interpretation can be tested. The researcher must present acceptable evidence to show that the author of the text did indeed have the purported intention. Empirical evidence must exist, in other words, supporting and making probable the interpreter's hypothesis.[14]

The attribution demand generally presents no difficulties for the interpretation of works by individual authors. However, there may be no preparatory texts at all, as often is the case with newspaper editorials. In such cases, an intentionalist interpretation contributes no more than a literal one; the intentionalist method is, in practice, useless.

The fact that the intentionalist method of interpretation can sometimes be quite impractical should not deter us from employing it to some ends. Our example concerning the law on municipal energy planning illustrates a field of application that conforms to our more general reasoning on the method's usefulness in the section on systematic interpretation. We can, of course, also use the method of intentionalist *interpretation* when we describe the meaning of decisions, e.g., decisions on national policies, for the purpose of explaining them later in accordance with the intentionalist approach to *explanation*.

3.6   *Intentionalist Interpretation and Intentionalist Explanation*

We have just touched upon a problem that requires a brief comment: the relationship between intentionalist interpretation and intentionalist explanation.

We have regarded intentionalist interpretation as a suitable method in content-oriented analysis of messages. Intentionalist explanation, on the other hand, is a form of function-oriented analysis. We emphasized in Chapter 1 that content-oriented analysis of political messages is something entirely different from function-oriented analysis; the two must be held separate. Does the distinction not break down at precisely this point? As even their labels indicate, both intentionalist interpretation and intentionalist explanation seem to focus on the intentions of actors. The two procedures seem to resemble one another closely; one might even claim that they are identical. If one admits intentionalist interpretation into an early stage of a content-oriented analysis, then one seems to be slipping an element of intentionalist explanation into the content-oriented research process. The distinction becomes impossible to maintain.

The answer to this objection is that the distinction does not break down at all. Making an intentionalist interpretation is something quite different from making an intentionalist explanation.

The intentionalist method, then, is a procedure used for disentanglement of intended meaning. It can be used in content-oriented analysis to cast light on the intended meaning of claims. These claims can, properly speaking, be put forth by a specific actor. In any case, though, it is their content that is interesting. One focuses, in other words, on *what* is said. In intentionalist explanation, interest is directed toward the fact *that* something is said or *espoused* by some actor. The practical difference can be difficult to see, but on the level of principle, the difference is extremely significant. Furthermore, in content-oriented analysis, attention is focused primarily on the content of various reasons and on how they justify the conclusion. In intentionalist explanation, expressed reasons are treated merely as indicators of something else—that the actor had certain motivations that induced him to act in the way he did. The reasons, in the case of intentionalist explanation, are never interesting per se, but only to the extent they can be grounds for inferring the actor's motives. We cannot simply assume that expressed reasons are indicators of actually held motives. This is clear if we keep in mind the fact that an actor may express reasons with the conscious intent to mislead observers as to his real motivations.

As we see, then, the result of an intentionalist interpretation is not identical to that of an intentionalist explanation.

3.7 *Reconstructive Interpretation*

A fourth group of interpretive methods differs from the literal, intentional, and even systematic methods in that it emphasizes that a text's meaning is reconstructed or corrected by the interpreter. The interpretation is freed from the text being interpreted in the sense that it need not agree with the original text's letter, contextual meaning, intent of the originator, or spirit of the message.

Opinions may differ as to what it is exactly that this kind of interpretation should agree with. An extreme view is that the interpretation is entirely the analyst's construction and so not an interpretation at all. In principle, then, it does not need to agree with any original message. Another possibility is that the rendering may accord with something in the interpreter's milieu, rather than with the meaning of the text or the originator's intent with the message. As a basis for discussion, an example of this method will be presented here.

This reconstructive perspective on interpretation marks Johan Galtung and Arne Naess's book on Gandhi's political ethic. The authors were not satisfied to merely describe Gandhi's doctrine of nonviolence, though this alone would have been a demanding task since Gandhi never made a serious attempt to summarize and clarify his pioneering doctrine. The authors wanted to make a more edifying contribution, to complement and ecumenicize Gandhi's doctrine. Their aim was to dislodge it from various political situations that existed in the past and that Westerners are unused to. They wanted to make the doctrine so general that it became valid vis-à-vis contemporary Western social and political issues.

In order to emphasize that they were not engaged in a history of ideas, the Norwegian authors called their method descriptive-constructive. By this they meant to emphasize that they were guided largely by the letter of the original texts and by Gandhi's intentions, but that their interpretation also included an important element of rational reconstruction. This goes beyond the postulate of the ameliorative systematic method of interpretation that states that a text should be purged of internal contradictions and that overlooked reasons should be added. The authors write:

> We may undertake to expand or modify the purely historical presentation. And guesswork will naturally bear much of the burden; we can never be sure that a specific generalization is the only one the material would allow. We must take care in never diverging from the spirit of the historical teaching—just from its letter, to the extent that this is possible at all. The researcher's goal must be that [Gandhi], if he were to read the presentation, would nod his head and say: "Yes, there is much here about which I have never expressed my opinion and much about which I could never even have thought. But under different

circumstances than those under which I actually lived, I could well have expressed myself like this without coming into conflict with things I said earlier.''

A criterion of whether the interpretation is reasonable, then, is whether it agrees with the spirit of Gandhi's teaching. As long as the authors were governed by this ambition, we can say they were employing the ameliorative method of systematic interpretation. They mention another point of comparison that indicates that they were going further in their construction than allowed by the ameliorative technique and the principle of charity. ''The criterion,'' they write, ''is simply to choose the reasonable interpretations which are most in tune with current debate and thinking in our cultural milieu.''[15] Thus, the interpretations go beyond not only Gandhi's intent or the spirit of his doctrine; they even transcend his milieu. Let us call this the transcendental feature of Galtung and Naess's work; it deserves the name ''reconstructive interpretation.''

The question, however, is whether interpretation is a fortunate label. Would it not be better to say Galtung and Naess were engaged in theory or hypothesis formation, which, in this special case, is of the normative variety? Note, for example, how the authors attempted to give the nonviolence doctrine as good a ''non-Indian'' formulation as possible. While it is true that the presentation should agree with the spirit of Gandhi's teachings, the authors did not hesitate to abandon this demand in order to achieve as good and relevant a formulation as possible. Perhaps if this feature of the construction were pronounced it would be better to say that the authors were engaged in constructing their own theory rather than in interpretation.

We find traces in both authors of a gnawing anxiety that the thoughts they present do not deserve to be called scientific. The method of interpretation is too arbitrary for that. ''The constructive method involves so much uncertainty that the results could not usually bear the name science,'' they write at one point.[16] This anxiety is easy to understand, especially against the background of their notion of the reconstructive method's purpose. If they were to formulate as the goal of their work the construction of their own theories and hypotheses, then their anxiety would be less appropriate. The reconstructive method could then generate results that were just as scientific as those generated by the two other methods of interpretation.

Their whole presentation is pervaded by the notion that they are presenting Gandhi's doctrine. They have reconstructed, deepened, clarified, and generalized the doctrine, to be sure, but they seem to be saying that the theory is still Gandhi's. We can, however, turn this reasoning on its head. One could argue that the philosophy presented here is Johan Galtung's and

Arne Naess's. What is the relationship between Gandhi's philosophy and that of the two Norwegian thinkers? Obviously, the authors were very much motivated by Gandhi's thoughts and actions as they developed their own doctrine. One might say that Gandhi's life and teachings served as heuristic tools for the authors in their attempt to formulate their own doctrine of nonviolence. One might say, in other words, that Galtung and Naess took some of their ideas from Gandhi's doctrine. However, some of their ideas came from other places, e.g., from contemporary debate and thinking in the western cultural milieu. Thus, the two Norwegian researchers' doctrine of nonviolence cannot claim to be a reflection of Gandhi's teachings.

The reconstructive method, then, would not be an interpretive tool in our sense, but would instead be a general recommendation to gather ideas from other thinkers in order to construct lines of reasoning that are as watertight as possible.

Finally, though, let us for the sake of argument say that the main purpose of the book was to present an exposition of Gandhi's opinions and ideals. This may even have been the authors' primary goal; the title of the book is, after all, *Gandhi's* Political Ethic. If the interpretation's validity is to be judged, then the points of view according to which the exposition was made must be clearly stated. The authors understood this, of course. From the quotation above, it is clear that one criterion was the "spirit" of Gandhi's doctrine. However, the statements in the quotation are not very precise; and the viewpoint is not developed more fully anywhere else. As we already pointed out, the authors do indicate another starting point: One must "choose the reasonable interpretations which are most in tune with current debate and thinking in our cultural milieu."[17] Two comments will be made on this. What is current western debate and thinking? This question is never clarified or answered. This transcendental criterion has thus been formulated in an extraordinarily vague way. Just because of this, this criterion is able to guide the interpretation in only a most general way. Further, how are we to balance the criterion "spirit of Gandhi's doctrine" with the criterion "current debate and thinking in our cultural milieu"? Above all, how are we to test the reasonableness of the balance? How, in other words, are we to validate the result of the interpretation? I would like this question to be answered in principle, because the reconstructive criterion means that agreement with Gandhi's teaching (its spirit) is not solely decisive. The authors provide no answer, and neither does their concrete presentation provide clues as to how validation was accomplished. Thus, the authors' presentation and application of the reconstructive method suffers from shortcomings. One might ask whether the method has led them to sit atop a fence—they are obviously not dealing with Gandhi's political ethic, yet they refuse to admit that they are dealing with their own political ethic.

3.8   The Complementary Nature of Interpretive Methods

All four methods of interpretation presented here seem to have some use in content-oriented analysis of political messages. To some extent it would seem more fruitful to let them complement each other rather than to view them as mutually exclusive alternatives.

An interpretive task can, for example, begin with the literal method, which later is complemented by the intentionalist method. This combination should find its primary application when we want to examine a position held by some particular, influential actor. This includes government decisions on policies for various sectors of society. These positions are so politically and socially significant that it may be justified to establish exactly what they mean.

The literal method can also be combined with the pure systematic method. This combination is useful for getting at deeper latent meanings than those that the literal method can uncover on its own.

The literal method can also be complemented by the ameliorative systematic method and the principle of charity. This combination is fruitful when we want to analyze a particular actor's position and we are more interested in the position itself than in that actor's actual formulation of it. In such a case we are so interested in the validity of the position that we can dismiss elementary inconsistencies as well as add reasons that the actor may have overlooked. The aim is to build up a position that is really worth attacking.

The constructive method, finally, recommends that we collect ideas from various sources in order to construct an argument of our own that is as valid as possible. This method may be used when our attention is focused entirely on the substance of the message and we can ignore who formulated the various stages in the argument. This procedure is used in part, for example, by political philosophers who attempted to construct justifications for the preservation of political institutions such as democracy or who give reasons in support of freedom, equality, justice, representative government, minimal state power, or the welfare state.

3.9   Validity of Interpretations

We said earlier that interpretations can also be classified according to their degree of validity, i.e., how well they accord with the meaning of the original message. Such a classification can yield three kinds of interpretations—correct, reasonable, and unreasonable.

3.9.1   *Correct Interpretations*

As we explained earlier, we mean by correct interpretation one that is so well supported that we can say with absolute certainty that it is an adequate rendering of a message's content. We must ask if this really is a fruitful notion in political message analysis.

Advocates of the literal method of interpretation are the ones, above all, who have maintained that their procedure yields correct interpretations of a text. They proceed from the assumption that (a) every well-written text has only one correct interpretation and that (b) the correct interpretation of every well-written text is evident from the text's wording.

These attempts to achieve correct interpretations have been subjected to severe criticism. The position is obviously entirely incompatible with the fundamental insight of modern semantics—that words and sentences are in general both equivocal and vague, even if the context in each individual case helps reduce these obscurities.[18] We cannot, then, produce correct interpretations. This objection is, in my opinion, a crushing blow. We must, therefore, dismiss as unfounded every claim that the only correct construal of a text's meaning has been established.

3.9.2   *Reasonable Interpretations*

The concept of a reasonable interpretation seems to be much more useful in political message analysis. As we all know, political messages are sometimes so fuzzy that it is possible to compose long lists of, at least in principle, different conceivable interpretations of a key sentence or term. We can, however, with the aid of our special knowledge about the sender of the message and the context in which it was sent, as well as our familiarity with normal usage, limit the list of possible interpretations to just *reasonable interpretations*. Reasonable interpretation, according to Arne Naess, is an entirely special kind of interpretation: It must be *common*, i.e., the persons or groups who accept the interpretation may not be too few or too special.

Actually, neither of these criteria is particularly illuminating. How many people must embrace an interpretation for it to be considered reasonable? Does Naess really mean that in this case a scientific issue is to be resolved by a majority decision? Which groups are too special to be counted? Is the group made up of political scientists among them? What if 100 randomly selected people interpret Rousseau's theory of the social contract in a way that makes him a precursor to liberal democracy while, at the same time, four internationally respected political scientists and Rousseau specialists regard him as a forerunner of totalitarian dictatorship? Naess offers no clues as to how this and similar problems can be solved. This difficulty in applying the criteria of reasonable interpretation is one of the weak points in his attempt to develop fundamental semantic concepts.[19]

A more useful method might be the one we can extrapolate from Karl Popper's work. Popper argues that the researcher should strive not only for interpretations that enjoy powerful positive support from the research material. He should also search for cases that might upend his interpretation. The interpreter, then, should consciously try to falsify his own interpretations. In this way, he should be able to create a set of interpretations with a degree of reasonableness that is dependent on how well they are supported by evidence. A researcher, then, can argue that one interpretation is more reasonable than another. The point is that disagreements about interpretations must be settled by argument. If he does this, the researcher has dispatched his obligation; it is then up to our scientific society to accept or reject his result.

3.9.3 Clarifications

To return to Naess, though, even the various reasonable interpretations may be rather numerous. If we are intent upon carrying our analysis beyond the semantic stage, then we need to clarify the content of the message. This means that we decide to accept one or more of the reasonable interpretations, but we do this in such a way as to exclude, implicitly or explicitly, at least one of the original interpretations. While we eliminate at least one reasonable interpretation of the message we are refining, we must choose as our refining alternative a formulation that does not give rise to any new reasonable interpretation of the original message. All reasonable interpretations of the refining formulation, then, must be reasonable interpretations of the original message.[20]

We can express the relationship between interpretations, reasonable interpretations, and clarifications in the Venn diagram illustrated in Figure 3.2.

The diagram shows what certainly is the most common case, where the set of reasonable interpretations is smaller than the set of interpretations. Note, however, that a special case can exist in which the set of reasonable interpretations can coincide with the set of interpretations. The set of clarifications, however, must always contain at least one element less than the set of reasonable interpretations.

We can use an argument in John Rawls's well-known book, *A Theory of Justice*, to illustrate how the notions of interpretation, reasonable interpretation, and clarification can be useful for practical research. It is typical of

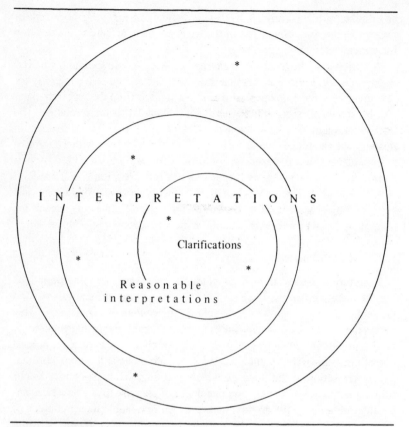

Figure 3.2 The Relationship Between Interpretations, Reasonable Interpretations, and Clarifications

Rawls's method that he used the mechanism to develop his own argument and not in order to interpret the doctrines of others. Unlike other philosophers with a constructive bent—e.g., Leo Strauss and his disciples—Rawls does not readily reference his arguments to previous thinkers, preferring instead to reason as if the thoughts were pulled from inside himself. The relevant example deals with the so-called second principle of justice in Rawls's theory—inspired by natural law—on just government. He formulates the thesis as follows:

> Social and economic inequalities are to be arranged so that they are both (a) reasonably expected to be to everyone's advantage, and (b) attached to positions and offices open to all.

Everyone's Advantage

		Principle of Efficiency	Difference Principle
EQUALLY	Equality as careers open to talents	I_1 System of Natural Liberty	I_3 Natural Aristocracy
OPEN	Equality as equality of fair opportunity	I_2 Liberal Equality	I_4 Democratic Equality

Figure 3.3 Rawls's Four Interpretations of the Second Principle of Justice

If the inequalities do not fulfill these demands, then they are not just.[21]

As Rawls is the first to point out, the phrases "to everyone's advantage" and "open to all" are ambiguous. Both of these expressions have two natural meanings. The principle, therefore, can be given four different interpretations (I_1, I_2, I_3, and I_4), which Rawls summarizes in Figure 3.3.

In the first interpretation (I_1), equality—in the sense that all careers in society are formally open to anyone who has the desire and ability—is combined with the so-called principle of efficiency. This latter is nothing more than what economists call the Pareto optimality, which states that a society is efficient if it is impossible to change it in such a way that one person's lot improves without some other person's lot becoming worse at the same time. If both of these conditions exist, then according to this first interpretation, a society is economically and socially just.

In the second interpretation, justice exists if the principle of efficiency is combined with a somewhat greater demand for equality. It is no longer enough that all potential careers are formally open to all; everyone must also have a reasonable chance to attain them. This means roughly that all who possess the same ability and the same skills should have an equal chance in life, regardless of the social class to which they happen to have been born.

The third interpretation says that justice exists if all careers are open to all in principle and if those people with greater natural endowments are allowed

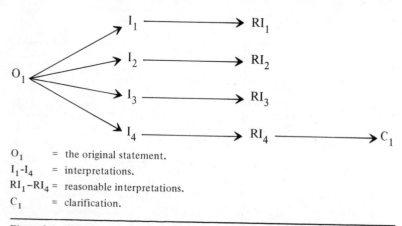

O_1 = the original statement.
I_1-I_4 = interpretations.
RI_1-RI_4 = reasonable interpretations.
C_1 = clarification.

Figure 3.4 Flow Chart of John Rawls's Interpretation and Clarification of the Second Principle of Justice

to advance only so long as this favors those members of the society who are worse off. Rawls calls this state "noblesse oblige."

The fourth interpretation, finally, holds that all people should not only have the same formal right to all careers, but they should also have the same opportunity to enter them. This should be combined with the thought that higher aspirations in those who are better off can be permitted only if this causes a rise in the ambitions of those who are the least advantaged. Only if there exists a situation in which everyone's lot improves is this to be preferred to the situation in which everyone's lot is equal.

Since Rawls clearly regards all four of these interpretations as equally reasonable, he goes on immediately to the clarification process. He does not undertake this clarification from a linguistic perspective; rather, he bases it on philosophical reasoning. The fourth interpretation is preferable, Rawls argues, because it would be the most rational choice if one were starting from scratch, assuming that one finds contract theory to be an agreeable perspective on society. Rawls refines the fourth interpretation as follows:

Social and economic inequalities are to be arranged so that they are both (a) to the greatest benefit of the least advantaged and (b) attached to offices and positions open to all under conditions of fair equality of opportunity.[22]

We can summarize Rawls's interpretive operations in the flow chart in Figure 3.4.

4

DESCRIBING MESSAGES AND JUDGING SUPPORT AND CLARITY

Having expounded on the meaning of interpretation and having chosen one or more methods of interpretation, we can now put these tools to practical use. We do this when we begin to interpret and describe the discourse to be examined. We must find answers to our basic research question.

The task of describing discourse may be divided into the following three consecutive states:

(1) identifying claims and reasons;
(2) working out their meaning; and
(3) portraying them.

4.1 Identifying Claims and Reasons

We must begin the process of identification by collecting material that we expect will contain information relevant to our basic research question. The material we collect, then, depends on the question we ask. I will not delve into various types of material here. Let it suffice to say that the material can consist of books, newspaper and magazine columns, papers in journals, parliamentary records, party publications, government publications, and the like. To begin, the researcher skims through the material in order to develop a sort of general feel for what it is about and whether it is relevant at all to the subject chosen for study. Once the researcher has found that the material seems pertinent, he can read it more carefully time and again in order to locate stated claims. The researcher also tries to uncover possible unstated claims.

The procedure is the same with regard to reasons. The researcher reads the material several times in order to identify reasons pro and con. He also looks for tacit premises.

Thus, an important first step in the description of an argument is the identification of claims and reasons relevant to the basic research question and the act of sorting them out from all other types of statements in the material. How do we do this? There seem to be two options. We can look for (a) placement cues and (b) indicator words.

The most obvious way to identify claims is to look for placement cues such as whether they are located at the beginning or end of a paragraph or passage. Such a cue, though helpful, is far from reliable. The order in which various parts of an argument are communicated to the researcher may not be that convenient for him at all.

It might be a good point of departure, however, to expect that reasons will be presented prior to claims. In the following examples, the claim "Sweden is a neutral country" follows the reason "Sweden has not joined any military defense alliance":

(1) Sweden has not joined any military defense alliance; thus (therefore, so, hence, consequently) it is a neutral country.

(2) Because Sweden has not joined any military defense alliance it is a neutral country.

From time to time, however, claims are stated before grounds:

(3) Sweden is a neutral country since it has not joined any military defense alliance.

Elementary logic textbooks also mention the case where a claim is sandwiched in between two elements of a reason:

(4) Since all nations that have not joined any military defense alliance are neutral, Sweden must be a neutral country for (the reason that) it has not joined any such alliance.

It is evident from our examples that an argument can be stated with its conclusions first, last, or in between several premises. Hence, conclusions and reasons cannot always be identified in terms of their positions within the statements of an argument. It is also evident that the locations of claims and reasons within larger units such as passages, articles, books, speeches, and so on are not reliable identification cues. Then how can they be recognized?

Certain terms or phrases serve typically to introduce an argument's premises or conclusion. Let us call these terms or phrases "indicator words." Irving M. Copi has distinguished between premise-indicators and conclusion-indicators.

In example 1, "thus," "therefore," "so," "hence," and "consequently" point to conclusions; they are conclusion-indicators. In examples 2, 3, and 4, we find the premise-indicators "because," "since," and "for (the reason that)"; no indicator-words signal conclusions in these cases.[1] These would seem by and large to be the two possibilities available to us in the identification of arguments.

4.1.1 Claims Must Be Supported by Reasons

As we begin to collect material in our search for relevant lines of reasoning, we may quickly find shortcomings in the discourse. These flaws may be elementary and concern the way the discourse was presented. The reasoning may simply be incomplete. Consequently, we must initiate a validity test while we are still trying to identify which arguments we are going to study.

The features of the complete description of the arguments are determined in part by how strictly we apply two basic criteria for validity testing in the description phase. This, in turn, is determined by the purpose of the study. In practice, then, it is impossible to erect a watertight bulkhead between the description and the rational assessment of political messages. A rational assessment must be executed just as the arguments are being described, not after the description is finished.

We can express the first criterion of rational argumentation as a require-ment that claims be supported by reasons. This rule suggests that there is a kind of absolute minimum requisite for valid discourse; if a line of reasoning does not satisfy this so-called rule of support, then it is useless to go on and examine whether it satisfies other standards for rational soundness. It is imperative that we reject any argument that does not fulfill the requirement of support.

It happens both in journalism and politics that unsupported claims are made. The theses may be repeated several times during a debate and be followd by idle talk which, while it may touch upon the subject, still does not constitute reasons to support the theses. Even though the person who proffers a thesis does not believe that his position will gain intellectual force by being repeated several times, he may think that his presentation will be more effective if he does this. However, effective and rational argumenta-tion are two different things.

To present a claim without reasons is to break the rule of support and this practice should be condemned forcefully. Bare claims regarding controver-sial affairs or political positions cannot be taken at all seriously. The mistake of supporting claims by repetition rather than by reasoned evidence — what is called the fallacy of *argument ad nauseam* — seems to be sufficient reason to dismiss an entire argument as incomplete.

4.1.2 Tacit Claims and Reasons Must Not Cause Unclarity

Valid argumentation must also fulfill a second demand, one which, reasonably, must be applied as soon as the researcher tries to identify an argument. This criterion suggests that claims and reasons must not be tacit in such a way as to give rise to unclarity. This is the first subrule under the general rule of clarity.

This yardstick, for example, becomes relevant once we have assured ourselves that grounds have been presented either for or against the claim we are studying, but that these grounds seem to be based partly on implicit empirical or evaluative assumptions. This is very common in political language. There can be several causes. Assumptions are sometimes excluded because they seem obvious. To express them would be superfluous; after all, everyone understands that they exist. Occasionally, they are excluded because they are controversial. This is particularly true of essentially contested value premises.

While transgression of the first general rule is a serious matter, breaking the rule of clarity can sometimes be overlooked. In some cases it may not even be necessary to point out that certain assumptions are implicit. In others it may be better to proclaim that premises are implied and then to hurry on and make them explicit. This procedure could, for example, be part of the general application of the principle of charity.

Tacit suppositions can also create genuine unclarity concerning the message's actual meaning. The context may be such that the researcher basically feels unsure of how the assumptions should be concretely formulated. In these cases, of course, violations of the rule of suppressed information must be clearly pointed out. Perhaps the analysis will have to stop at this. In other cases we might be able to present reasonable interpretations of the tacit assumptions. Then, in accordance with the principle of charity, we can select those assumptions that lend the line of reasoning the greatest possible weight and let the continued analysis be based on this.

4.2 *Working Out the Meaning of Arguments*

In the second phase of discourse description, we try to understand more penetratingly what is being communicated. If the claims or reasons that have been proffered contain poorly known technical jargon, then we may have to deepen our understanding through outright conceptual analysis. Furthermore, political language abounds with vague and ambiguous words and sentences. Whenever we run across such obscurity we must try to determine the exact nature of it. Here, we immediately run up against the question of how it is to be judged. There is an interplay between interpretation and validity testing.

4.3   Words Must Be Clear

The third standard for judging political argumentation is included, as is the second, in the general rule of clarity. It states that claims and reasons must not be phrased in such a way that they cause confusion. Ambiguity and vagueness must be avoided (see Chapter 2). The background to this rule is that fuzziness impedes communication because interpretation is made more difficult. To some extent, unclarity in political argumentation must always be condemned. At the same time, this demand must not be taken too far. We must remember that clarity and precision are not ends in themselves but only means for achieving more effective communication. If there are too many clarifications, the presentation can become very difficult to read and so make the message more difficult to understand. The point is that comprehension can be obstructed by both excessive muddiness and excessive precision. It is necessary to balance the two extremes when we judge clarity.

4.3.1   Unconscious Obscurity . . .

Many factors influence the clarity of political messages. Knowledge of the sources of obscurity can help us trace and take a stand toward abstrusity.

We should differentiate between unconscious and conscious obscurity. A statement may be unclear because the speaker lacks insight into the properties of the language he is using. He may also not know enough about what he is saying. In these cases the speaker uses ambiguous and vague expressions because he does not realize that they give rise to obscurity.

One common form of unconscious muddiness occurs when a speaker shifts between different senses of the same term. He thus may reach apparently reasonable conclusions that in fact are entirely untenable. Gunnar Fredriksson gives an example of how the equivocity of the word ''monopoly'' was put to energetic use in the Swedish debate on commercial radio and television. Vilhelm Moberg once wrote in an article:

> Dismal experience should tell us in Sweden how easily a radio monopoly can be turned into the mouthpiece of a country's government. And how important that monopoly is in the formation of public opinion, say, during an election! . . . It is significant that it is primarily the country's power brokers who want to preserve the monopoly of the word.

In the first sentence, Moberg uses the word to mean ''technological monopoly,'' while in the second, he shifts over to a new sense of the word, i.e., ''regulated public opinion formation.''[2]

In one of the classic critical works of Swedish political science, *Conservative Ideas,* Herbert Tingsten reveals how renowned ideologues like Treitschke, Maurras, and many others commit grandiose errors when they shift back and forth between different meanings of words like "people," "freedom," "democracy," and "the public interest."[3] Typical is Fichte's use of the terms "German" and "German character" in his *Speeches to the German Nation,* a boundless glorification of all things German, published during the French occupation of Berlin in 1807-1808. For Fichte, the words did not just denote a particular nationality or a people living within certain boundaries. They were used in an ideal sense as well: all who believed in and worked for the good of mankind were "Germans," regardless of nationality, and Germans who did not belong to this army of progress were "un-German." In the fourth lecture, though, Fichte talks about Germans as a Germanic tribe, while in the seventh lecture he again says that a person is German if he believes in the new and the original qualities of the human being, in freedom, boundless possibilities for improvement, and in the eternal progress of our species. Tingsten points out that the exploitation of the equivocity of words is one of the most common methods used in the formation of ideology.[4]

We differentiate unconscious from conscious obscurity because from a moral perspective, they must be judged differently. Unconscious, unintentional obscurity is not morally objectionable in the same way as is conscious or intentional obscurity.

Rational assessment must expose obscurity, of course, regardless of whether it is conscious or unconscious. When we find unconscious obscurity, we cannot go on and pose the moral question of whether it is right to make use of obscurity. After all, no one *makes use of* unconscious obscurity, and so, it is not subject to moral judgment.[5]

4.3.2 . . . and Conscious Obscurity

From the moral point of view, then, conscious obscurity is the interesting kind. In the hands of a skilled political manipulator, the fuzziness of political language can, in fact, be of inestimable value. It can be used in many different ways. A cunning joke based on an ambiguity surrounding a political opponent can be a political weapon. Obscurities can also be perfect devices for avoiding deserved attack. As a defense, the person being attacked gives equivocal key words some other, more advantageous sense. We will often discover specific strategic considerations behind a use of obscurity for political manipulation. Obscurity is used to gain political advantage.

It is worthwhile for us to call attention to a few cases of conscious, calculated obscurity:

(1) obscurity to produce a witticism aimed at generating interest;
(2) obscurity to keep open a respectable path of retreat;
(3) obscurity to make something more morally acceptable;
(4) obscurity to hide actual disunity; and
(5) obscurity to hide actual unity.

We can mention political jokes as examples of morally inoffensive obscurity. Jokes, slogans, and other political witticisms often gain their potency from some hilarious ambiguity. They may be used to focus attention and make listeners more amenable to the real message, which will come later.

During World War II, the expression ''save soap and waste paper'' was coined in the United States. Because of its inherent ambiguity, this slogan eventually became wholly unsuccessful. Gerald Ford demonstrated considerable irony at his own expense with a witty characterization of himself during his inaugural speech: ''I am a Ford, not a Lincoln.''[6]

Politicians sometimes lay down linguistic smokescreens in order to get aides to take morally or politically reprehensible action while, at the same time, they deny to some other audience all knowledge of these actions and so abdicate any responsibility for them. The goal is to get some dubious act carried out while simultaneously keeping open a morally respectable path of retreat.

A government's relationship to its intelligence organizations can be especially sensitive. It became evident in a U.S. Senate committee report in November 1975 that the CIA had developed advanced plans to assassinate several foreign leaders, including Patrice Lumumba, Fidel Castro, and Salvador Allende. The report also said that the CIA had been directly involved in the murder of Rafael Trujillo and Ngo Dinh Diem. From the point of view of political responsibility, it is important to ask whether the president and other leading politicians knew of or, in the name of the national interest, even ordered these acts which, from the common moral perspective of the individual, were entirely indefensible. The committee reports, however, that it had a remarkably difficult time obtaining unequivocal evidence.[7] It seems that in their dealings with each other, politicians and those inside the CIA were very calculating in their use of the so-called principle of credible denial. The intelligence community argued that politicians should not be told all the gory details so that they could categorically deny all knowledge of and responsibility for the assassination plans if, contrary to expectations, the naked truth should one day come to light. At the same time, though, the politicians should acquire enough approximate information so that they generally know what is going on. The president and his closest aides seem to have been entirely satisfied with this procedure and in some cases even employed it in their dealings with CIA officers. Written communication was entirely forbidden. Fuzzy circumlocutions, evasive expressions, euphemisms, and mimed allusions were everyday occurrences.[8] Both the CIA and the president's men used expressions that could be interpreted as "murder," "kill" or "execute," but that could also be interpreted to refer to other much more respectable measures. They talked about "removing" Lumumba, saying that he required "forceful actions" or that he must be "gotten rid of." It was necessary to "keep Allende out of office" and to "knock down," "eliminate," or "remove" Castro. One CIA officer was given the expressive order: "get off your ass about Cuba!"[9]

After all this, the committee's conclusion was that lacking clear evidence, it could not unequivocally tie any president to the assassination plans.[10]

A third form of conscious obscurity is aimed at taking advantage of the emotive side of language. Something that actually is disgusting is described in strictly neutral or even positively charged terms. The goal is to get the audience to accept what it otherwise would not. In the same way, phenomena that are not repulsive are given very negative labels. The point then, of course, is to get people to loathe what they otherwise would have liked.

Supporters of American involvement in Vietnam during the 1970s were extraordinarily inventive in developing a language with which to describe the horrors of the war. In his *Logic and Contemporary Rhetoric*, Howard Kahane offers a whole list of examples of this kind of official doublespeak. A sample from that list, with translations:

EUPHEMISM	TRANSLATION
Pacification center	Concentration camp
Incursion	Invasion (as in "Cambodian incursion")
Protective reaction strike	Bombing
Surgical strike	Precision bombing
Incontinent ordinance	Off-target bombs (usually used when they kill civilians)
Friendly fire	Shelling friendly villages or troops by mistake
Specified strike zone	Area where soldiers can fire at anything—replaced "free fire zone" when that became notorious
Waterborne logistic craft	Sampan (as in "waterborne logistic craft sunk")

Strategic withdrawal	Retreat (when our side does it)
Adviser	Military officer (before we admitted "involvement" in Vietnam) or CIA agent
Termination	Killing
Enemy infiltration	Movement of enemy troops into the battle area
Reinforcements	Movement of friendly troops into the battle area
Selective ordinance	Napalm (also similarly "selective" explosives)

Here are a few other examples from Kahane of doublespeak, with emphasis on language used in the Watergate scandal:

Inappropriate	Illegal
Entry	Burglary (as in "the entry into Democratic headquarters")
Electronic surveillance or Intelligence gathering	Wiretapping or Illegal eavesdropping
Indicated	Said (usually when what was said was a lie or politically risky)
Destabilize	Overthrow (as in "We intended to destabilize the communist government in Chile")
Termination	Any kind of ending (for example, of a relationship; in military and spy circles generally restricted to death)[11]

This manipulation of language occurs, of course, in all political contexts in all countries, but dictatorships tend to be particularly systematic in these machinations. In his book, *The Politics of Communication,* Claus Mueller gives many examples of language manipulation in the Third Reich. One instrument of manipulation was the Office of the Press, which stipulated many terms to be used instead of others in newspapers. These orders were originally called Language Regulations, but the name was later changed to Daily Directives from the Secretary of the Press. Among the examples of directives Mueller offers in his book are these:

DATE	DIRECTIVE
Mar. 20, 1934	"It is requested that the term 'People's Day of Mourning' be replaced by the term 'Memorial Day for the Heroes.' "
Sept. 1, 1936	"The following has definitely been decided upon for the

names of the different powers in Spain: The 'Franco Government' has to be called the 'Spanish National Government'; the others can never be mentioned in connection with the term 'government.' Their name is simply 'Bolsheviks.' "

Sept. 1, 1939   "The word 'war' has to be avoided in all news coverage and editorials. Germany is repulsing a Polish attack."

Oct. 16, 1941   "There should be no more references to Soviet or Soviet Russian soldiers. At most they can be called Soviet army members [*Sovietarmisten*] or just simply Bolsheviks, beasts, and animals."

Mar. 16, 1944   "The Secretary of Propaganda and People's Enlightenment has requested that the term "catastrophe' be completely deleted from the German language. It has therefore been decided that the word "catastrophe' be replaced by the term 'large emergency' and 'catastrophe aid' by 'air war aid.' "[12]

The purpose of the fourth form of obscurity is to hide actual disunity. Unclear formulations can be used this way in international treaties or in communiques. Sometimes this is admitted openly, e.g., when it is said that at all costs a "formula" must be found upon which all parties can agree. The formula is a linguistic disguise that barely hides the disunity from the eyes of the layman, but that does not prevent the parties from maintaining their divergent opinions.

A telling example is Resolution 242 of the UN Security Council, adopted unanimously on November 22, 1967. The resolution dealt with the Arab-Israeli war. One passage said:

The Security Council, . . . Emphasizing . . . that all member-States in their acceptance of the Charter of the United Nations have undertaken a commitment to act in accordance with article 2 of the Charter,
(1) Affirms that the fulfillment of the Charter principles requires the establishment of a just and lasting peace in the Middle East which should include the application of the following principle . . .:
(i) Withdrawal of Israeli armed forces from territories occupied in the recent conflict. . . .

The key words, "withdrawal . . . from territories occupied," appear in the last paragraph of the quotation. One of the points of this formulation is that it does not refer to "withdrawal . . . from *the* territories occupied" or "*all* territories occupied." The phrase could be interpreted, then, in such a way that a just and lasting peace in the Middle East could be achieved if Israel were to withdraw from some of the occupied territories, e.g., Sinai, though not necessarily from all of them. The wording also makes it possible for Israel and its allies to claim that Israel does not have to withdraw from, for example, the Arab section of Jerusalem in order to achieve a just and lasting peace.

At the same time, though, Israel's enemies have been able to say that the resolution means that Israel must withdraw from all occupied terrirories if there is to be peace. Territories are either occupied or they are not. Israel occupied Sinai, the Gaza Strip, East Jerusalem, the West Bank, and the Golan Heights in the Six-Day War of 1967.

This interpretation is also supported by the Russian version of the resolution. The Russian language does not have a definitive article: thus, the Russian text makes possible the interpretation "from the territories occupied," even though there is no definitive article.[13]

Sometimes, evasive formulations can have the exactly opposite purpose, i.e., to barely cover over basic shared values. In some situations, politicians or government officials may find it unpleasant or at least tactically ill-advised to publicly appear to agree with, say, a foreign government or a domestic opposition party. They may want to avoid being judged according to the company they keep; they want to avoid guilt by association.

In his writing on the death of ideology in the fortunate, highly developed welfare democracy, Tingsten offers many splendid examples of such duplicity, as he considers it. The parties are essentially united on all the old issues, he writes, but in their competition for votes, they try to mobilize all the resources of the old political language so as to appear to be engaged in great battles on a field of silent desolation. "The words of honor live on, fragile and shimmering. On political holidays, at demonstrations and elections, veterans of long since disbanded armies go on parade, speaking of liberalism and socialism as if the words were important, as if they were thoughts for the future rather than epitaphs."[14]

It is the job of rational assessment, of course, to find and destroy obscurities, regardless of whether they are unconscious or conscious. However, we then limit our criticism strictly to the messages' content.

With respect to conscious obscurity, however, we can also ask whether these shifts between unclear meaning, conscious formulae, euphemisms, defamation, and allusion are morally defensible. A significant portion of political debate deals with exactly this. Note that we are no longer judging the content of the messages; we are appraising their *pronouncement*. We have thus departed from rational assessment of the intellectual content of messages and turned to assessment of the *acts* of pronouncing them. In spite of this, we will offer some views here on this latter form of assessment as well.

The moral question has been discussed since antiquity. Machiavelli, Metternich, and Talleyrand are well-known advocates of manipulative statesmanship. Bismarck made changes in the Ems Dispatch in order to lure France into a war that might unite the German states under Prussian leadership. Is such conscious obscurity defensible?

The first answer to the question must be no. The main rule should be that politicians should use clear language, but this is not enough. They should follow all other rules for rational political discourse. I would like to call this basic presumption in favor of the rules of rational political discourse *the principle of message rationality*.

The really interesting question may be whether we can accept exceptions from this principle. Can we conceive of political situations in which clear language would have such catastrophic or serious consequences that obscurity would be preferable? The question is important, but it is far too large for us to deal with in this context. Let us merely say that every deviation from the principle of message rationality must have a special justification. Following this principle requires no special justification, but ignoring it does. This does not necessarily mean that all conscious obscurities must be condemned. Situations may exist in which gobbledygook, con artistry, and doublespeak are morally defensible. Special justification may weigh more heavily than the basic principle of message rationality. However, the principle does fundamentally limit the conscious use of political obscurity: In every situation where an unclear formulation is a possible alternative, we must first check to see whether the clear formulation could be used instead.[15]

4.4   *First-Order and Second-Order Disagreement*

Our reasoning so far concerning the description and assessment of claims and reasons has been based on the tacit assumption that all who participate in rational political discourse accept the basic rules governing the analysis. Everyone, we presume, accepts the desirability of clarity. All participants, we assume, agree on what meaning is and which methods of interpretation should be used to elucidate it. If two interpreters arrive at two different interpretations of the same text, then this is because the passage in the text was so indefinitely framed as to leave room for two expositions. Their disagreement is entirely within the rules of the game. It is a first-order quarrel.

Conflicts between two analysts or between an analyst and someone being analyzed may be more profound and may relate to the very rules used to determine whether a political message is valid or not. Some thinkers do not accept the rule that the wording of messages must be clear. Others may not accept the prescription that statements proffered as reasons must be relevant to the claim, that statements should be consistent with each other, that inferences from reasons to claims should be validly derived, or that statements of fact should be true. These disagreements concern the constitutive rules of the game. They are second-order quarrels.

Two thinkers may agree superficially to maintain, say, the rule that words must be clear. Both assert that the meaning of what is said should be clear. However, the agreement on this standard may be illusory. The two may differ profoundly on what "meaning" means. They thus demonstrate that they are not in agreement on one of the fundamental rules of rational political discourse.

The two may also disagree on rules other than those used directly as yardsticks of validity. The disagreement may have to do with which method of interpretation should be used to describe the message and so create a basis for applying the clarity rule. One analyst may have used the intentionalist method to interpret the text, while another may have used the literal method or the systematic method.

We can leave the problem of choosing a suitable method of interpretation; we discussed it in an earlier context. We will, however, say a few words about the meta-conflicts that stem from differing notions of what "meaning" means and that, as such, have to do basically with the meaning of the clarity rule.[16]

4.5 Second-Order Disagreement on the Essentialist Theory of Meaning

There is a clear conflict about the rule of clarity between those who largely advocate the analytic position that pervades this work and those who adhere to the so-called classical tradition in political philosophy. The conflict is evident in Karl R. Popper's *The Open Society and Its Enemies* and even more dominant in T. D. Weldon's work, *The Vocabulary of Politics*.

The classical political philosophers commit a serious mistake, says Weldon, when they believe that words—and especially political terms such as "state," "citizen," "law," "freedom," and "right"—have an essential meaning. A word like "state," according to this view, is actually the name of a thing. The word has meaning in the same way that a child has parents. Assume, says Weldon, that a little boy is found abandoned in a telephone booth. No one knows who his parents are, but everyone understands that the lad's parents must be somewhere. We should, therefore, begin to search for them. The search may succeed. If, however, there are no clues or if they do not lead us anywhere, then the result of the search is negative. Nonetheless, we all know in principle how to conduct such a search. The situation is analogous with respect to the search for the meaning of words, argue the classical political philosophers.[17]

According to this view, the task facing political philosophy is to ascertain the essential meaning of words. This is achieved when we gain insight into the immutable essences of which the political words are imperfect reflections. The essentialist theory of meaning is connected, then, to the ontological notion that there are real essences. To ascertain the meaning of words is to gain knowledge of these essences. At the same time, this theory of essence is tied to a normative theory that states that these essences are also absolute yardsticks with which we can judge the soundness of existing political institutions and polities. When we know what "state" means, then we know something about the nature of the state and we can then also decide which state is the best—the communist, the socialist, the liberal, or the conservative. Once we have discovered what "justice" means, then we also know what justice essentially is and so we can determine which state is the most just.[18]

How do we go about gaining knowledge about the meaning of words and so about the ideal and inner nature of things? Simply through the analysis of words. By merely processing the material with his thoughts, man can gain knowledge about the true meaning of words and about the true nature of those things that the words reflect. The essentialist theory of meaning, in other words, is also combined with a verification theory that is more intuitionist than empirical. Observations of reality and empirical evidence are not needed to gain knowledge about facts; philosophers can gain insight into the innermost nature of things with nothing but the aid of reason or intuition.[19]

Let us not get caught up in ontology, the normative theory, or the verification theory; let us return instead to this perspective on the meaning of words and the notion of interpretation that flows from it. What is the difference between the essentialist notion and the perspective advocated by, for example, Weldon and Popper and adopted by modern science? According to the modern perspective, the essentialist theory confuses two issues that must be kept separate: the semantic question of meaning and the empirical question of truth. One might also say that the semantic questions that the essentialist theory of meaning poses are related to the term to the left in the definition "human being = thinking animal." The essentialist reads the definition from left to right. He believes then that he answers both the question of the term's meaning as well as the question of its underlying nature. According to Weldon and Popper, though, the definition should be read from right to left. One asks what one should call a thinking animal and the answer is a human being. The job of the definition in this case is not to convey knowledge about essences, but to make a long linguistic expression shorter and so easier to handle. Instead of describing anything, the definition stipulates a use of language. Thus it can be neither true nor false.[20]

The essentialist view of definitions is untenable. Plato and Aristotle thought that human beings had an ability, called intellectual intuition, with the help of which they could uncover essences and discover which definition is the true one. We may admit that certain of our intellectual experiences can sometimes be described as results of intuition. Anyone who understands an idea in the sense of having a feeling for what it means can be said to understand it intuitively. No matter how powerful these psychological experiences may be, they can never serve to establish the truth of a scientific hypothesis or theory. Such hunches cannot serve as evidence in a scientific discussion, since someone else may have an equally strong feeling that the same theory is false. Intuition undoubtedly can inspire a researcher to make important discoveries, but it can also lead him astray. Science is not primarily interested in how one came upon one's ideas, but in what the ideas are and how they can be tested. To tie this in with an important theme of this book—which returns on many different levels in many different contexts— the question of the origin of a conviction is irrelevant to the intellectual validity of that conviction. The questions of origin and validity must be logically separated. The classical essentialist theory of the meaning of words is based on an unfortunate confusion of origin and validity.[21]

There is every reason to agree with Popper that every branch of knowledge that professes this theory of meaning has never become anything more than phrasemongering and barren scholasticism. Science has progressed only to the extent that it has freed itself from the strait jacket of the essentialist method.[22]

5

ASSESSING RELEVANCE

The third main assessment criterion suggests that messages ought to be relevant. This means, roughly, that they should be important and substantively pertinent to the matter at hand.[1]

5.1 Two Types of Relevance Assessment

The rule of relevance can, as we saw in Chapter 1, be broken down into two subrules. The one holds that statements actually proffered should be pertinent to the subject matter of the discussion. Whatever is said must belong to the topic; idle chatter adds nothing to the subject in an orderly discussion. The other subrule says that relevant aspects of the case should be acknowledged and presented. Relevant facts should not be suppressed or excluded. Biased selection of facts must be banned from every rational debate. In this second case, we can talk about comprehensiveness testing.

Clearly, the twin requirements of relevance are logically related to each other. Whereas first degree relevance testing means identifying and discarding *irrelevant* information in what *is* actually communicated, second degree testing implies identifying and collecting *relevant* information that *is not* communicated. We can sketch the difference in the diagram in Figure 5.1.

Obviously, four kinds of information are involved. Relevance assessment of the first type focuses entirely on what is actually communicated (1 and 2 in the diagram). Irrelevant information included in the message (1 in the diagram) is discarded, and relevant information included in the message (2 in the diagram) is retained. Assessment of comprehensiveness focuses on what is not communicated. In the set of information not included in the message (3 and 4), one subset is deemed relevant (3) and brought forward, while the other subset (4) is left out.

5.2 Type 1 Relevance Estimation

We can also discern two aspects of the first type of relevance assessment. First, an answer may be irrelevant to a question. If a journalist asks a question, for example, and a politician answers by offering claims and

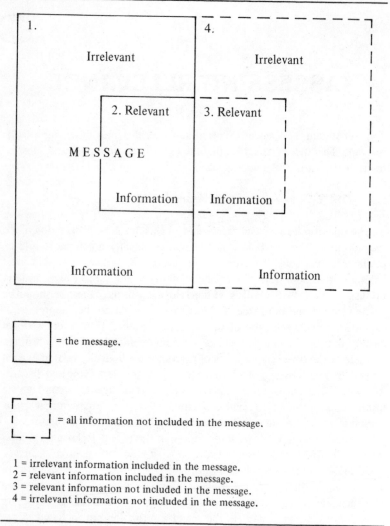

Figure 5.1   Relevant and Irrelevant Information

reasons about something totally different, then his answer is beside the point and irrelevant *in relation to the question*. Notice that in this case, both claims and reasons are irrelevant. We can formulate a second-order subrule as follows: An assertion made in answering a question should be germane to the content of that question.

If an author offers reasons for a claim, and another writer tries to refute it on the basis of grounds that have nothing to do with the topic, then the reasons are irrelevant *in relation to the first author's claim*. A second subrule holds that statements put forth as reasons for or against a claim must be pertinent to that claim.

We must take seriously violations of the first rule of relevance. We must ruthlessly eliminate irrelevant pronouncements from all further assessment.

The debates between presidential candidates Jimmy Carter and Gerald Ford in 1976 have been examined from the point of view of relevance. The researcher tried to determine the extent to which the candidates' answers addressed the questions put to them. The questions were posed in order to extract statements from the candidates revealing their positions on given issues. An answer was deemed satisfactory if it pinned down the candidate's position, unsatisfactory if it did not. In our context, the latter type of answer is considered irrelevant.

The researcher refined his categories further. Satisfactory answers were subdivided into direct answers that were short and to the point, and other answers that were merely responsive in the sense that an answer could be constructed, though perhaps with some effort, from the materials in the response. (Let us disregard here the fact that this subdivision is a bit vague.) We shall examine an irrelevant answer, but first, for comparison's sake, let us look at two relevant answers, one direct and one responsive.

Satisfactory answer, direct (as to which constitutional amendment he would work hard for if he were president):

> CARTER: I would not work hard to support any of those. We've always had, I think, a lot of constitutional amendments proposed, but the passage of them has been fairly slow.

Satisfactory answer, responsive (as to new legislation for controlling agencies like the FBI):

> FORD: You are familiar, of course, with the fact that I am the first President in 30 years who has reorganized the intelligence agencies in the Federal Government: the C.I.A., the Defense Intelligence Agency, the National Security Agency and others.
>
> We've done that by executive order. And I think we've tightened it up; we've straightened out their problems that developed over the last few years.
>
> It doesn't seem to me that it's needed or necessary to have legislation in this particular regard. I have recommended to the Congress, however—I'm sure you're familiar with this—legislation that would make it very proper, and in

the right way, that the Attorney General could go in and get the right for wiretapping under security cases.

This was an effort that was made by the Attorney General and myself, working with the Congress. But even in this area, where I think new legislation would be justified, the Congress has not responded. So I feel in that case, as well as in the reorganization of the intelligence agencies, as I've done, we have to do it by executive order.

Unsatisfactory answer, irrelevant (as to his concept of the national interest and the role of the United States in the world):

CARTER: Well, I'm not going to name my Cabinet before I get elected. I've got a little ways to go before I start doing that.

But I have an adequate background, I believe. I am a graduate of the United States Naval Academy, the first military graduate since Eisenhower. I have served as the Governor of Georgia and have traveled extensively in foreign countries and South America, Central America, Europe, the Middle East and in Japan.

I've traveled the last 21 months among the people of this country. I've talked to them and I've listened. And I've seen at first hand, in a very vivid way, the deep hurt that's come to this country in the aftermath of Vietnam and Cambodia, Chile and Pakistan, and Angola and Watergate, the C.I.A. revelations.

What we were formerly so proud of the strength of our country, its moral integrity, the representation in foreign affairs of what our people or what our Constitution stands for—has been gone. And in the secrecy that has surrounded our foreign policy in the last few years, the American and the Congress have been excluded.

I believe I know what this country ought to be.

I've been one who's loved my nation as many Americans do, and I believe that there's no limit placed on what we can be in the future, if we can harness the tremendous resources, militarily, economically, and the stature of our people, the meaning of the Constitution, in the future.

Every time we've made a serious mistake in foreign affairs, it's been because the American people have been excluded from the process.

If we can just tap the intelligence and ability, the sound common sense and the good judgment of the American people, we can once again have a foreign policy that will make us proud instead of ashamed.

And I'm not going to exclude the American people from that process in the future, as Mr. Ford and Kissinger have done.

This is what it takes to have a sound foreign policy—strong at home, strong defense, permanent commitments—not betray the principles of our country and involve the American people and the Congress in the shaping of our foreign policy.

Every time Mr. Ford speaks from a position of secrecy in negotiations and in secret treaties that have been pursued and achieved in supporting dictatorships, in ignoring human rights, we are weak and the rest of the world knows it.

The first statement by Jimmy Carter is a direct, concise answer to the question posed. It must be classified, therefore, as satisfactory or relevant.

Ford's statement was also considered satisfactory. It is undoubtedly an answer to the question. It is not as concise and straightforward as Carter's, so the author characterized it as responsive rather than direct.

Carter's answer to the question about national interest and the U.S. role in the world does not deal with the question at all. It concerns Carter's background and his qualifications for conducting foreign policy, the problems facing the country, his affection for it, his plan for an open foreign policy, and the mistakes of the current administration. The answer evades the question through digression. It is not relevant.[2]

In connection wih our second-order subrule, which says that statements put forth as reasons for or against a claim must be pertinent to that claim, we can formulate a more specific rule with the aid of the basic distinction between rational assessment and explanation. We can formulate it as a proscription: We must not assess the validity of a claim by reference to those factors that explain why it was enunciated or entertained. In other words, the rational soundness of a claim must be decided by assessing the reasons offered for or against it, and not by determining what led the speaker to make it.

Proximity may cause these two things to be confused. This has even left its mark in the language. The word "reason" can be used both in the sense of justification as well as motivation. A motivation is a type of explanatory factor. Thus it can happen that one asks for reasons in the sense of justifying statements and gets instead an enumeration of various motivating forces. This notion was dealt with thoroughly in Chapter 1 in the section on intentionalist explanation.

Reference to factors explaining why someone has enunciated or entertained a claim, then, should not be acceptable features of an assessment of its rational soundness. One reason for this is that we can study the motives why political messages are enunciated or entertained regardless of whether their content is clear, relevant, consistent, or true. Unclear, irrelevant, inconsistent, or false messages may have been very influential. We can explain the origin of Vidkun Quisling's ideology with reference to various factors in the man's psychological make-up, but this does not answer the question of the ideology's clarity, consistency, or truth.

Based on the newly described relevance rule, we can criticize political actors for presenting irrelevant reasons. We might say that they resort to unfair methods in the rational political interlocution. We find a classic Swedish example of this in an exchange between Bengt Lidforss and Harald Hjärne. In an article in January 1905, Hjärne spoke up for the Russian monarchy, which he considered a bulwark against pure and naked licentiousness. He also expressed anxiety over what would happen when warmongering parties were no longer reined in by the czar. Lidforss retorted:

> Without playing psychologist in any deeper sense—there is no reason to—one might nevertheless dare to make the assumption that this impairment of Mr. Hjärne's powers of judgment is connected to some shock suffered during the past few years; and one would probably not be incorrect to trace this shock to the pompous fiasco which became of Mr. Hjärne's membership in Parliament. Mr. Hjärne has been so naive as to think he could impress the peasants in Parliament with the same subtle devices he uses to garner the applause of students—with antitheses, paradoxes and blather—and this naiveté has been his downfall. Still, he might have saved himself if the driving force in his political work had been zealous concern for some cause, if his heart had beat for some ideal. But one need not be particularly receptive to see the sick ambition, the unrelenting self-aggrandizement, which so evidently marks all of Mr. Hjärne's public behavior. He is as power hungry as Bishop Billing, though not as able to adapt, and so things turned out as they did.[3]

This magnificent lampoon clearly has nothing at all to do with Harald Hjärne's Russian articles. It is an unusually clear example of an extremely irrelevant argument.

It is a logical fallacy to dismiss an argument for reasons like Lidforss's. There are many such fallacies, discovered long ago and dutifully recorded in the literature. Some are so common as to have been endowed with their own Latin names. Lidforss's fallacy is called *argumentum ad hominem,* since it entails an attack on a person and not on what that person said. It can also be regarded as a special case of the genetic fallacy of trying to weaken or support the validity of a statement through reference to the statement's origin.[4]

The fact that a statement provides reasons for a claim is not identical to the fact that it constitutes a reason for accepting or expressing the claim. Many of the classic fallacies spring from the fact that these things are not kept separate. As examples of such fallacies we can mention *argumentum ad verecundiam* and *argumentum ad ignorantiam.* The former is appeal to authority, i.e., to the respect in which famous people are held. The latter exists if we come to the conclusion that something is true because we do not know if it is false, or vice versa. Let us examine an example of a fallacy called *tu quoque*. The Latin expression means "you also," and the fallacy consists of answering an accusation not by discussing its merits, but by making a counteraccusation.

In 1976, a Swedish government was formed which, for the first time since 1932, did not include any Social Democrats. When the three governing nonsocialist parties presented their statement of purpose, an intense debate arose as to whether the new prime minister, Thorbjörn Fälldin, had broken a promise or not. The new leader of the opposition, Olof Palme, said at a press conference that Fälldin—who strongly opposed nuclear power—had promised during the campaign that he would under no circumstances participate in a government that permitted the loading of nuclear fuel into the second reactor at the Barsebäck power station. Fälldin's position had been uncompromising—rather liberating and un-Swedish. Nevertheless, Fälldin accepted into the goverment's statement of purpose a formulation that meant that Barsebäck would be loaded with nuclear fuel. This was, Palme charged, not only a breach of promise, but pure and simple fraud.[5]

The conservative newspaper *Svenska Dagbladet* retorted that it is common that the victors are accused after an election of breaking promises. Olof Palme would likely have exercised more caution in his accusations, the paper went on to say, if he had looked back 44 years into Swedish political history. In their 1932 campaign, the Social Democrats had clearly supported free-trade agricultural policies. However, in a crisis agreement with the Farmer's Party in 1933, the Social Democrats' leader, Per Albin Hansson, retreated almost totally from the agricultural policies he had advocated a year earlier in the election. Grain and milk production were regulated, the price of butter was raised, and an excise tax was levied on margarine. Both of the historic shifts of power—in 1932-33 and 1976—were accompanied by accusations of broken campaign promises. Added *Svenska Dagbladet:* "Politics is called the art of the possible. Why should the Social Democrats have an exclusive right to take advantage of any possibilities present in a difficult political situation?"[6] This refutation of an accusation with a counteraccusation is clearly similar to an *argumentum tu quoque*.

5.3   Comprehensiveness Testing

Political messages are often biased and misleading. They may contain very detailed and relevant information, but only about things deemed positive for the position held. All negative aspects of the case may be hidden. Stated differently, all reasons for a claim may be presented while most conceivable reasons against are left out. Testing for comprehensiveness implies finding out whether some points of view that are germane to the subject matter have been left out.[7]

Exposing incomplete analysis can mean two things. One possibility is that the analyst introduces reasons the advocate left out, even though they support his position. This was dealt with earlier in connection with the ameliorative systematic method of interpretation. This is a flaw in the analysis, of course, and attention should be drawn to it, but it should not be judged too severely. In some cases, overlooked reasons ought to be brought up in order to build up a position really worth attacking.

The second possibility is that the analyst looks for counterevidence and counterreasoning that the advocate did not deal with. The investigator tries to overthrow the advocate's case by introducing negative reasons that weaken, contradict, or cast doubt on it.

The nuclear power debate in Western Europe and North America in the seventies has been marked by attacks by opponents of nuclear power against the flaws and holes in the earlier arguments of nuclear power advocates. The opponents claim, for example, that insufficient attention was paid to radioactive wastes, reactor malfunctions, and the risk of nuclear weapons proliferation.

It is very difficult to say what constitutes a complete analysis of a given topic, but this does not mean the criterion is useless. Even if we cannot define the outer limit, we have, in many cases, a good basis for arguing that a certain aspect is part of the subject. We can, of course, also claim that an argument is incomplete against the background of what is said on the subject in some well-defined place, e.g., in specific books, in a previous parliamentary debate, in an earlier policy study, or in a statement by some foreign body.

5.4 Conflicting Rules of Relevance

The first type of relevance agreement is usually assumed to mean just what we have described: Based on one or more criteria of what is relevant, the various reasons proffered in support of a thesis are divided into relevant and irrelevant ones, and the latter are dismissed. Suppose, however, one party to a debate refuses to accept one of the criteria. He may argue that the causes from which an ideology originates are acceptable reasons for deciding whether that ideology is valid or not. If we argue that his argument is irrelevant, he will not accept this since he does not accept the rule on which we base our assessment of relevance. We must climb to a higher level of argument in order to deal with this type of reasoning. We must defend our relevance rule or criticize the debater's reasons for not maintaining and applying the distinction between reasons in the sense of evidence for a claim, and reasons in the sense of motives that explain the enunciation or entertainment of that claim. Once again, we are faced with conflicting fundamental rules in rational assessment.

As an example of an advocate for an alternative view of criteria for relevance assessment, we may look to advocates of that school of Marxism that is usually associated with Georg Lukács. We might also look to some representative of the Frankfurt School, e.g., disciples of the so-called Apel model of knowledge. Or we may consider a work like Thomas Kuhn's on scientific revolutions. In this context, I will instead draw on a classic body of work, Karl Mannheim's sociology of knowledge.

5.4.1   Mannheim's Theory of the Origin and Validity of Knowledge

In his main work on ideology and utopia, Mannheim argues that what in a given time in a given society is considered logically and empirically true is determined by economic, social, or other extralogical circumstances. There exist no statements and theories that are valid in and of themselves; they are valid only in relation to certain values and perspectives. What was true for a proletarian in 1850 was not necessarily true for a worker today. This is not just a matter of the rather obvious insight that the origin of some specific piece of knowledge is caused by, say, the researcher's social perspective. Mannheim says that the social perspective determines whether the piece of knowledge is true or false, consistent or inconsistent, and perhaps also whether it is clear or unclear. There is an imperative logical connection between the origin of a set of ideas on the one hand, and its validity on the other. To render an opponent's argument invalid, one has only to "uncover" its sociological, psychological, or genetic roots. One might also say that Mannheim's position takes a systematic *argumentum ad hominem* and makes of it a respectable tool for demonstrating the invalidity of an opponent's views. We can call his form of relativism *epistemological*.[8]

5.4.2   Does Epistemological Relativism Lead to a Logical Paradox?

Mannheim's theory has been subjected to much sharp criticism from many important social researchers and philosophers. The criticism has proceeded along two main lines.

Perhaps the most common objection suggests that the theory must be rejected because, if it is applied to itself, it contains a damaging logical contradiction. If it is really the case that true knowledge exists only in relation to different values and perspectives, then this must also have consequences for the thesis of epistemological relativism. If the thesis were true in all milieus, regardless of time and place, then it would itself be a magnificent example of true knowledge that is independent of all social perspectives. And so it contradicts itself. If, on the other hand, the theory that all doctrines are relative is also relative in relation to specific social perspectives and values, then any critical person would naturally ask what these perspectives and values are. If this question could be answered, then all researchers with other values and perspectives could simply ignore the thesis. It would not be valid for them. In addition, one must ask whether this modification of the original relativistic thesis—the modification that states that the thesis is valid only for those who hold certain social values and perspectives—is true. Should the modified thesis express a general truth, then even it is self-contradictory. If, on the other hand, it too is said to be relative to certain social perspectives and values, then we must once again ask what they are. The argument can be carried on to infinity without ever freeing itself of the logical problem.[8]

There are reasons for us to assume that this objection is not at all as important as the critics would like to think. We can demonstrate this through a line of reasoning that uses the following diagram:

> Every proposition within
> this rectangle is false.

Now assume that the proposition inside the rectangle is true. It would be true, then, that every proposition inside the rectangle is false. But since there is only one proposition inside the rectangle and since it says it claims to be false, then it must be false. Let us assume instead that the proposition is false. Then, the proposition that every proposition within the rectangle is false would be false. Then the proposition must be true at the same time as it says it is false. This seems to be a genuine paradox. Furthermore, it seems to be analogous to our interpretation of Mannheim's argument that true knowledge exists only in relation to different values and perspectives. As we just showed, Mannheim's thesis is also paradoxical or self-contradictory.

Bertrand Russell offered a solution to this paradox in his theory of types. The reasoning is actually very simple. Russell argues that a class cannot be a member of itself. This means that if one makes a statement about all statements in a certain class, then this statement that is made about the others cannot be considered to belong to the same class. It is this principle that is violated in the case above and in the criticism of Mannheim.

We might also say that the paradox arises because of the ambiguity of the term "proposition" in the rectangle. This term refers sometimes to itself and other times to actual propositions. The paradox arises because the term is confused with its reference, in this case, itself, among other things. We can eliminate the ambiguity by distinguishing between object language and meta-language. If we call propositions containing the terms "true" or "false" meta-language, and propositions that do not contain these terms object language, then we avoid the paradox. The rectangle must now include the words: "Every proposition on the object language level inside this rectangle is false," which, in turn, is a proposition on the level of meta-language. Since there is no proposition on the object language level in the rectangle, the proposition on the meta-language level must be false. There is no contradiction and the paradox is solved.[9]

5.4.3 Epistemological Relativism and the Genetic Fallacy

If this "paradoxical" critique of epistemological relativism hardly measures up, the second objection is all the more tenable. It says that Mannheim is guilty of what philosophers commonly call the genetic fallacy. He confuses the question of the genesis of knowledge in its widest sense with the question of the validity of knowledge.

When a researcher formulates problems, hypotheses, and theories, when he applies various methods and bases his presentation on some and not on other material, he is forced to constantly make choices that, in turn, are governed by evaluative attitudes, motives, intentions, and the like. The fact that these values can be both intra- as well as extrascientific is of little interest here. The important thing is that social science in this sense cannot be "value free." On the contrary, it must be "value governed," or, to use Max Weber's term, "*wertbezogen.*" Most people would also agree that a researcher should strive to be aware of which values, attitudes, motives, and intentions govern his research, since in this way he can question values that should not be allowed to influence the research process. The outlook for achieving this awareness is not too good. Just getting a rough but somewhat complete understanding of the values is practically impossible, not to mention the more difficult problem of obtaining a detailed understanding of how these values influence the research. So, it is not entirely obvious that any increase in the degree of awareness is worth the considerable trouble it takes. If in spite of everything, the individual researcher moves toward complete awareness, it is still not entirely obvious that he should account for that awareness. On the contrary, this accounting should be done only in those cases where one might presume that openness can be of interest to the public one seeks.[10]

We should understand, though, that no matter how much soul-searching the researcher subjects himself to and how much he "socioanalyzes" himself in order to find hidden values in the research process, he still has not at all answered the question of the validity of the results of the process. The fact that the research process is obviously governed by, say, evaluative motives, does not mean—as Mannheim seems to argue at times—that the results put forth are valid or invalid only in relation to some specific perspective. The question of the validity—e.g., the logical consistency and truth—of values judgments and statements of fact is decided on grounds different from those on which an inquiry into their origin and consequences is based. To establish causal relations between, for example, political ideas and their environment is as legitimate a scientific pursuit as appraising their validity, though the latter task can be carried out logically independently of the former. When Mannheim refused to accept this, he committed the genetic fallacy.[11]

By expressly rejecting epistemological relativism, I want to emphasize as clearly as possible that a rational assessment of a set of messages and an explanatory analysis of the same set are two enterprises in political science; the execution of the one is logically independent of the other. I do not mean that the genetic, social, or psychological context is of no *practical* significance to rational assessment. Obviously, we cannot understand some kinds of political arguments unless we study their environment. Mannheim was, of course, conscious of this. Right at the beginning of the book on ideology and utopia, he says that "the principal thesis of the sociology of knowledge is that there are modes of thought which cannot be adequately *understood* as long as their social origins are obscured."[12] From one point of view this statement is extremely surprising. Mannheim suddenly states that the main thesis of the sociology of knowledge is not the empirically testable (at least in principle) notion of the *Seinsverbundenheit* of knowledge, or the philosophical notion that the question of the validity of knowledge can only be decided through reference to its origin. He argues instead that the social context must be taken account of if one is to understand and so interpret an idea's semantic meaning. If I understand him correctly, Mannheim is recommending that social researchers use the context of ideas as an interpretive aid in attaining a deeper understanding of their meaning, not in order to relativize their logical consistency or empirical truth.

That this should be the principal thesis of the sociology of knowledge is, against the background of other of Mannheim's statements, completely unreasonable. He must have formulated it because he did not clearly differentiate between, on the one hand, the *semantic* question of the meaning of words and sentences, and on the other hand the *logical* question of the consistency of statements and the *empirical* question of their tenability and truth value. This is a flagrant example of obscurity in *Ideology and Utopia*.

In fact, though, Mannheim's statement is entirely reasonable and should be acceptable to even the most inveterate opponent of epistemological relativism. The argument against this relativism says that the origin of knowledge has no relevance for an assessment of the question of the logical or empirical validity of knowledge. Few people would argue that the context of statements is not relevant to the semantic question of how statements are to be interpreted and refined. On the contrary, the only way of uncovering the deeper, latent meanings of messages is by placing them in various contextual situations.

CHECKING CONSISTENCY

Logic, like whiskey, looses its beneficial effect when
taken in too large doses.
Max Black, *Critical Thinking*

Once we have tested whether all the statements presented as reasons for
the claim really are relevant to it and whether some relevant reasons have
been suppressed or overlooked, then we can go on in our test to the fourth
main rule, the rule of consistency. We recall that this rule suggests that the
message should be consistent and free from contradictions. We also recall
that it may be split up into two subrules. The one deals with the relation in
each individual argument between claims on the one hand and reasons on the
other. It says that inferences from reasons to claims should be validly
derived. The other subrule has to do with the case as a whole or the
relationship between several cases. It focuses on the relation among claims
themselves and among reasons themselves. It prescribes that claims should
be consistent with other claims and reasons with other reasons.

The discussion of consistency assessment will be divided into the following sections:

(1) exposing deductively invalid inferences;
(2) exposing inconsistent propositions;
(3) exposing inconsistent value judgments;
(4) exposing inconsistent commitments; and
(5) refuting charges against the very rule of consistency.

6.1 What Is an Inference ?

We remember that an argument is a series of statements where one
statement, the claim or conclusion, is said to follow from one or more others,
the reasons or premises. An inference concerns the relationship between
reasons and conclusion. It is that part of an argument that applies or carries

the reasons to the conclusion. To make an inference is to assert that one statement is true because it is well supported or rendered certain by another.[1]

We pointed out in Chapter 3 that logical analysis of inferences entails three preliminary steps:

(1) Arguments must be identified; in particular, one must separate isolated statements from statements that are followed by evidence.
(2) One must indicate which statements are premises and which is the conclusion.
(3) If the argument is not complete, tacit premises must be uncovered and accounted for.

Only once an argument has been written out in this form can we apply the fourth rule for rational political discourse.

6.2   When Are Inferences Valid ?

Because inferences are not individual statements in the usual sense, but are the derivation of one set of statements from another, it is said that truth and falsity cannot be ascribed to them. According to this usage, we cannot investigate whether inferences are true or false, since truth is not at all an issue. This does not mean that inferences cannot be subjected to some qualitative appraisal; we can determine whether they are logically or deductively valid or not. To maintain a clear distinction between validity in general and the validity of inferences, we will in the latter case persistently talk about *logical* or *deductive* validity.

The question of logical validity of inferences is not independent of the truth of those premises and conclusions from which they are constructed. There is a complicated indirect connection, which the following presentation will discuss.

Let us assume that we have an inference with a number of premises and a conclusion, such that if the premises are true then the conclusion must also be true; to assert that the conclusion is false would involve a contradiction. By definition, this is exactly what a deductively valid inference is. Logical validity is defined in terms of contradiction and avoidance of contradiction.[2]

Reflect on the following, consciously simplified example:

(1)
All Nordic countries are members of the United Nations.

Finland is a Nordic country.

Ergo, Finland is a member of the United Nations.

Can the premises in this inference be true and the conclusion false? Obviously not. If we know that the premises are true, then we can certainly conclude that the conclusion is also true. Furthermore, this is a case of valid inference where both the premises and the conclusion actually are true.

Let us look further at the determination of logical validity by considering a couple of other examples:

(2)
All European countries are members of the United Nations.

Switzerland is a European country.

_____

Ergo, Switzerland is a member of the United Nations.

Is this inference also valid? Many would be inclined to say that it is not, since one of the premises and the conclusion, considered individually, are false. The inference is, in fact, valid. It is not conceivable that the premises would be true at the same time as the conclusion is false, and so the inference must be valid.

The third inference may also be somewhat perplexing in the beginning:

(3)
All European countries are members of the United Nations.

Denmark is a European country.

_____

Ergo, Denmark is a member of the United Nations.

This inference is valid, even though the first premise is obviously false. If the premises were true, then the conclusion would also have to be true.

So far we have seen three examples of valid inferences: one with true premises and a true conclusion, one with a false premise and a false conclusion, and one with a false premise and a true conclusion. The question of whether the premises or the conclusion are true or false thus does not seem to have had much to do with the logical validity of the entire inference. There is only one remaining possibility. Can an inference be logically valid if it contains true premises and a false conclusion? Let us look at the following argument:

(4)
All Nordic countries are members of the United Nations.

Israel is a member of the United Nations.

_____

Ergo, Israel is a Nordic country.

Both premises are true, while the conclusion is false; thus the entire argument is also invalid. An inference is valid only in the case where, if its premises are true, the conclusion must also be true. An inference with true premises and a false conclusion, therefore, cannot be valid. When we test the logical validity of political arguments, then, we are interested in tracking down this interesting combination of true premises and a false conclusion. If we find such a combination, then we can be certain that the inference is invalid.[4]

What we have said concerning the relationship between the logical validity of an argument and the truth of the premises and the conclusion on which it is based can be summarized in the following manner:

Truth value of premises and conclusion	*Can the inference be valid?*
True premises True conclusion	Yes
True premises False conclusion	No
False premises True conclusion	Yes
False premises False conclusion	Yes

We can draw one certain conclusion from this arrangement. If an inference contains true premises and a false conclusion, then it is necessarily invalid. In the other three cases, the inference may be valid, but we cannot really be sure. We see further that inferences need not contain a true conclusion to be valid. The premises need not be true, either. It is entirely possible to take horrible premises and make a splendid inference that leads to a crazy conclusion. For the purposes of our discussion of the relations between deductive validity and truth, we can state that there seems to be an indirect connection between the two. This connection is between, on the one hand, possible (as opposed to actual) truth values of the premises and the conclusion, and, on the other hand, the validity of the inference. An inference is certainly invalid if it is not possible that it has true premises and a false conclusion.[5]

Some readers may be irritated by the way logic treats inferences with false premises. Could we not stop splitting hairs and deal only with arguments that we know have true premises? No, that would not be very well considered. The fact is that both politicians and political researchers are interested in, and even depend on, hypothetical premises with an unknown truth value. A politician may have to choose between alternative courses of action. Before making his decision, he tries to determine the conceivable consequences of each possible course. One thing happens if he chooses one alternative, and something else happens if he chooses another, and so on. Finally, he will likely choose that course that offers the most pleasant consequences. If we were to deal only with true premises, though, we would be unable to carry on this hypothetical reasoning. The purpose of the whole decision-making process is to decide which premise we want to realize, and this is something quite different from beginning with a true premise.[6]

There may be logicians who argue that our natural logical intuition sometimes needs the support of technical aids in order to achieve satisfactory assessments of the deductive validity of inferences. The common tool in logic is the truth table method. Some elementary knowledge of symbolic logic is needed to understand it. One should be familiar with the so-called truth tables for the five fundamental sentential connections ''not,'' ''and,'' ''or,'' ''if/then,'' and ''if and only if/then.'' We shall not present the truth table method here. I agree with Stephen Toulmin that formal, idealized logic is of little help in practical, rational assessment.[7] What is needed, most and always, is not expert knowledge of symbolic logic, but unspecialized logical wariness.

6.3 *Inconsistent Propositions*

The machinery of deductive reasoning can only be used for exposing contradictions between reasons and the claim they are supposed to weaken or support. It cannot be employed for ascertaining inconsistencies among reasons themselves or among different claims. Another, simpler type of logical technique—consistency testing proper—comes into the picture here. In practice, this is a much more useful tool for analysis than the deductive gear.

A consistency test is aimed at establishing whether a discourse contains formal contradictions. An inconsistency should not be regarded as a case of obscurity, since it can be perfectly clear. It is always unclear, on the other hand, what a speaker who wraps himself in inconsistencies actually wants to say. An inconsistency exists, for example, when someone both claims and denies the same thing. ''Richard Nixon was forced to resign as U.S.

president," and "Richard Nixon was not forced to resign as U.S. president" is an example of an abnormally clear contradiction. What is asserted one moment is denied the next. Intuitively, an inconsistency means that two propositions cannot be true simultaneously. If we intend to convey information or suggest measures, therefore, we cannot make inconsistent pronouncements, since the person we are addressing would then not know what the information or measures consisted of.[8]

The inconsistencies presented so far have been so obviously contradictory that they seem to lack realism. In both politics and political philosophy, inconsistencies can be embedded in such long, abstract, and perhaps complicated discourse that we need days or months of reading and reflection to track them down. An example of this deeper kind of inconsistency exists between Plato's earlier philosophy, i.e., the *Republic,* and his later thinking such as in the *Laws.* If the theory in the *Republic* on the ideal form of government were correct, then the philosopher king would need no laws. But if, on the contrary, laws are necessary, as Plato later realized, then the principles of the ideal state must be changed.[9]

6.3.1   Contraries and Contradictories

Inconsistencies between propositions are commonly divided into two kinds: contraries and contradictories. A political sociologist may assert in a class of undergraduates that, "the greater the cross-pressure a person is subjected to by conflicting political and social interests in his milieu, the less will be his involvement in politics." The same sociologist may also say, in a textbook, that a more severe cross-pressure results in greater political involvement. His two assertions are said to be contraries. Notable for such an inconsistency is the fact that (a) both propositions cannot be true, although (b) both propositions can very well be false. We see in our example that both cannot be true simultaneously. We also realize that the two propositions could be false; it is conceivable that no matter how much cross-pressure is put on a person, his political involvement could remain unchanged.

Contradictories are stronger than contraries. Two propositions are contradictories if one is the denial of the other. This means that they (a) cannot both be true and they (b) cannot both be false.

A simple change can transform the two propositions above into contradictories: "The greater the cross-pressure a person is subjected to by conflicting political and social interests in his milieu, then the less will be his involvement in politics," and "It is not at all true that the greater the cross-pressure a person is subjected to by conflicting political and social interests in his milieu, then the less will be his involvement in politics."

We see immediately that both these propositions cannot be true. The second sentence also precludes the possibility that political involvement might remain unchanged. Both propositions, therefore, cannot be false.

6.3.2 Why Should Inconsistencies Be Avoided?

Why is it so important to avoid inconsistencies? The first reason is that a person who first asserts one thing and then denies it has not managed to make any assertion at all. Claiming and denying something cancel each other out. But this is not all. A student of Duns Scotus made the shocking discovery that from a contradiction any statement whatsoever can be validly derived. If we are inconsistent, then we have said everything logically possible but also simultaneously denied it all. The person who expresses an inconsistency has thus managed to say both everything and nothing all at once.[10]

6.4 Incompatible Value Judgments

In the early part of 1920, the then leader of the small Italian fascist party, Benito Mussolini, condemned in an article in his newspaper, *Il Popolo D'Italia,* the exercise of state power. His words were vehement: "Down with the state in all its forms, the state of yesterday, today, tomorrow. The bourgeois state and the socialist state. For us, the last champions of individualism, there remains in the face of the gloomy present and an awful tomorrow nothing but an admittedly absurd but always consoling religion: anarchy." It does not take much imagination to envision the bewilderment and consternation experienced by simple members of parliament when, a few months later, the same writer coined the slogan that with time would become the motto of Italian fascism: "Everything for the state, nothing against the state, nothing outside the state."[11]

It should be obvious that the two statements are inconsistent. The contradiction exists because Mussolini in the one case expresses himself very negatively and in the other case very positively about state power. His pronouncements contain value judgments and we can test the consistency of these by investigating whether a person in various contexts has expressed himself on the same subject with solely positive, negative, or indifferent judgments.

We can expand the logical test of value judgments much farther, opening unimagined perspectives for rational assessment. In political life, we generally have to deal with significantly more complex value judgments than those that evaluate one phenomenon at a time. Politicians and political philosophers are forced to set priorities among many different phenomena at once. Faced with large numbers of alternatives, they must order their preferences. Even in those cases, logical rational assessment can examine whether the actors are consistent in their preference hierarchies. The so-called transitivity principle is fundamental to this.

Let A stand for anarchism, B for Manchester liberalism, and C for social liberalism. In order for someone choosing between these three classical theories of state to have a consistent order of preferences, the following conditions must be fulfilled:

(1) if he is indifferent with regard to A and B and with regard to B and C, then he must also be indifferent with regard to A and C;

(2) if he prefers A to B and B to C, then he must also prefer A over C;

(3) if he prefers A over B and is indifferent with respect to B and C, then he must prefer A over C.[12]

Inconsistencies of this type have long been known in economic and political theory. A famous example is the so-called paradox of voting. Since the eighteenth century, philosophers have wondered how, on the basis of individual preferences, one might arrive at a decision that is rational for the entire society. A vote is one of the most obvious ways of aggregating individual values into a collective choice. But Condorcet made the remarkable discovery that, in an election between three candidates, a majority could prefer A over B and B over C, as well as, astonishingly enough, C over A. This peculiar fact clearly violates the transitivity principle; so, the result of the vote must be inconsistent. Later, this paradox was refined further in Kenneth Arrow's famous theorem. Arrow presented some very reasonable criteria of a collective choice and showed that there is no method for aggregating individual preference orders in such a way as to always fulfill the criteria.[13]

The fact that older theories of the state, group theories, and class doctrines contain serious inconsistencies between assumptions on the interests of the individual and the collective has most recently been demonstrated by Mancur Olson in *The Logic of Collective Action*. Both Marx's theory of class and, for example, Arthur Bentley and David Truman's group theory assume that the interests of the individuals coincide with the collective interest of the group. But according to Olson, this is not true at all of large groups. It is certainly rational for an individual to have an organization that looks after the interests of the group to which he belongs. But for the individual group member, it is actually not particularly rational to join the organization or to work for the interest of the whole. His contribution tends to disappear in the mass. His efforts have no noticeable effect on the advantages that the organization provides him. As long as everyone else works, he will still enjoy these benefits. For the individual, then, it is most rational not to bother about the general good and to work with all his strength just for himself.[14]

6.5 Inconsistent Commitments

Political documents sometimes contain pledges or promises of future actions that are inconsistent with each other. These seem especially common in international agreements between states. One state wants to advocate a certain principle for future action, but the other state will not agree. In order, nevertheless, to reach an agreement, the states simply agree to write into the treaty or communiqué that the principle both does and does not obtain.

We can take one example from the Treaty of Peace and Friendship between China and Japan, signed in Beijing on August 12, 1978. The treaty contains only five operative paragraphs. Two of them read as follows:

> Article II: The contracting parties declare that neither of them should seek hegemony in the Asia-Pacific region or in any other region and that each is opposed to efforts by any other country or countries to establish such hegemony.
>
> Article IV: The present treaty shall not affect the position of either contracting party regarding its relations with third countries.

The clause rejecting hegemony was included because China insisted on it. "Hegemony" is a term used in China to denounce what it regards as Soviet aspirations to world domination. The last part of Article II is undoubtedly aimed at the Soviet Union.

The Japanese opposed this clause in part because they wanted to sign a similar peace treaty with the Russians. In conjunction with this treaty, the Japanese demanded return of the southernmost of the Kurile Islands, occupied by the Soviet Union after the end of World War II. The Japanese did not want to challenge the Russians unnecessarily by signing an antihegemony clause.

In part due to this disagreement, the negotiations dragged on. The Japanese finally accepted the antihegemony clause in Article II. At the same time, the Chinese accepted the Japanese demand for a disclaimer, which would take the edge off the antihegemony clause. They agreed to insert Article IV, which says that the present treaty shall not affect the position of either contracting party regarding its relations with third countries. Thus, the parties said simultaneously that the treaty was aimed at a third party—the Soviet Union—and that it was not. Thanks to these inconsistent commitments, the treaty was signed.[15]

6.6   Conflicting Rules of Consistency

We have repeatedly stated that argument-criticism can be carried out not only as first-order, but also as second-order assessment. As emphasized strongly in Chapter 4, we can criticize writers who argue *ad hominem* and commit the genetic fallacy; when in their defense some of them contend that such steps are fully compatible with their views of what is permissible in science, then we must take up this second-order challenge and subject it to criticism. Many political ideologies can be criticized for being unclear and for containing incorrect interpretations of other writers' theories; when some writers try to defend this kind of thing by saying that they embrace an alternative theory of meaning, then we must examine this second-order notion, too. So we are forced to discuss opposing ground rules for rational message assessment. The same kind of meta-confrontation can appear, of course, within the framework of inconsistency assessment. Sometimes we find not only invalid inferences, inconsistent propositions, and incompatible preferences, but we are also faced with writers who espouse an alternative logic which they say is impervious to ordinary consistency appraisal. They say, in other words, that their ideology is the child of a special logic and must be assessed accordingly. They usually advocate some form of dialectical logic; we then have to subject this logic to methodological assessment.

This confrontation about the applicability of the very rule of consistency can assume a defensive or offensive posture. One might be interested in defending traditional logic or in describing and attacking the alternative, dialectical logic. As an example of such a confrontation between logical perspectives we might again examine Alasdair MacIntyre's study of Herbert Marcuse's political philosophy.

Marcuse assumes that logic's content neutrality—the fact that logic distinguishes and classifies statements and arguments solely according to their form—is a distortion of reality. This subjects thinking to some sort of unnatural control. It arose at a certain time in the history of Western civilization, and it is possible to compare and contrast thinking as it was before this controlling instrument took effect with thinking as it became afterward.

MacIntyre correctly says that both of these statements are wrong. To be sure, formal logic was discovered as a discipline at a certain point in human history: People thought in syllogisms before Aristotle; they had to if they were to think at all. Logic articulates the rules that govern the use of ordinary language and that enable us to argue correctly and to avoid the curse of inconsistency. Marcuse seems to maintain that symbolic logic is doing something special when it says that thinking should be purged of inconsistencies. MacIntyre admits that it has made us more aware of the penalties of inconsistency. But even if logic were not an academic field, contradictions would still be contradictions and the disadvantages associated with them would be the same. What are these disadvantages? MacIntyre repeats the view of modern logic that by being inconsistent, one manages to say everything and nothing all at once. In order to be able to say that this is the case and not this other, then, we must follow the laws of logic.[16]

Marcuse's mistake is that he contrasts thinking that is entangled in the strait jacket of logic with thinking that is free of it. But thought that does not accord with the laws of logic would have no coherent language to express itself in. There cannot be and has never been such thinking, and there can never have been a point in history when thinking was subjected to the control of formal logic. The entire control metaphor is ill-conceived, therefore, since it is based on the erroneous contrast between logical and nonlogical thinking.[17]

Marcuse also accuses symbolic logic of being sterile. MacIntyre argues that Marcuse has misunderstood what logic is and what it can achieve. Logic is not a set of rules with which to make discoveries. It is not a heuristic tool. There are no logical rules for how to make discoveries. Discoveries are the fruit of imagination, talent, fortune, and hard work. Only once the discovery has been made can logic enter in as an aid in testing it. To return once again to one of the main themes of this book, logic belongs in the context of justification, not in the context of discovery.[18]

7

TESTING TRUTH

A true proposition describes a state-of-affairs that
occurs; or, in the case of a proposition about the past,
a state-of-affairs that did occur; or in the case of
the future, that will occur.

John Hospers,
An Introduction to Philosophical Analysis

Our last major rule for rational political discourse holds that propositions
should be true. The term "proposition" can be used in several ways. We
have used it here to mark an extremely important distinction—between
sentences and propositions. A sentence has a meaning. When we have talked
about propositions, we have been talking not about sentences, but about
what sentences mean. A sentence, or part of a sentence, expresses a proposition if it is used to *assert* something. A proposition may be true or false, a
sentence only meaningful or meaningless. We see that a proposition is not
identical with the sentence that expresses it. As synonyms to "proposition"
we will use "assertion" or combinations like "factual assertion." The terms
"statement" and "statement of fact" have been, and will be used to express
either the proposition or the sentence entailing it.[1]

Truth is a property of propositions, not sentences. The question is now
how we carry out a test of truth.

7.1 Four Steps of Truth Testing

Before he can conclude whether a proposition is true or not, the researcher must:

(1) Ascertain the meaning of the sentence;
(2) establish that he is dealing with a proposition;
(3) decide how, in principle, he will assess its verity; and
(4) execute the test.

165

The four steps are presented in logical order. Obviously, he must determine if the sentence really expresses a proposition, as well as how to test it, before he can operationalize it and collect evidence of its truth or falsity. Otherwise he would not know what was being operationalized or why the data were being collected.

The first and second steps, then, have to do with separating sentences expressing propositions from sentences expressing, e.g., questions, imperatives, or exclamations. Propositions can be of many different kinds. Consider the following pronouncements by politicians, editorialists, and political philosophers:

(1) On the ninth of April, 1940 the Germans began a military attack on Denmark and Norway.

(2) The long tenure of the Social Democrats in Swedish politics cannot be explained by saying that the emergency economic policies they inaugurated in the early 1930s were decisive in sparking the economic boom. Rather, the party had the advantage of coming into power in 1932, just as the world began to rebound from the Depression on its own; the depreciation of the Swedish crown contributed as well. Per Albin Hansson took the helm a few months before unemployment figures peaked in 1933. By the time the emergency economic agreement (between the Social Democrats and the Farmer's Party) was reached in the spring, the economy had turned around. The upswing had begun with improved exports and diminished unemployment. It is possible that the emergency economic measures during the later stages of the economic cycle reinforced the trends toward expansion which already existed when the emergency economic program was put into effect (Nils Lundgren).

(3) If growth in energy use continues at anything approaching historic rates, nuclear power will play a major role, because it seems clear that other sources of energy cannot be expanded at the rate required to meet the needs that would develop (argument in energy controversy).

(4) If the Western powers had not yielded to Hitler's Germany in Munich in 1938, then World War II probably could have been avoided.

(5) The history of popular war in China and other countries offers conclusive proof that the development of the people's revolutionary forces from initially small and weak to large and strong follows a general law of development in popular war. A popular war inevitably faces many difficulties and meets success and adversity as well as defeat, but no force can change its general trend of development toward the great victory (Lin Piao).

(6) The monopoly capitalism of industrialized countries exploits the fruits of the people's work in its own and in other countries. It craves raw materials, markets and cheap labor in other countries and continents. It uses

political pressure and infiltration. It supports reaction and fascisms. It protects its interests with armed force and war. Profitable military expansion devours labor, research and technology. Militarism erodes and suspends democratic freedoms and rights. Opinion is regimented. Armament and war are the markets of the weapons manufacturers. Today the United States is imperialism's center and its armed police (the program of the Swedish Left Party Communists).

(7) Policy is the adoption of one among several courses of action (P. R. Kaim-Caudle).

We see that these quotes differ quite a bit. We have a pronouncement on a single, delimited occurrence (1); a sentence that contains explanations (2); one that indicates a conceivable developmental trend (3); or even a law of development (5); one that embodies a counterfactual assertion (4); and one that expresses generalizations (6). Many of them are complicated, others are simple, but they have one thing in common: They are all indicative sentences that normally would have to be interpreted as describing a set of facts. Since they assert something, they can be true or false, at least in principle.

One pronouncement—7—differs from the others. This one is also in indicative form and seems to entail a proposition. Actually, it does not. It is a stipulative definition of the word "policy." Stipulations may be deceptive, because they often take the same form as propositions. They do not describe language. They regulate it. They prescribe how words will be employed. Therefore, they cannot be subjected to truth assessment. In the context of tenability testing, then, they must be set aside (see pp. 80ff).

The purpose of first and second steps in a complete truth assessment, then, is to clarify the intension and extension of the sentences, and to sort out from the collected set of statements those that express propositions. As we see, this falls under semantic analysis or interpretation. It will not be discussed further here, since we dealt with it in great detail in an earlier section of the book.

The remaining two steps, however, are part of the actual truth assessment as it has been conceived and delimited here. The third step means first of all that we must form an opinion as to what we mean by "true," "false," "verification," "falsification," "confirmation," "degree of confirmation," and similar expressions that are commonly used in the context of truth assessment. It also entails deciding which evidence we shall consider as contributing to a determination of truth as well as deciding how this evidence will be sorted out. The fourth step, finally, is to collect the relevant data and judge the result.

Both steps three and four lead us into difficult and much-debated problems, e.g., the question of different theories of the meaning of truth, the role of empirical observation versus theoretical assumptions in science, as well as historical source assessment, statistical analysis, and interview techniques. We must also take a stand as to whether it is really possible to determine a proposition's truth value. So far I have assumed that truth assessment is a matter of trying to determine truth value. The expression "verify" is applied to those operations that are carried out in order to determine whether an assertion is true; "falsify" is applied to corresponding operations to determine if an assertion is false. Obviously, though, there are statements of fact that cannot be verified or falsified even in principle. Counterfactual propositions fall into this category. There does not seem to be any way to verify or falsify the content of the sentence 4: "If the Western powers had not yielded to Hitler's Germany in Munich in 1938, then World War II probably could have been avoided." It dealt with circumstances that never existed. It is also impossible to conclusively verify unrestricted universal statements such as: "A popular war inevitably faces many difficulties . . . but no force can change its general trend of development toward the great victory"; they deal not with past and present cases, but also with future instances that cannot be investigated empirically, even in principle. There are also many scholars who argue that it is even practically impossible to conclusively prove the truth of theories that, at least in principle, are accessible to verification. So many sources of errors arise during operationalization and testing against empirical cases that we can never be really certain that the theory has been verified.[2] With this in mind, falsification has been considered a more useful strategy; this was Popper's answer to the impracticability of the verification method. Now it is argued that theories cannot even be falsified for certain.[3] One can, therefore, only say that theories are well or not so well supported. Thus, when we use words like "verified" or "falsified," we should keep in mind that they actually are approximate synonyms of "confirmed" and "disconfirmed."

7.2 Truth Assessment as Criticism

Analysts of political ideas sometimes hesitate to test the tenability of propositions because they feel the task is overwhelming. In the introduction to his study of revolutionary theory from Marx to the Russian revolution, Reidar Larsson tries to justify why he chose not to subject the assertions of Marxist theoreticians to truth analysis. His argument is primarily pragmatic and practical:

> Such an examination would, if it were feasible, demand an investigation of almost the entire social and political history of Europe during more than a century.[4]

This practical dissociation from truth assessment is understandable only if it is based on the tacit assumption that all truth analysis means the collection of evidence in order to confirm or disconfirm statements. There is no doubt that it can be extraordinarily demanding to try to verify or falsify certain kinds of generalizations. It would likely require a large amount of trying work to prove generalizations 2, 5, and 6 above. As a demonstration, we may examine the following rather limited generalization, first formulated by Edvard Bull and later refined and tested by, among others, Walter Galenson and William Lafferty: "It is true of Denmark, Norway and Sweden that the more rapid the transition from agricultural to industrial society, the more radical the country's labor movement became." As we see, the generalization deals with three cases, and in principle, we could try to confirm it through a complete investigation of all three. We could break the generalization down into three sentences and place them in the following confirmation table:

Denmark has had the slowest transition from agricultural to industrial society, and its labor movement became the least radical.

Sweden has had a more rapid transition from agricultural to industrial society than Denmark, and its labor movement became more radical than Denmark's.

Norway has had a more rapid transition from agricultural to industrial society than Sweden, and its labor movement became more radical than Sweden's.

Ergo, it is true for Denmark, Norway, and Sweden that the more rapid the transition from agricultural to industrial society, the more radical the country's labor movement became.

The inference is logically valid. But since we are to test tenability, we must also determine if each of the premises is probably true or well founded. What we need, in other words, is an inference that is not only valid, but also sound.

Common methodology holds that we must define the meaning of fundamental concepts like "agricultural society," "industrial society," and "radical." When does an "agricultural society" become an "industrial society"? Are both communist and social democratic organizations included in the "labor movement"? Shall we include both political parties and trade unions? We must then operationalize—specify the reference of—these concepts so they can be measured empirically. We may need to construct some sort of index of radicalism and an index of what constitutes an agicultural and an industrial society. This is no simple task, of course. We must also determine the relationship between the hypothesis's dependent and independent variables. Shall we interpret the hypothesis causally? In other words, is a slower transition from agricultural to industrial society a sufficient, necessary, or both a sufficient and necessary condition of a less radical labor movement in the three Scandinavian countries? Or does the hypothesis merely indicate a covariation between the two macrophenomena?

Finally, we must determine whether the hypothesis as formulated can be empirically tested at all; if it can be tested, we must determine what type of source material will be relevant. Last but not least, we must collect the material and check to see if it confirms our hypothesis. The gathering of information may necessitate archive research in all three countries. Thus, the operationalization and, above all, the adduction of evidence requires a large investment of labor. To convince ourselves of this we need only look at Lafferty's book, which contains the latest attempt to wrestle with this still rather simple generalization.[5]

Reidar Larsson thus seems to be right in his dissociation from truth assessment, assuming that it is equated with verification or falsification. In my opinion, this premise does not always hold true. I would even like to go a step further and say that, in the context of rational assessment, *criticism* is often the most suitable strategy for truth assessment. Criticism does not imply that we have to verify or falsify propositions. It suggests something less demanding. It entails demonstrating that the author of the propositions has not verified or falsified them.

When we scrutinize political pronouncements, ideologies, doctrines, reports, or whatever, we are not primarily interested in parading our own statements of fact. Instead, we examine what others have communicated. In this context, it would seem that attempts at criticism of what is stated are more appropriate than attempts at verification or falsification of it. The advantage to this method is that we can subject the propositions to a powerful truth test without having to collect our own data on social or political life. We save time and labor without actually losing anything. We can pose and answer a few questions that are connected to the above-mentioned first step in truth assessment: Are the propositions operationalized? If so, what is the quality of the operationalization? We can also pose and answer questions concerning the third step: Are the propositions at all testable? Do they refer to ultimate causes, the nature of things, or counterfactual events that make them inaccessible in principle to empirical testing? And we can pose and answer questions with regard to the fourth step: Are the propositions supported by evidence? Is the evidence relevant? Is there enough evidence to decide the question of confirmation/disconfirmation?

We subject a writer's statements of fact to a substantial truth critique if we can show that they cannot be tested empirically. We also reduce their power if we point out that they are not supported by evidence. If the writer, like Lin Piao in our example 5, claims to have conclusive proof that his statement is true, but if we can show that the evidence is too weak for such a conclusion, then this too is a substantial criticism of tenability. We can do all this, obviously, without undertaking any empirical studies of our own. Because the questions are formulated on the basis of a methodological foundation, we hardly need to fear that we will achieve nothing more than impressionistic and uninteresting comments on empirical reality.

A very instructive example of a forceful tenability assessment, which does not include any data-gathering by the assessor, is found in Brian Barry's *Sociologists, Economists and Democracy,* where he criticizes Gabriel Almond and Sidney Verba's famous study, *The Civic Culture.*

Almond and Verba subtitled their investigation *Political Attitudes and Democracy in Five Nations.* They claim to have something to say about the conditions for stable democracy in five nations and they try to demonstrate the values that the people living in the countries in question must hold. In spite of this, they actually have very little to say about the connection between attitudes and democracy.

Barry offers the following outline of the structure of Almond and Verba's argument.

> First, the authors consider the possible attitudes . . . that people might have towards their country as a whole and to various political institutions within it (parties, branches of government, and so on). They suggest in the course of this discussion that a certain combination of such attitudes is conducive to the maintenance of a democratic political system. Then, using this as a guiding thread, they examine how far the combination of attitudes postulated as favourable to democracy is actually found in the five countries where their survey was carried out, namely, Britain, the U.S.A., Italy, Germany and Mexico.
>
> The combination of attitudes which the authors believe to be most supportive of democratic government they call the "civic culture." Summarising drastically, it might be described as a judicious mixture of respect for authority and sturdy independence. The ideal democratic citizen, according to this, would believe in the legitimacy and the general competence and goodwill of the political authorities while at the same time believing that he has the right . . . and also the ability to exert influence on what they do, so as to secure redress of grievances for example. These two components are called "subject competence" and "citizen competence" respectively.

Brian Barry admits that, in theory, this all sounds fairly plausible. But what is the connection between various citizens' attitudes and the existence of democracy in a country? A wealth of survey data notwithstanding, the authors do not answer the question. They conclude that of their five countries, Britain comes closest to the ideal balance that constitutes the civic culture. The United States follows, while the other three countries are not ranked. However, according to Brian Barry, the authors have nothing to say about the relationship between civic culture and democratic polity.

To get the beginnings of an answer, says Barry, we need three things:

> We should first need an hypothesis relating the prevalence in a country's population of the "civic culture" (to a specified extent) with the existence in that country of (a certain amount of) democracy. (The criteria of "democracy" would, of course, have to be spelt out.) Then we should have to test this hypothesis by seeing whether the two kinds of variable — "cultural" and "institutional" — were related in the data in the way required by the hypothesis. And, finally, we should have at least to face the question of causality. To put it crudely, even if the relationship does exist, is this because the "culture" influences the working of the "institutions," or is it merely that it reflects them?

Barry continues:

> We look in vain to Almond and Verba for any of these items. The nearest approach to a hypothesis is the question: "Is there a democratic political culture — a pattern of political attitudes that fosters democratic stability, that in some way "fits" the democratic political system?" . . . Now, "fits" says so little that the statement that a certain culture fits a certain system might be interpreted as immune to empirical disproof. . . . [However,] it is fairly clear that Almond and Verba do mean that certain attitudes actually affect the attainment or maintenance of democracy. Beyond that, though, it would be hard to go. Assertions of various kinds might be made: some level of "civic culture" could be held to be a necessary condition for the possession of a certain degree of "democracy," or a sufficient condition, or a necessary and sufficient condition. Or it could simply be said that, other things being equal, a country with more "civic culture" is more likely to be democratic than one with less; and this would imply that, unless there were special reasons to the contrary, the "other things" should tend to cancel out, leaving a positive correlation between the amount of "civic culture" and the amount of "democracy."
>
> These hypotheses would require, in order to be tested, that we should have either a criterion for the presence of relevant amounts of "civic culture" and "democracy," or a scale for them on which at least ordinal positions could be established. As we have noted, Almond and Verba do make it clear that they think the order of their five countries in "civic culture" is led by Britain and the U.S.A., but that is all. As for the other side of the relationship, it is an extraordinary fact that they do not address themselves to the question of how "democratic" their five countries are. . . .
>
> But this raises the final question, of the direction of causality, which Almond and Verba discuss only incidentally. . . . Suppose that some hypoth-

esis or other connecting "civic culture" and "democracy" is confirmed for the five cases studied . . . —would we be much further ahead? Might one not argue that a "democratic" political culture—such as the "civic culture"—is the *effect* of "democratic" institutions? The prima facie case for saying this is not without force. If you ask people whether they expect to get fair treatment from civil servants . . . it is possible that their replies add up to a fairly realistic assessment of the actual state of affairs. . . . This interpretation of the data has some support, in that many differences in response from one category of person to another look as if they could be accounted for as accurate perceptions of reality. . . .

Obviously, if this interpretation is correct, there are no grounds for saying that the correlation arises from the conduciveness of the "civic culture" to "democracy," but rather for the unexciting conclusion that "democracy" produces the "civic culture." But this interpretation can no more be established from data for a single point in time than can the other.[6]

As we see, Barry has carried out a thorough tenability assessment without doing his own empirical investigation and without lapsing into mere impressionistic commentary. Both Almond and Verba assert that they want to say something substantive about the relation between cultural attitudes and political democracy, but Barry demonstrates convincingly that their test is seriously flawed. The relationship between the two variables is inadequately specified. It is not clear whether there is a causal connection or only some kind of covariation between them. Neither variable is satisfactorily operationalized and substantiated. The countries are not ranked according to how "civic" and "democratic" they are. The latter problem is, surprisingly, not even touched upon by the authors. And finally, according to Barry, there are reasons to believe that democracy produces civic culture, not the other way around as Almond and Verba claim.

The conclusion must be that the authors' thesis—that a certain civic culture is conducive to democracy—has not been proved. Brian Barry cannot prove that it is false, of course, but he can show that its truth has not yet been made probable.

7.3   Conflicting Criteria of Truth

Tenability analysis as discussed so far has been based on the tacit assumption that the researcher, the originator of the analyzed text, and all other participants in the rational political discourse mutually accept a common criterion of truth. However, this is far from always the case. There are strongly contrasting opinions as to what "truth" may mean and, consequently, what relationship is being tested in tenability analysis. Before I get into these conflicts about the very rule of verity, I want to briefly present the notion of truth that underlies the reasoning in this book.

7.3.1   Truth as Correspondence

There are three classical theories on what "truth" may mean: (1) the pragmatic theory, (2) the coherence theory, and (3) the correspondence theory.[7] Either consciously or unconsciously, most social researchers today align themselves with the last of these. It holds that truth is correspondence. A proposition is true if and only if it indicates that certain facts exist and if it also is such that these facts do exist. If a proposition is true, there is agreement, or correspondence, between what the proposition asserts and the facts. Truth is correspondence with facts.

At first glance, it may seem reasonable to assume that the propositions should correspond to events, situations, and other factual circumstances. It does not seem unreasonable to assert that the statement "In 1974, during his term of office, Richard Nixon was forced to resign as president" corresponds to the factual event of that politically dramatic summer. But the assumption is much less convincing if we are faced with true negative statements of the type "Richard Nixon was not nominated as Republican candidate for president in 1964"; or possibly true statements of the type "Without the Vietnam war, there would have been no Watergate and Richard Nixon might have had the most successful presidency since Harry Truman's; with Henry Kissinger as his point man, he would have achieved his stunning diplomatic successes in China, the Soviet Union, and the Middle East and be a president who is revered today"; or necessarily true statements of the type "Richard Nixon either narrowly lost the presidential election of 1960 to John Kennedy or he did not." In all of these latter cases, there is still a fact which is related to the true or probably true proposition. It is just as much a fact that Nixon was not nominated as Republican candidate for president in 1964 as that he lost the presidential election in 1960. This shows that the fact to which a proposition corresponds may not be confused with the object, the situation, the event, or the possibility that is the subject of the statement. That correspondence which modern variants of the correspondence theory of truth refer to is one between propositions and facts, where facts are not the same as concrete events.[8]

What is it that makes one fact correspond to a proposition while another corresponds to another? This is a very difficult question. Some argue that it is a matter of a copy or a reproduction; others say that it is a matter of so-called structural agreement. None of these notions are really satisfactory. Mental pictures are not *like* the physical things to which they refer, and words are not the least similar to the things they represent.

A better way of putting it would be that a true proposition corresponds to a fact in the way names of books on library cards correspond to books themselves, i.e., for every book a card and for every card a book. There may well be a correspondence in this sense. But what is gained by this explication? It seems that it is at least as clear to say that a true proposition is one that *describes* an actual state of affairs. I agree with John Hospers that this way of regarding it is less misleading than the use of the word "correspondence" may be.[9]

7.3.2 Truth as What "Functions" or "Works"

It is not easy to depict the pragmatic theory of truth since there are several versions, developed by, among others, Pierce, William James, and John Dewey. In general, the theory holds that an idea—by which these writers mean any opinion, belief, statement, or pronouncement—is an instrument with a particular function. A true idea is one that fulfills its function, that works in a certain way; a false idea is one that does not function or work.

William James said that religion and metaphysical statements and systems could not be judged by whether they depicted reality or were logically consistent, but rather on the basis of whether they satisfied the people who held them: "The true is the expedient in the way of our thinking, just as the right is the expedient in our way of behaving."[10] His comparison of truth and right shows that the pragmatic theory can be considered an extension of the utilitarian way of thinking from ethics to epistemology. The parallel between utility and truth stands out even more clearly in a statement by Dewey:

> [I]f ideas, meanings, conceptions, notions, theories, systems are instrumental to an active reorganization of the given environment, to the removal of some specific trouble and perplexity, then the test of their validity and value lies in accomplishing this work. If they succeed in their office, they are reliable, sound, valid, good, true.[11]

The pragmatic theory, which of course is more complicated than it appears here, includes the entirely reasonable observation that our ideas are used in many different ways and that they therefore must be accepted or rejected for varying reasons. But as a theory of truth, the pragmatic theory has serious flaws. One weakness is that it overlooks the distinction between accepting something in general and accepting something as true. Advice, decisions, values, suggestions, plans, proclamations, assertions, excuses, promises, and utopian schemes can all be accepted or rejected. They are accepted or rejected for varying reasons precisely because the rules that govern their pronouncement vary. In precisely the same way that these "ideas" are normally expressed with different words, so their acceptance or rejection is clothed in various linguistic terminology, e.g., "good" or "bad," "right" or "wrong," "reasonable" or "unreasonable," "wise" or "unwise," "suitable" or "unsuitable." But lumping together all kinds of positions we take on all that we say and think under headings like "truth" and "truth assessment" leads to needlessly muddled thinking. Accepting an idea as beneficial has to do, among other things, with its consequences; stating that it is true means asserting that it says what the facts are when the facts also are as they are said to be. We can conceive of an idea functioning well in society even though it is false. It is this important distinction between function and truth that the pragmatic theory never manages to deal with.[12]

Another flaw in the pragmatic theory of truth is that it tends to overlook the distinction between the fact that something may be acceptable or accepted as true and the meaning of the term "truth." The theory more squarely addresses the practical problem of discerning and testing what is said to be true rather than the theoretical problem of the nature of truth. Advocates of the theory, therefore, tend to reduce the notion of "being true" to "being held as true" or even "being tested for truth." Thus, Charles Pierce could say: "The opinion which is fated to be ultimately agreed to by all who investigate, is what we mean by the truth." We can say that pragmatic criteria like benefit and satisfaction are reasons for holding something as true rather than elements in a definition of "true" or "truth."[13]

To summarize, the pragmatic theory of truth tells us much about the various kinds of positions we take on the various things we say. But it does not help us to separate these conclusions from the issue of what it means to say that propositions are true.

7.3.3   Truth as Coherence

The coherence theory seems to have won more support from professional philosophers. It was characteristic for the great rationalistic, system-oriented metaphysicians Leibniz, Spinoza, and Hegel; but it was also embraced by some earlier logical empiricists like Neurath and Hempel.[14] According to the proponents of this view, truth consists in coherence. It is not always clear what "coherence" means exactly; we can say at least that coherence is not a relation between propositions and events, situations, states of nature, or facts, but rather, a relation among propositions themselves. To say that something is true, then, is to say that it is coherent with a set of other propositions. When we test whether a statement is true, we determine whether it is coherent within a larger system of propositions. This system of statements, which it must be coherent with, may be, to take an example from those advocates of the theory who are logical positivist, that which is accepted in modern science.

What kind of relation to a set of propositions makes a given proposition true? According to one interpretation, propositions are coherent when they are consistent with each other. Then, truth assessment would be entirely reduced to consistency appraisal. This is a very queer solution. A proposition may be consistent with, i.e., not contradicting, numerous other propositions without therefore being true. The statement ''C. B. Macpherson is England's most well known political philosopher'' is not contradicted by the statement ''England has spawned many prominent political philosophers.'' We nevertheless know that the former is false. Consistency, then, does not seem a sufficient condition of truth.[15]

According to the second interpretation, a true proposition must be connected to the rest of the system by logical implication. A proposition is true if it logically follows from a set of other propositions. To establish a proposition's truth, in other words, would be the same as determining if it is a conclusion of a logically valid inference. However, as we recall from the section on logical validity, a statement can be logically derived from other statements without necessarily being true. A false conclusion can be logically derived from false premises. Thus, logical consequence is not a really adequate criterion of truth in the empirical sense.

Proponents of truth as coherence usually draw their best examples from a priori reasoning in mathematics, logic, and metaphysics. Note that there is a close connection between meaning and truth in the analytic reasoning that characterizes these sciences; the truth of a proposition is actually established through analysis of the meaning of the sentence expressing it. But this is also the decisive weakness of the coherence theory: It provides criteria of truth and falsity only for analytic statements, but not for synthetic statements. It is a theory of coherence between statements and other statements, but not a theory of coherence between propositions and facts from our world of experience. It is insufficient, therefore, as a theory of truth for experiential knowledge.[16]

7.3.4 Marxist Rejections of the Correspondence Theory

Conflicts about the rule of truth may come up when we study, for instance, certain Marxist, conservative, and fascist political philosophies. Alasdair MacIntyre's book on Herbert Marcuse's social thinking contains a confrontation between an adherent and a critic of the correspondence criterion. From the outset, MacIntyre notes that Marcuse rejects certain criteria of truth. But what is Marcuse's own view of truth? He never explains which criteria of truth he accepts himself or which criteria he appeals to when inviting his readers to accept his own propositions. This is MacIntyre's first objection.

Marcuse gets into two difficulties when he speaks about truth. He contrasts what is true with what is merely factual, and he rejects as empiricist any theory that views truth as correspondence with facts. To be limited to the facts as they are, Marcuse argues, is to be untrue. But he never tells us what the facts are that make his own view true — even though his own theory is true or false depending on what these facts are. Further, all discussion is dependent upon the participants having common criteria for what is true or false. When these criteria are called into question, says MacIntyre, it becomes all the more important to indicate clearly how truth can be attained.

There is also a third difficulty. Marcuse sometimes writes as if every epoch had its own criteria of truth. But if truth is relative to time and place, how are we to judge between theories which arose at different times in different places? There is an obvious need for a nonrelative notion of truth, says MacIntyre.[17]

Judging from MacIntyre's analysis, Marcuse dismisses the correspondence theory; on the other hand, it is not possible to say with certainty what perspective Marcuse does embrace. There exists, in any case, a clear conflict of rules of discourse between MacIntyre's and Marcuse's views.

7.3.5   Pragmatic Theories of Truth in Conservatism and Nazism

Other political philosophers have committed themselves to a pragmatic concept of truth. Within the conservative tradition, Louis Gabriel de Bonald seems to have embraced a pragmatic view of truth. He sometimes seems to equate true with useful. On this Tingsten writes in *Conservative Ideas:* "All truths are beneficial to the people: this thesis is essentially true, and the reason for this is evidently that whatever is beneficial to the people is a truth." Tingsten is satisfied to point this out and does not intimate that we might have here a more fundamental conflict — a conflict of rules — between his own analytic position and the French ideologist's.[18]

Many Nazi thinkers adopted a pragmatic conception of truth. Generally, they tended to measure a theory's value according to how well it stimulated action, says Tingsten in his work of 1936 on Nazism and fascism. In particular, we find the idea that all results of spiritual work are true in a more profound sense since they serve life. Alfred Rosenberg, in *Der Mythos des Zwanzigsten Jahrhunderts,* says more clearly than any other National Socialist thinker that thoughts should be judged with reference to their effect. Having quoted Goethe's words, "only what is fruitful is true," he maintains that even a delusion can be organically true, "since it makes fit for action people who are unfit with respect to their reason, views, or will, and so it increases their creative power." For National Socialists, writes Rosenberg, truth is "not a question of logic, correctness or falsity; truth means that an organic answer is required for the question: fruitful or unfruitful."

From the pragmatic perspective, Tingsten continues, Nazism's victory in 1933 must seem to be proof of the truth of these theories. This, he points out, was the conclusion drawn by the movement's leaders. Thus could Goebbels assert that Nazi ideology had stood the decisive test of truth by seizing power in 1933.[19]

APPRAISING VALUES

Controversies among advocates of naturalism,
intuitionism and subjectivism seem likely to continue
indefinitely.
                    Robert A. Dahl, *Modern Political Analysis*

Observe the following statements:

It is clear . . . that the best form of political society is one where power is
vested in the middle class (Aristotle).

In taking a state, the conqueror must arrange to commit all his cruelties at once
(Machiavelli).

Constitutions and common laws . . . should be adapted to the country's
character, to a cold, hot or temperate climate, to the country's situation and
size, to the people's style of life as farmers, hunters and shepherds (Montes-
quieu).

The greatest evil is unlimited government power (Friedrich von Hayek).

Ours is a democratic dictatorship. . . . Its first task is to suppress the reactionary classes and elements and our country's exploiters who are opposed to the
socialist revolution, to suppress all who try to thwart our work of socialist
construction (Mao Zedong).

The fact that these sentences deal with things that are best and worst and
things that should be done shows that they express judgments of value.
"Value judgment" refers to that which is expressed by sentences like: (1)
"this is good," "this is valuable," "this is bad," "this is desirable," "this
is better than"; or (2) "this should be done," "this is right," "this is
wrong." Sentences of a rather different grammatical form may also express
value judgments, e.g., "The first task of a democratic dictatorship is to
suppress the reactionary classes." It seems that this utterance, at least in
some cases, could be formulated as an "ought to" sentence without change
in meaning. Therefore, it seems that it may be construed as a value judgment.

181

8.1 *Some Distinctions*

Political value statements must be appraised on the basis of the same five
major standards of rationality that apply to political discourse in general.
However, statements of value are commonly regarded as having a special
position. They cannot be judged in exactly the same way as statements of
fact. This justifies our discussing assessment of value statements in a
separate chapter.

For such a discussion to be illuminating, we must carefully differentiate
between a few things that are not always kept separate. The following list
suggests that we should distinguish between:

(1) value sentences;
(2) value judgments;
(3) value statements;
(4) those phenomena in the world to which value judgments refer and that we can
    call ''values'' or ''value characteristics;''
(5) the enunciation of value sentences;
(6) the espousal of value judgments;
(7) the evaluative attitudes or feelings behind the enunciation of value sentences
    or the espousal of value judgments;
(8) the effects of the enunciation of value sentences or of the espousal of value
    judgments.

''Value judgment'' in this case, then, signifies what is expressed by value
sentences. In our introduction to this chapter we gave a host of examples of
both of these phenomena. ''Value statement'' can mean either the judgment
expressed or the sentence expressing it. Further, the sentence and what is
expressed by it must be differentiated from its extension. According to some
thinkers, value judgments can refer to values or value characteristics in the
real world. It is also important to distinguish between, on the one hand, the
actual sentence and, on the other hand, the linguistic act of enunciating the
sentence and the psychological espousal of whatever the sentence says.
Furthermore, the enunciation of value sentences and the psychological
espousal of value judgments can be caused by evaluative attitudes and
feelings, which may be referred to as evaluations. Such attitudes and
feelings constitute parts of motives that may explain enunciations or espousals. Enunciations and espousals may also affect their environment, of
course, and these effects must be distinguished from whatever factors are
causing them. In my terminology, finally, ''questions of value'' will signify
a wide-ranging group of problems that in some way are connected with the
phenomena enumerated above.[1]

How researchers should relate to questions of value has sparked controversy like few other methodological issues have. The most memorable battle was the so-called *Werturteilsstreit* (the value dispute), fought in Imperial Germany in the decades before World War I. Its climax came on January 4, 1911 at a meeting in Berlin of the enlarged committee of the *Verein für Sozialpolitik* (Association for Social Policy). The atmosphere at the meeting was conspiratorial and passionate. The more than 50 participants agreed on extraordinary precautions to preserve the intimate character of the discussions. Minutes were not to be taken, and the stenographers were sent home. Each participant formally promised not to disclose anything about the proceedings to outsiders. Publication of papers submitted by eminent scholars was formally forbidden. The fears behind this secrecy proved justified. The discussion ended in a violent clash between, among others, Max Weber and Werner Sombart on the one hand, and a majority that included Joseph Schumpeter, Leopold von Wiese, and Eduard Spranger on the other. Max Weber, the foremost advocate of the so-called value-free approach, informed his opponents in the end that they did not understand what he was talking about, whereupon he angrily stormed out of the meeting. German social scientists were split into two camps that exist, to some extent, to this day.[2]

The issue of whether social science should be value free has never ceased to concern its students and practitioners. Interest in the issue surged in the late 1960s and throughout the 1970s due to criticism of the value-free approach inspired by Marxism and hermeneutics.

Several broad approaches to the appraisal of value judgments in political reasoning have been advanced. The standard value-free approach draws a fundamental distinction between ends-statements and means-statements. It suggests that statements about means can be translated into ordinary propositions that can be assessed for truth or falsity. As far as ends-statements go, though, it is not possible to decide in a scientific way whether they are true or false, right or wrong, good or bad. From this it has been concluded that valuational questions do not at all come within the purview of science.

A second approach implies an all-out attack on the means-end philosophy. It holds that argumentative study is inherently evaluative, since selection of problems, concepts, schemes of classification, data, and critical lines of reasoning is determined by evaluative attitudes. Given this, then, the best a rational assessor can do is to make himself aware of his evaluative attitudes and to try to keep inappropriate motives from influencing important choices.

A third approach implies avoiding the value issue altogether by denying that statements of value play any significant role in the language of politics. Political language consists mainly of statements of fact.

We will now treat these three approaches in order.

8.2   *The Value-Free Approach*

The dominant position in international social science has long been that science cannot establish the validity of (ultimate) value judgments. Having nothing to say, social scientists qua scientists should not engage in reasoning in ethical matters. Several Scandinavian political scientists still maintain this position. "Political science is a science *about* politics, not a science *of* politics," Ingemar Lindblad writes, without batting an eye, in his much-used introduction to the methodological problems of political science. The same position recurs in Jörgen Westerståhl's *Studying Politics*.[3] On the Scandinavian scene, we can trace this position back to Axel Hägerström's famous inaugural lecture of 1911, *On the Truth of Moral Propositions*. Said Hägerström: "Since science has only to establish that which is true, and since it is nonsense to consider as true a notion of what should be, then it can be the task of no science to establish how we should act." Science, he concluded, "has no business setting values. Just as little as it can show that given rules should be followed, so it cannot show that they should not be followed and that other principles of action should replace them. The opinion presented here . . . maintains . . . that moral science cannot be a science *of* morals, but only a science *about* morals."[4]

It is not difficult to find proponents of this view in the international social science community. T. D. Weldon's *The Vocabulary of Politics* falls close to this position, even if his conception seems to me to be a bit more sophisticated than is commonly assumed.[5] The most extreme enunciation along these lines I could find, though, is in Ludwig von Mises's book from before World War II on capitalism and socialism. In answer to the question of whether liberal ideology, which Mises embraces himself, is optimistic or not, he answers that:

> for an ideology so thoroughly based in science as that of liberalism, the question cannot even be discussed as to whether the capitalist social order is good or bad, whether we can conceive of a better one or not, and whether for some philosophical or metaphysical reason we should reject it or not. Liberalism is based on purely scientific grounds, on economics and sociology, which within their systems do not recognize values and have nothing to say in the question of whether something is good or bad and how it should be. It has only to establish what is and how it is.[6]

My opinion is that this position is too cautious and restrictive. The goodness or badness of different social orders *can* be discussed in social science. Social scientists *can* argue questions of value without abandoning their professional standards. Social science is *not* entirely impotent with respect to assessing the validity of value judgments. We must distance ourselves from the doctrine that political science is no more than a science *about* politics.

The value-free approach takes its point of departure in specific meta-ethical considerations. To show this, we will make a brief presentation of the main theories of meta-ethics.

8.2.1 Normative Ethics and Meta-Ethics

Contemporary ethicists take points to cut out a distinct boundary line between normative ethics and meta-ethics. *Normative ethical statements* are actual value judgments. They tell us what is right or wrong, good or evil. They prescribe what people ought to do. In normative ethics, value language is used in what might be considered a first-order way.

Meta-ethical statements, on the other hand, are *about* the uses or meaning of normative ethical words and statements. Meta-ethicists speak about the ways in which value terms like "right," "wrong," "good," "bad," are used in normative ethics. What are people doing when they talk about what they should do or say that something is good? This is a question that belongs to the sphere of meta-ethics. Meta-ethics also inquiries into another, even more important problem: How and in what sense can value judgments be proved, justified, or shown valid? Meta-ethics is talk *about* value judgments. It might be considered second-order discourse on value language.

Before embarking upon a discussion of meta-ethical theories, we should distinguish between (1) value-ontological theories and (2) theories on value sentences. An ontological proposition holds that certain objects, properties, and relationships exist or do not exist. Value-ontological theories contain statements about whether values really exist or not. Theories on value sentences, on the other hand, deal with how value sentences should be interpreted and clarified so that their meanings can be made more precise than in their original formulations.[7] We see here that the value theories are firmly tied to the question of the meaning of moral language. And so, we have to return to the various notions of what meaning is.

In light of this brief conceptual elucidation, we can interpret classical meta-ethical theories as various combinations of different kinds of value sentence theories and value ontologies (see Figure 8.1).[8]

8.2.2 Value Cognitivism

There seems to be no end of controversy in meta-ethics, and to condense this extremely complicated area of discourse into a small diagram no doubt is to commit oneself to gross oversimplification. However, a basic distinction can be drawn between cognitivism and noncognitivism. *Cognitivism* holds that value judgments can be true or false whereas *noncognitivism* expressly

		Value Ontology	
		Positive	Negative
Value Sentence Theory	Cognitivist	Ethical Descriptivism: (a) Naturalism (b) Intuitionism	Ethical Descriptivism: (c) Subjectivism
	Noncognitivist		Noncognitivism (Value Nihilism, The Emotive Theory)

Figure 8.1 Meta-Ethical Theories

denies this. Three comprehensive cognitivist positions are entered into the diagram: naturalism, intuitionism and subjectivism. It does not seem unfair to assert that ethical naturalism and ethical intuitionism are both based upon a combination of a referential theory of meaning and a positive value ontology.

According to *ethical naturalism,* value terms such as "good," "bad," "right," and "wrong" are considered to mean something in the sense of *referring* to something. Sentences containing such words can be translated into statements expressing factual assertions. When we pronounce a statement of value, it can be translated without change of meaning into another pronouncement, or set of pronouncements, that do not contain any value terms at all. The expression "x is right" may be translated into: "The majority of people approve of x" or "x will promote the maximum happiness." These translations are considered assertions about an objective reality. Value sentences are, in effect, disguised statements of fact that may be true or false.

Ethical naturalists further maintain that value judgments translated into propositions may be justified by empirical inquiry in the same sense as ordinary and scientific factual statements can. To find out whether x is right—according to the translation, "The majority of people approve of x"—we have to take a poll. Then we will know how many approve of the act in question, and once we know this, we know whether it is right. We can have a purely empirical knowledge of good and evil, right or wrong.[9]

Intuitionists agree with naturalists that at least some value terms refer to or stand for properties of things. However, intuitionists deny that all ethical words are definable in nonethical ones. At least some of them are verbally undefinable. But if there are ethical sentences that have meaning that is not reducible to that of nonethical sentences, what is their meaning? Nonnaturalists answer that it is just different from the meaning of any other sentences. Their meaning is simply unique.

Some nonnaturalists also argue that value properties referred to by value terms are not natural ones. They are characterized as nonempirical and nonnatural. This means that we cannot discover the truth of statements of value by empirical observation or logical calculation. Their truth is self-evident. They can only be justified through a kind of immediate experience, reflection, or intuition.[10]

Value cognitivism in its two classical versions has been strongly criticized with respect to both the underlying referential theory of meaning, and the theories about how one might justify judgments of value.

It is doubtful whether naturalists offer an adequate account of what value sentences mean. They hold that such sentences constitute an alternative vocabulary for reporting facts. In actual usage, however, this seems evidently not to be the case. When we are maintaining factual assertions, we are not thereby taking a pro or con attitude toward what we are talking about. We are not commending it, prescribing it, evaluating it, and so on. But when we make value judgments, we are not neutral in this way. We seem to do something more than make factual assertions when we issue judgments of value.

The naturalist view of justification is also insufficient. William E. Frankena offers the following argument against it. If we accept a certain definition of "right" we will also know how to justify judgments about what is right. But we may still ask why we should accept this particular definition. When a person tries to persuade us that "x is right" means that "the majority of people approve of it," he is in fact persuading us to accept the ethical principle that what the majority of people approve of is right. He cannot establish his definition first and then show us that this principle is valid because the latter is true by definition. He cannot establish his definition unless he can convince us of the principle. Concludes Frankena:

> To advocate the adoption of or continued adherence to a definition of an ethical term seems to be tantamount to trying to justify the corresponding moral principle. Appealing to a definition in support of a principle is not a solution to the problem of justification, for the definition needs to be justified, and justifying it involves the same problems that justifying a principle does.

The first argument against naturalism can also be raised against intuitionism. Even the latter is based on an insufficient theory of meaning. Value sentences do not seem to be merely property-ascribing statements. They express favorable or unfavorable attitudes; they recommend, prescribe, and the like. Furthermore, intuitionism's theory of justification seems odd, weird, and difficult to defend. What does a nonnatural value property look like? And why should we stick to self-evident truths in social science? There seem to be no satisfactory answers to these questions.[12]

As an alternative to naturalism and intuitionism, a group of theories has been proffered that bears the name of *ethical subjectivism*. According to one characterization of subjectivism, value sentences express the proposition that the person enunciating the sentence experiences a certain emotion or assumes a certain attitude vis-a-vis the object he is talking about. Value sentences do entail factual assertions, but not about the object. They convey psychological information about the subject or the speaker. Thus the label "subjectivism." Meta-ethical subjectivism also implies a negative value ontology. It expressly denies that there could be objects in the world that, beside all their empirically ascertainable natural properties, are also equipped with a set of value properties that the human being might gain knowledge of through his senses or more immediately through intuition.

It is even more true of subjectivism than of naturalism and intuitionism that it is patently insufficient as a comprehensive meta-ethical theory. One argument against it should be enough. Assume that person A says: "I like revolutionary wars of liberation against colonial oppressors," and that person B exclaims: "I dislike revolutionary wars of liberation against colonial oppressors." According to ethical subjectivism, "I like X" means the same thing as "X is right," and "I dislike X" means the same as "X is wrong." Since the I-like sentences are uttered by different persons and therefore do not contradict each other, and since they are supposed to mean "X is right" and "X is wrong," respectively, then "X is right" and "X is wrong" should not contradict each other. Thus it should be possible to assert simultaneously that "X is right" and "X is wrong." However, this is an unreasonable consequence. It is inconsistent to assert that one and the same act is both right and wrong. And so, meta-ethical subjectivism must be untenable.[13]

8.2.3   Value Noncognitivism

Of the classical value theories, we are left with value noncognitivism. Noncognitivists differ greatly among themselves. One well-known school maintains that it is misleading to say that judgments of value are true or false, since they are not factual assertions at all. They are neither propositions about value characteristics of the real world nor about the speaking subject. Value judgments are considered entirely atheoretical, and so criteria of truth or falsity are not at all applicable to them. Value sentences are direct and immediate expressions of emotion much like ejaculations. Uttering that conservatism is good is like saying "Conservatism, hurray!" Statements of value may also express an order, advice, or a recommendation. They should not be interpreted, however, as describing that the speaker experiences an emotion, gives an order, gives advice, or makes a recommendation. Value statements fill expressive, evocative, and maybe even other noncognitive functions, but they do not report anything. In the words of Alfred Ayer:[14]

> In saying that a certain type of action is right or wrong, I am not making any factual statement, not even a statement about my own state of mind. I am merely expressing certain moral sentiments. . . . If a sentence makes no statement at all, there is obviously no sense in asking whether what it says is true or false.

It is this conception that has led to the conclusion of our value-free approach: Social sciences are sciences about, but not in questions of value. Value judgments cannot be justified in any rational way at all.

This rather extreme version of noncognitivism has long had a powerful grip on Scandinavian and to some extent even Northwest European and North American social science. In Sweden, it has even been graced with a particular name—value nihilism. In general, however, noncognitivism contains reasonable as well as contestable tenets. There seem to be good reasons to maintain that ultimate value sentences express something other than propositions. This claim is not generally accepted but is still relatively well established among social philosophers and ethicists.

Accepting this, however, is not identical with jumping to the conclusion that ultimate value judgments are purely arbitrary, that they cannot even be reasoned about, or that social science cannot be a science in politics, only about politics. We can reason in questions of value and justify ultimate judgments of value in various ways.

Another important counter-argument hits a particular version of noncognitivism that is based on a causal, psychological, or pragmatic theory of meaning. The meaning of value sentences is said to be their disposition to be caused by, or to cause, the occurrence of certain psychological processes in the sender and the receiver. Can these psychological processes really be equated with the meaning of the value sentences? It is clear that the term "meaning" can, in fact, be used in this way. But a statement's meaning can also be related to the fact that language is a calculus in so far as it is guided by rules. It is this meaning that is of greatest interest in this context. We can maintain that the meaning of a speech act is one and the same regardless of what psychological processes preceded it or what psychological effects it has had. As I have pointed out so many times, the question of meaning should be resolved with the help of content-oriented analysis; some noncognitivists make the mistake of trying to resolve it by means of a function-oriented analysis of the statements' origins and effects.[15]

We can take as an example the pronouncement, "Abolish agricultural regulation!" As is clear to everyone, the pronouncement of this statement may be caused by many different psychological processes or states, e.g., anger, hate, fear, sorrow, distress, loss, resignation, joy, or indifference. The enunciation of the statement can also have several different effects, e.g., surprise, delight, and disgust. Regardless of the causes or effects of the enunciation of the statement, its meaning in the specific linguistic context is the same. The meaning remains constant regardless of causes or effects. It follows from this that the meaning of a statement cannot be equated with the psychological processes causing or caused by its enunciation. This is exactly what certain noncognitivists do when they claim that value statements have expressive or evocative functions. While they believe that they have answered the question of what value statements mean, in reality they have answered a completely different question, i.e., the question of the origin and consequences of value statements. It is undeniably odd that our simple rule of thumb—that we must keep separate the questions of origin and effect on the one hand and validity on the other—has not been obeyed in practice even by several of our century's foremost philosophers.

8.2.4   Prescriptivism and Neonaturalism

Partly under the influence of this burden of criticism, two new meta-ethical schools have recently emerged. They go under the names prescriptivism and neonaturalism (descriptivism). *Prescriptivism* is a form of value noncognitivism. Its leading proponent is R. M. Hare. According to him, all forms of cognitivism are patently wrong. However, he refuses to regard value judgments as mere expressions or evocations of feeling or attitude or as mere arbitrary decisions. Value expressions express evaluations, advice, recommendations, prescriptions, instructions, or some other kind of guidance in the choice among alternatives. Hare also maintains that we can reason in questions of value.[17]

Neonaturalism is not nearly as unified as prescriptivism. Two of its best-known proponents are Philippa Foot and G. J. Warnock. In some respects, this theory seems to be a return to value cognitivism. At least some neonaturalists claim, for example, that it is not always logically possible to distinguish between the descriptive and evaluative meaning of moral pronouncements and that the criteria applied in value judgments are not only a matter of free choice.[17] Clearly the most interesting current discussion in meta-ethics is between descriptivists and prescriptivists. Both schools have been subjected to extensive criticism; we do not have the space to go into it in detail here. However, it seems difficult to accept that ultimate value judgments can be true or that an Ought could be derived from an Is, as some neonaturalists maintain. Prescriptivism seems much more commendable.

8.2.5   The Ends-Means Solution

Let us summarize: Meta-ethics offers no definitive answer to questions of what value sentences mean and how value judgments may be validated. Meta-ethics is still an area of stormy controversy. There certainly seem to be good reasons to reject meta-ethical subjectivism as well naturalism and intuitionism in their old, classical forms, but cognitivism is far from refuted in any stronger sense of the word. Modern, less extreme versions of noncognitivism seem to be on the right track. Although maintaining that value sentences do not express propositions, they conclude that value judgments can be reasoned about and justified in various rational ways. However, not even this position is generally accepted. And so, our hopes that meta-ethics could provide us with definitive advice and clear guidance have been frustrated. But this is no reason for melancholy and resigned self-effacement. The strategy of rational political assessment must instead be to decide from case to case how value sentences should be interpreted and justified. Let us see how far this maxim—in combination with what we have learned from meta-ethics—can carry us.

We should, however, interject a few additional distinctions here. The process of assuming a position vis-à-vis values could be divided into the following four questions:

(1) Which goals shall we choose?
(2) Have the goals been achieved?
(3) Which means shall we choose to attain the goals?
(4) Have the means contributed to the attainment of the goals?

We should differentiate, then, between choice of goals, measurement of goal achievement, choice of means, and assessment of the effects of the means.[18]

How can science help us answer these four questions? The first and third questions differ substantially from the second and fourth. When answering questions 1 and 3, we express value judgments, but in answering 2 and 4, we say something *about* value judgments. It is important to keep this distinction in mind. Not even the most inveterate noncognitivist has ever argued that assertions *about* value judgments must be excluded from scientific discourse.

In 1975, the Swedish Parliament set as a goal an average yearly increase in energy consumption of no more than two percent between 1973 and 1985.

If in 1986 we were to measure how well the goal was met, we would carry out an ordinary empirical investigation. We would be measuring goal achievement, to be sure, but the study itself consists of describing the goal of 1975, describing actual energy consumption for the period 1973 through 1985, and comparing the numbers in order to ascertain whether actual energy consumption *really was* as the goal prescribed. Similarly, we might investigate whether the appropriate administrative, economic, and informative policy instruments devised in 1975 to contribute to the achievement of the goal actually influenced energy consumption as intended. We would then be evaluating the effects of the means, but the investigation itself would focus on demonstrating whether the means actually were influential or not.

Assertions *about* value judgments are not value judgments at all. They are propositions that can, in principle, be confirmed or disconfirmed. They can also be of another kind than those indicated by questions 2 and 4. We can, for example, determine which value sentences were pronounced at a specific time and in a specific context. We can investigate why a certain person or group of people have embraced certain value judgments, e.g., we can try to determine which evaluative attitudes underlie the entertainment of these value judgments. We can also try to establish what functions value statements have for the political system, party, group, or personality. In all of these cases, we are conducting ordinary empirical investigations.[19]

Questions 2 and 4 entail the two fundamental problems that public policy evaluation or evaluative research try to resolve. Apparently, they need not give rise to value judgments on the part of these researchers. The questions can be answered in plain descriptive language. They do not cause us any difficulties that are peculiar to value judgments.

Let us go on, then, to the first and third questions posed above. Both require an answer that contains directly expressed value judgments.

The questions: "Which goals shall we choose?" and "Which means shall we choose to attain them?" rest on the assumption that questions of ends must be kept separate from questions of means. The distinction is significant because the answers contain two entirely different types of judgments of value. We can call them *categorical* and *instrumental* judgments of value. We sometimes also contrast intrinsic against extrinsic value statements. Categorical statements express that something is valued "as an end" or "for itself" or "in its own right," whereas instrumental statements say that something is valued "merely as a means" or "for something else."[20]

Assume person P claims that any information concerning his country's espionage organization should be kept secret—i.e., a limitation of freedom of speech is desirable—since this would reduce the risk that secrets about his country's intelligence activity against other countries would be revealed. Assume further that person Q dislikes such a measure precisely because it is assumed to have this effect. Here we are faced with a conflict concerning how we should evaluate a possible action. At the same time, there is agreement concerning the consequences this action will have. Statements of the second kind express instrumental value judgments. Their logical structure is that a certain act A (limiting the freedom of expression) is good (or better than alternatives B and C), if a certain end E (reducing the risk that secrets about one's own country's intelligence activities would be revealed) is to be attained. Claiming this is the same as asserting that a limitation of freedom of expression will result in a decreased risk that secrets about one's own country's intelligence activities will be revealed, or that if there is no limitation of freedom of expression, the risk of intelligence revelations will increase. The instrumental statement of value says, in other words, that act A is a means to achieve end E. An instrumental value judgment can thus be reshaped into a *proposition about* an empirical means-end relationship. This proposition contains no value judgments at all. Even the most inveterate value noncognitivist should agree that an instrumental statement of value can be given such a factual interpretation.

The point of the argument is that most political-ethical discussions include both agreement/disagreement about an end as well as about means to attain the end. But since statements about means are entirely descriptive, they can, without any doubt at all, be subjected to ordinary truth assessment. Given the end, social science can thus point out suitable means to that end without suffering pangs of conscience.

Let us develop the example further. Why does person P believe that secrets about his country's espionage organization should not be revealed? Perhaps he thinks that a secret intelligence service must be able to gather information concerning threats to his country's national security in order that his country might defend itself against those threats. Why does person Q regret that the secrets are not revealed? He may think that this leads to decreased public access to the way various authorities act. In both of these cases, then, we are faced with instrumental statements of value that can be tested against empirical reality.

We can go further. Person P may assert that threats to national security must be averted in order to preserve national independence, which, in turn, is necessary if work to preserve and deepen the democratic form of government is to continue, which, in turn, is a prerequisite for an increase in the influence of the people. So we are faced with a series of new lines of reasoning about means. These can be translated into propositions and so be subjected to ordinary truth testing.

Decisions having to do with the validity of normative judgments are thus time after time turned into questions of the truth of statements of fact. Thus, empirical science is able to contribute indirectly to the solution of questions concerning the validity of value judgments. The better the support for our theories on the various links in the means-end chain, the more certain we can be when we make value judgments. Good empirical theory helps us to take a stand on the validity of value judgments. This means that applied science, normative theory, or what in political science is called ''policy science'' or ''policy analysis'' becomes a fully respectable occupation.[21]

If there is agreement on the effects of the means but not on the desirability of the end, then the issue is raised to the level where the end-statement can be interpreted instrumentally in relation to a higher end. We are led to the conception of a series, or hierarchy, of ends, where an end on a lower level becomes a means for reaching the end on the immediately higher level. In principle, it is difficult to see any end to this process.

We have now answered the third of our four questions about value judgments. Pronouncements about which means are good for the attainment of which ends can be translated into statements that say that the means will lead to the achievement of the ends. These means-statements can be subjected to scientific truth assessment. Like statements *about* value judgments, they must be characterized as propositions. Thus, the validation of instrumental value judgments does not differ from the justification of ordinary propositions.

We are now left with only the first question: ''Which ends shall we choose?'' Here we run into a problem that distinguishes categorical value judgments from factual assertions. We said above that it is difficult to see, in principle, any end to the process of interpreting a given value judgment instrumentally in relation to a higher value judgment. In practice, however, there is always an end. Person P may conclude his line of argument by saying that preserving and deepening the democratic policy increases the influence of the people, but the consequences of this are never indicated. An illustration of person P's entire chain of argument appears in Figure 8.2.

Person Q, on the other hand, may argue that decreased public control of the actions of state authorities will increase the position of power of the privileged groups, and this in turn means that the people's influence decreases. Q's line of reasoning ends here. The whole chain of argumentation appears in Figure 8.3.

P's and Q's argument chains end with two different propositions: Popular influence will, in the one case, increase and, in the other, decrease. The same ultimate value underlies both: Popular influence should increase. In both cases, we have an intrinsic value that is not further justified. We are

Limitation of freedom of speech.

$\downarrow$

Decreased probability that secrets concerning his country's intelligence activities will be revealed.

$\downarrow$

Increased probability that the intelligence service will be able to work well and gather information on threats to national security; increased probability that national security will be preserved.

$\downarrow$

Measures will be taken which will avert threats to national security.

$\downarrow$

A condition for continued work to preserve and deepen the democratic polity.

$\downarrow$

The people's influence grows.

Figure 8.2 Person P's Chain of Arguments

faced, in other words, with a categorical value judgment, and the criterion is that it is not considered instrumental in relation to any other value. It cannot be translated into a statement of means to attain another end. The question is how science should deal with such categorical value judgments.

Obviously, what is expressed by the statement: "Popular influence should increase" cannot be tested by means of an ordinary truth assessment. We do not seem to be dealing with a proposition that can be shown to be true or false in the usual way. We might say, rather, that it expresses a yardstick for political evaluation or a norm for how we ought to act. It can be neither confirmed nor disconfirmed in the ordinary empirical way. It is impossible,

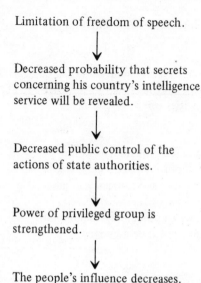

Limitation of freedom of speech.

Decreased probability that secrets concerning his country's intelligence service will be revealed.

Decreased public control of the actions of state authorities.

Power of privileged group is strengthened.

The people's influence decreases.

Figure 8.3 Person Q's Chain of Arguments

in this sense, to determine scientifically the truth of categorical value judgments.[22]

We will hardly deny that this is a serious limitation. We should, however, be careful not to draw the conclusion from this that science is entirely paralyzed in the face of categorical value judgments. There are a couple of other criteria of validity besides truth that are applicable to categorical judgments of value. With their aid, social science can accomplish much to facilitate a rational choice between different ultimate ends. It can, of course, (a) address the semantic clarity of categorical value judgments. It can (b) establish inconsistencies between various categorical value judgments held by an actor by establishing which intrinsic values are physically impossible to achieve simultaneously. Science can also provide us with other facts that help us to take a stand vis-à-vis categorical value judgments. It is legitimate for science to discover (c) if the object of a categorical value judgment can in any way be realized physically; (d) if so, which alternative means exist and how great the probability is that they will lead to the end; and (e) which side effects and ultimate consequences result from the choice of means beside the fact that they probably result in the attainment of the end.[23]

By conveying this information—which seems wholly indispensable if we are to make rational and responsible decisions—science can actually weaken or strengthen our confidence in categorical value judgments. If we were to find that a much-praised end were in all likelihood not at all realizable, then it would in practice be pointless to ask the question of whether it is desirable or not.[24]

At this point it should be clear that the rational assessment approach must in no way be limited to dealing with pronouncements *about* value judgments. It can also give reasons for and against value judgments. Instrumental statements of value can be rewritten as propositions and tested empirically in the usual way. The significance of this should not be underestimated, since most value judgments in political language are of this character. Categorical value judgments also occur, and not even in the face of these is the rational assessor forced to stop. He can present a number of scientifically supported viewpoints on them. There is, however, one thing he cannot do: He cannot confirm or disconfirm them in the same way he does statements of fact.

8.3 The Evaluative Choice Approach

Proponents of the evaluative choice approach are extremely critical of the basic thought behind the means-ends approach. They argue that there does not exist any objective study of value judgments or even of social phenomena at all. Not even reasoning on appropriate means for reaching desired ends can be objective. All acts of research are inherently evaluative because the researcher must make up his mind to pursue one question rather than another. More specifically, the advocates of the evaluative choice approach argue as follows: A researcher has a limited amount of time, energy, and money at his disposal; since there are innumerable questions that he might conceivably seek to answer, he must allocate his resources to a small sample of these questions; in other words, he must choose to scrutinize some things. He may, for example, choose to study the controversy surrounding nuclear power rather than the controversy about public housing, public transportation, or health care. By necessity, his choice must be governed by evaluative attitudes. The same can also be said about his choice of concepts, schemes of classification, data, and techniques for processing data. An assessment of propositions about value judgments or pronouncements of means for attaining ends cannot, then, be carried out in the objective way that the proponents of the means-ends philosophy claim.

True, it is very reasonable to assert that the choice to pursue one research question rather than another most often reflects a choice on the inquirer's behalf. It is also obvious that to some extent such a choice must be governed by evaluations. This emerges from the fact that the selection of a research problem, e.g., the controversy on nuclear power, seems to be identical with endorsing a statement like: "I ought to study the controversy on nuclear power." The endorsement of normative statements presupposes at least one normative statement as a premise, since normative statements cannot be derived from factual ones. Thus, it is reasonable to assert that the selection of a question is a consequence of the researcher's evaluations. What we are saying here is that the researcher's allegiance to a research question is explained by a certain motive containing an evaluative component.

These evaluative motives may be of several kinds. Maybe his choice was made because energy problems struck the investigator as more interesting than, say, housing problems. His choice was a matter of personal taste. Or his choice may have been a consequence of evaluations pertinent to what is valuable from a theoretical, intrascientific point of view. His choice may also have been influenced by evaluations of what is socially or politically important. According to a method recommended by Gunnar Myrdal, among others, the investigator should be conscious of his evaluations and should make them specific and explicit in order to be able to appraise them critically and so avoid allowing inappropriate evaluations to govern his choices.[25]

As the researcher performs such research-psychological or research-sociological acts, or as he studies them ex post facto, the issue of how evaluations influence his choices is salient. We may ascertain that a certain evaluation caused the researcher to choose a certain problem for study. In this way, we make an intentionalist explanation of the investigator's choice. But we have said nothing at all about whether the choice is good, interesting, fruitful, important, or worthwhile. The fact that certain evaluations *caused* a researcher to pursue one question rather than another is not relevant as a *reason* for the pertinence, salience, importance, fruitfulness, and so forth of the question.

We realize this more easily if we make the following assumption: Two West German experts on the Soviet Union decide simultaneously and independently that they wish to study the relationship between the Communist Party and the labor union movement in the Soviet Union. Researcher A, a decided anticommunist and an astute critic of the Soviet system of government, chose this topic because of an intense personal wish to demonstrate that the party dominates everything in Soviet society. Researcher B, who defends the Soviet system, chose this particular subject because he believes that the union movement is somewhat more independent and Soviet society considerably less totalitarian than generally thought in the West. In judging the relationship between party and union movement in the Soviet Union, does it make any methodological difference that the researchers' motives are quite different? No. The truth or falsity of the hypothesis that the party does not exert decisive power over the union movement in all substantive matters

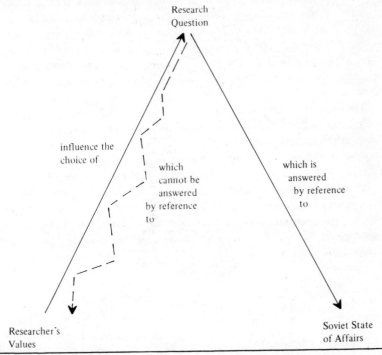

Figure 8.4   The Logical Independence of Scientific Criteria of Validity from Researcher's Values

must be determined by looking at the actual relationship between the two in Soviet society, not by referring to the researchers' ideological preferences. Ideological motives can explain why the researcher chose the subject. They may also be used to explain, say, why the hypothesis was tested against one type of evidence and not against another. But ideological motives are entirely irrelevant as reasons or evidence in controversies about political structure in the Soviet Union. The logic of our argument is represented in Figure 8.4.

The researcher's values influence his choice of research question, and they can be a part of the explanation of this choice. However, the research question cannot be substantively answered through reference to the researcher's values, but only with reference to Soviet reality.

The question of whether the researcher is influenced by values is a very interesting psychological problem, but its solution should have nothing to do with assessing the importance of the researcher's question, the fruitfulness of his concepts, or the force of his arguments. How he invented his question (or his scheme of classification or his critical argument) is logically independent of how the validity of the question, scheme of classification, and argument are to be assessed. That evaluative motives might have caused a researcher to make certain choices is irrelevant as evidence for the assessment of the validity of the choices. What the effects of his scientific results will be, once they are made public, e.g., who will gain from them, is also irrelevant.

The question of how to assess the validity of political value judgments — in the sense of that which is expressed by political value sentences — must be kept apart from how values — in the sense of mental acts, psychic states, or motives — work in the research process, e.g., how they govern the researcher's choice of problems, concepts, schemes of classification, data, and critical arguments. Furthermore, the problem of assessing the validity of statements of value must also be distinguished from the problem of finding out how the pronouncement of those same value statements influence various parts of the environment, e.g., readers and listeners. If these simple distinctions had been observed, many fruitless pseudo-discussions of the "value problem in science" could have been avoided.[26]

8.4 Avoiding the Value Swamp: Statements of Fact "Play the Main Role"

In a programmatic foreword to the book *Conservative Ideas*, Herbert Tingsten in the late 1930s energetically proffered the thesis that ideologies mainly consist of statements of fact. Since values play only a very insignificant role, then we hardly need to raise or assign any practical importance to the question of how we can test their validity. Tingsten wrote:

> My accounts of various political ideologies try, . . . to the extent that it can be considered necessary, to demonstrate the arbitrariness or misconceptions which have been essential to their formation. This is not, of course, a matter of criticizing values — the issue of truth does not exist in their regard. But ideologies — i.e., systems of thought which are considered to incite to political action or are generally assumed to play this role — are not, as is sometimes thoughtlessly asserted, essentially series of values. Statements of fact play the main role.

Political ideologies often start from a conception of reality, Tingsten continued. Sometimes they appear to be consequences of metaphysical systems.

> Catholic social theory is considered to include those rules for human social life which were layed down by God in the Bible or by the leadership of the

Catholic church. . . . Natural law, which likewise has been the basis for a number of ideologies, is a profane metaphysic. . . . In general, notions of the "true nature" of the world and of human beings have been extraordinarily important in the formation of political doctrines. In proximity to this type of ideological point of departure we find conceptions of history and predictions of the future which are based on them.

As examples, Tingsten offered Hegel's and Marx's philosophies of history, as well as Nazism's theory of race.

Tingsten was forced to admit, however, that there in fact was a group of political ideologies that took as their point of departure a stated, subjective value judgment.

Typical is utilitarianism when it claims to be based on the pursuit of welfare, utility or happiness. . . . Maurras says he is a relativist and is fully aware of his subjectivism when he sets up the good of France as the goal for his political activity. . . . What these ideologies claim they can achieve is an illumination of the means which should be used to attain an end strived for by all or by a certain group. . . . In this context we shall only emphasize that it is not possible, based on the general value premises mentioned above, to arrive at any directive at all for political activity without presenting some notion of the reality which is to be changed.

Thus, even these subjectively founded ideologies were, Tingsten argued, essentially attempts at establishing empirical relationships.[27]

Tingsten's approach to the value problem, then, assumes that it is meaningless to talk about truth and falsity of "values." Unlike statements of fact, values cannot be tested for truth. This is not a great obstacle in our attempt to assess the validity of political ideologies, Tingsten argues. Values, after all, play such a little role. Statements of fact occur significantly more often and play a significantly more crucial role in political ideologies than do value judgments.

If we look to that part of an ideology that usually is expressed explicitly, Tingsten's thesis seems to contain a certain measure of truth, even though the information element must be allotted a somewhat less pronounced role than he would argue. This is due to the fact that political language can have many other purposes besides conveying information. In practice, we often find that the evaluative or prescriptive use overshadows the informative use, even if the sentences are cloaked in the indicative form and seem at first glance to be nothing but descriptive.

It is, however, unreasonable to base a study of ideologies only on their explicit parts. We pointed out earlier in this book that we must also consider that which is tacit but still communicated. This would seem in most cases to mean that we take note of value judgments. The end result, then, would be a further attenuation of the thesis on the dominance of statements of fact in political ideologies.

Tingsten defines ideologies as systems of notions that are considered to incite political action or are generally assumed to play this role. This would probably mean that they can be regarded as a kind of reasoning in favor of some sort of practical conclusions. Tingsten would probably have agreed with this, but he wanted to maintain that the reasons for the conclusion consisted of statements of fact. In order for a practical argument to be complete, and in order for it to be valid at least in principle, it must contain at least one value premise. We can agree with Tingsten to the extent that value premises are often implicit in practical reasoning. Only the conclusion and the descriptive premises, or actually only the latter, are presented. This pattern is extraordinarily common. This should not lead us to the conclusion that the participants in the interlocution did not have any value premise. Either it is considered too obvious to need to be stated explicitly (freedom is good), or else it is regarded as so controversial that it is better to exclude it (lower inflation is better than increased employment). In such cases, the researcher should not hesitate to work out the tacit normative premises. This type of ameliorative systematic interpretation was treated above in Chapter 3. Tingsten tended to underestimate the significance of interpretation. He was often satisfied with literal interpretation of ideological pronouncements and so obviously overlooked the fact that value premises are usually tacit. Pointing this out undermines his thesis entirely. If ideologies are regarded as chains or clusters of reasons for practical conclusions (which can, of course, be very general), then the evaluative element will occur just as often as the descriptive.

A caveat is in order here. As we pointed out earlier, arguments often form chains in the sense that the conclusion in one argument becomes the premise in the next, and so on. As we have seen, value judgments that occur at lower levels in such a chain can be reformulated as assertions about means to ends. They can, in other words, be considered statements of fact. Only the ultimate end in such a chain cannot be reformulated as an assertion about a means. There is reason to assume that political ideologies to a rather great extent consist of such argument chains. These chains are common in other forms of political language, e.g., in discourse about individual policy instruments or broad policy programs. This offers strong support for a conclusion along the lines of Tingsten: Political language to an overwhelming degree consists of statements of fact or pronouncements that can be reformulated as statements of fact, and therefore we do not need in practice to be so concerned with the problem of testing the validity of value judgments.

8.5 Clashes Between Incompatible Standards for Assessing Value Judgments

> We hold these Truths to be self-evident that all Men . . . are endowed by their
> Creator with certain unalienable Rights. . . . That to secure these Rights,
> Governments are instituted among Men.

These famous words from the Declaration of Independence may be interpreted on two levels. Obviously, the framers of the Declaration meant to propound the moral rule that governments ought to secure these rights for their citizens. A rational assessment of this value judgment constitutes talk on the first normative level. The American rebels and freedom fighters also wanted to claim that these particular moral "truths" are "self-evident." This presupposes that principles of political ethics have an objective existence. They subsist somewhere and must be apprehended by man. They indicate the kind of positive laws that ought to be enacted, implemented, and obeyed by worldly government. It is these principles that constitute natural law. The term "law" in "natural law" is used in the sense of moral laws. Supporters of the natural law doctrine also hold that these laws, like laws of nature, can be discovered. Natural law is not enacted by people as is positive law—a legal rule or a system of legal rules. Natural law has an existence of its own, entirely independent of people. It describes and prescribes at the same time.

A rational assessment of the natural law doctrine is on the secondary normative level. This doctrine entails a cognitivist meta-ethical theory. It is not compatible with the meta-ethical position adopted in this work. According to the latter, it is not possible by scientific means to ascertain in an objective way ultimate rules that can guide lawmakers and ordinary citizens. Granted, certain other values such as the act of depriving people of their political freedoms and rights can be demonstrated to be wrong. But taken as categorical statements of value, their truth or falsity cannot be ascertained. There seem to be no objective criteria by means of which the truth of such ultimate principles may be assessed.[28]

In several places in this work we have pointed out that two kinds of conflicts can arise between the analytic position adopted in this book and the position taken in the political language that is the object of the analysis. The conflict may have to do with the specific application of one of the five major rules of assessment. It can also concern a rule as such. In our present case, we are faced with one more conflict of the latter kind. The conflict does not concern the validity of a certain value judgment. It has to do with how the actual validity assessment should be carried out.

These conflicts of rules can be of many different types also in the area of values. Here, it suffices to provide one more example. It is the confrontation between Felix E. Oppenheim's noncognitivist meta-ethical theory and Carl J. Friedrich's cognitivist conception in the former's excellent *Moral Principles in Political Philosophy*. The criticism leveled by Oppenheim is, in my view, quite acceptable. In his voluminous work on *Man and His Government*, Friedrich affirms, in a vein similar to precursors like Plato and Rousseau, that values are discovered in objects. He writes:

> The valuer's role is to discover the value, not to create or constitute it. . . .
> [Values] are facts in the sense of being experienced as being there. In other
> words, the values exist, whether there is someone to recognize them or not.
> . . . An act of moral goodness is good independently of any person present to
> appreciate it.

Both facts and values are a matter of experience. "The experiencing of value is as much a primary experience as observation of facts devoid of value." And just as the basic colors are nearly universally experienced, so the basic values are experienced by most persons. Hence, "the occasional occurrence of value blind persons need not disturb us unduly."

Friedrich uses the term "experience" to refer to the discovery of values as well as facts. However, his use of the expression "value blind" suggests the view that values and facts are not experienced in the same way. The latter seems to be apprehended by our five senses, whereas the former is grasped by a sixth, moral, sense. Any of the senses may deceive us and lead us into making mistaken judgments, whether of fact or of value. Both kinds of judgment are, nevertheless, objectively either true or false.

> Experience may deceive, and often does. This patent observation applies to all
> kinds of experience, and therefore, does not provide a basis for contrasting
> value experience with other kinds of experience. That something may be
> believed to be valuable when it is not parallels the fact that something may be
> believed to be straight when it is not, such as the well-known optical illusion of
> a broken stick seen in a glass of water.

This parallel between statements of fact and value judgments, however, does not hold, according to Oppenheim. That this rose is real and that those who deny that are colorblind can be established by an objective, i.e., intersubjective, procedure. Similarly, there is an operation by which anyone can confirm the hypothesis that a stick submerged in water is straight; pull it out of the water and it will appear straight. On the other hand, take a situation in which the majority and the minority in a given society disagree as to what is politically best. There is no way of determining whether the former experienced the objective value entity and the latter were deceived by their value experience. "It seems to me," Oppenheim concludes, "that this form of intuitionism does not provide an objective criterion by which to assess the truth of fundamental principles of ethics in general and of political ethics in particular."[29]

8.6 Epilogue

This presentation ends with this conflict surrounding rules for a rational discourse on political statements of value. Point by point, I have tried to show that an objective scientific attitude toward political messages does not preclude sharp criticism. Scientific objectivity should not be understood to mean that we should be satisfied to describe what is said but desist from closely appraising the messages. Criticism is not only admissible; it is desirable. The point is that it should not be done in just any fashion. It must follow certain rules. I have tried in this work to present these rules for rational political discourse.

Notes

Chapter 1

1. Sabine, 1939: 10f.
2. See, for example, Strauss, 1962: 232ff. and possibly also Stark, 1958: 213.
3. Certain writers, such as Levine, 1963: 6ff.; Naess et al., 1956: 1ff.; and Mannheim, 1968: 155ff. have tried to construct trisections of the fields of political theory, political argument analysis, or ideology analysis. Others, for example, von Beyme, 1969: 12, have even suggested dividing the field five ways. But all of these can be referred back to the fundamental distinction between content-oriented and function-oriented analysis.
4. The figure is based on a diagram in Ole R. Holsti's well-known book, *Content Analysis for the Social Sciences and Humanities,* 1969: 24ff. The version of this figure presented in the Swedish edition of my book has been subjected to constructive criticism by a number of people, including Gunvall Grip, 1979 and Anders Westholm, 1980. I have incorporated some of their main points into the following exposition.
5. Consider, for instance, Holsti's 1969: 14 definition, which goes as follows: "Content analysis is any technique for making inferences by objectively and systematically identifying specified characteristics of messages." For other definitions of content analysis, see Holsti, 1969: 2ff. and Krippendorff, 1980: 21ff. For a fresh overview of various uses of content analysis, see Rosengren, 1981.
6. On functionalism and functionalist explanation, see, for example, Nagel, 1961: 522ff.—the phrase in the text is adapted from p. 525—Merton, 1967: 73ff.; Meehan, 1967: 112f.; Stinchcombe, 1968: 87ff.; Elster, 1978: 121f.
7. The questions reflect a very rough division into sociological, political, psychological, geographic, and intellectual background factors. See the figure in Vedung, 1971: 35. We find this division in more or less the same guise in, for example, Myrdal, 1970: 3f. and von Beyme, 1969: 12. For another classification, see Wiener, 1961: 538.
8. Graber, 1976: 68f.
9. Holsti, 1969: 88.
10. Holsti, 1969: 69f. and references provided there. The inference problem is also treated in an interesting fashion in Graber, 1976: 68ff. and in George, 1959: 3ff., 13ff., *passim.*
11. Holsti, 1969: 72ff.
12. Holsti, 1969: 85ff.
13. Rescher, 1970: 2, 11. For an outline of various meanings of explanation, see Brown, 1963: 41ff.
14. The figure is slightly adapted from Hadenius, 1979.
15. For an interesting typology of rules for political interlocutions that differs in several

respects from the one presented here, see Midgaard, Stenstadvold, and Underdal, 1973: 19ff. and Midgaard, 1980: 86ff. In his incisive review of my book in the *Swedish Journal for Political Research*, Knut Midgaard (1980b) suggested several ameliorations, which I have tried to incorporate in this edition.

16. See, for example, Andrén et al., 1977: 67ff.

17. See, for example, Fischer, 1970: 302.

18. Fischer, 1970: 302.

19. Another good example is Sverker Gustavsson's impressive assessment in Gustavsson, 1971 (English summary) of Max Weber's, John Bernal's, Michael Polanyi's, and Jürgen Habermas's views of the relationship between government and the research community. His own reasoning develops into a defense of the so-called classical doctrine on the freedom of research from the state. For an interesting reformulation and extension of his ideas, see Gustavsson, 1981a. Another excellent contribution is Barry Holmstrom's critical review of broad Swedish opinion concerning the Korean War. He treats, among other things, the outbreak of the war in 1950, the military goals of the UN forces, the role of the Soviet Union, and China's entry into the war. See Holmstrom, 1972 (English summary).

20. Robert Goodin's *Manipulatory Politics* (1980) contains interesting examples of assessment of politically manipulative acts. Sissela Bok's *Lying* (1978) contains fascinating arguments about how political lies should be assessed. Holsti, 1969: 53ff. and Krippendorff, 1980: 38ff. contain sections on the use of content analysis for the purpose of auditing, e.g., press performance, against standards. However, they do not distinguish clearly between assessing message content per se and judging actions related to communication of messages.

21. Cf. von Wright, 1971: 11.

22. The figure is adapted from Conway and Feigert, 1972: 319.

23. Some of these expressions may be found in Donnellan, 1967: 85ff.; von Wright, 1971: 2ff., 1976: 373f.; Brodbeck, 1968: 59 (motive explanations); Geach, 1976: 3f.

24. Dray, 1957: 124, 122. Donald Davidson, 1980: 3 calls them "rationalizations." See also Hempel, 1965: 469ff., and Lewin and Vedung, 1980: ixf.

25. See, for example, Donnellan, 1967: 86.

26. See, for example, Davidson, 1980; Moon, 1975; and Nordenfelt, 1974. See also the general discussion in Donnellan, 1967.

27. Developed in von Wright, 1971, 1976. See also Melden, 1961 and Taylor, 1964. For good overviews over the contending positions, consult Moon, 1975 and Donnellan, 1967.

28. Davidson, 1963: 685f. The essay is reprinted in Davidson, 1980: 3ff.

29. Von Wright, 1971: 96ff. Later, von Wright admits that far from all human actions flow from this peculiar combination of an intention and a cognitive attitude which the practical syllogism schema embodies—von Wright, 1976: 394. Explanations in the social sciences usually do not have the character of intentionalist practical inference (PI) schema. But the PI schema is pivotal in the sense that the other explanatory mechanisms seems to revolve around this schema. See von Wright, 1976: 413.

30. von Wright, 1971: 97.

31. Concerning the distinction "prescriptive-descriptive decision theory," see, for example, Rapoport, 1964: 5f.; Raiffa, 1968: 77f., 289ff.; or Stokey and Zeckhauser, 1978: 13ff.

32. Luce and Raiffa, 1957: 13; Rapoport, 1964: 12ff., 1980: 44f.

33. This schema is adapted from, among others, Lindblom, 1968: 13; Quade,1975: 46ff.; and Anderson, 1979: 9ff.

34. Cf. Hadenius,1981: 28.

35. Lave and March, 1975: 123.

36. Hempel, 1965: 466.

37. Luce and Raiffa, 1957: 278f. and Hempel, 1965: 467.

38. Harsanyi, 1976: 40 and Hempel, 1965: 467. Among other decision rules proposed in the literature, we can note the maximax rule and the principle of insufficient reason.

39. The methodology for confirming the existence of motives is not well developed. Several of the ideas presented briefly here are treated in Hadenius, 1981: 15. See also Goldmann, 1971: 51ff. For a typology of reasons why actors conceal their motivations, see Goffman, 1959: 141ff.

Chapter 2

1. Popper, 1974: 222. See also Myrdal, 1958: 22f., 31ff., 50ff., 128, 254f.; Myrdal, 1970: 51; Easton, 1953: 52f., 92ff.

2. Brecht, 1959: 30f.

3. Scriven, 1976: 39.

4. Bunge, 1967: 168.

5. SIPRI, 1979: 388.

6. Galtung, 1969: 9ff.

7. Galtung, 1969: 10.

8. Galtung, 1969: 11.

9. For a presentation of the Swedish party system, see Hancock, 1972: 108ff.

10. Ogden and Richards, 1923: 14.

11. Cf. Lyons, 1977: 95ff.

12. Carney and Scheer, 1974: 68. Cf. Føllesdal and Walløe, 1977: 114.

13. Sartori, 1981: 9.

14. Carney and Scheer, 1974: 68.

15. Carney and Scheer, 1974: 68. For further comments on word, intension, and extension, see Black, 1952: 193; Black, 1968: 151f.; Brody, 1973: 12f.; Alston, 1964: 13ff.; Russel, 1921: 191; Cohen and Nagel, 1934: 30ff. Cf. also Føllesdal and Walløe, 1977: 115.

16. Brody, 1973: 12-13.

17. Cf. Føllesdal and Walløe, 1977: 118.

18. This reasoning is drawn from Sartori, 1981: 23ff., 27ff.

19. Sartori, 1981: 12.

20. Avineri, 1968: 36f.; Plamenatz, 1954. Cf. Sabine and Thorson, 1973: 795.

21. Black, 1952: 185.

22. This point is brought out in Sartori, 1981: 6f. On equivocity and ambiguity in general, see Brody, 1973: 32ff. and Copi, 1972: 92ff.

23. Sartori, 1981: 7. My terminology, though, differs from Sartori's.

24. Lyons, 1977: 5ff. and Brody, 1973: 36ff.

25. See, for example, Brody, 1973: 36ff. and Black, 1952: 190f.

26. Quade, 1975: 5.

27. Black, 1952: 195.

28. Black, 1952: 199.

29. See, for example, Black, 1949: 30ff; Brody, 1973: 40ff.; Alston, 1964: 84ff., 1967c: 218.

30. The figure is a modified version of the one found in Sartori 1981: 7.

31. Compare Alston, 1967c: 218; Brody, 1973: 40ff.; Ullman, 1962: 116ff.

32. See, for example, Brody, 1973: 43; Alston, 1964: 84ff.

33. Copi, 1972: 118. See also Oppenheim, 1975: 290, 1981: 179; Brody, 1973: 22.

34. Riggs,1970: 92.

35. The quotation is from Hempel's famous *Fundamentals of Concept Formation*, 2. Actually, Hempel prefers the term "nominal" instead of "stipulative." The meaning, however, is the same as far as I can see.

36. Oppenheim, 1975: 290; Hempel, 1952: 2ff.

37. Hempel, 1952: 4.

38. Cf. Hempel, 1952: 2ff.

39. Oppenheim, 1975: 291. For the synonym "lexical definition," see Copi, 1972: 120.

40. See, for example, Hempel, 1952: 11ff.; Copi, 1972: 121ff. ("precising definition"); and Oppenheim, 1981: 1, 177ff. See also Sartori, 1981: 40ff. and Graham, 1971: 89ff. For examples of explications see, Deutsch, 1966 (nationalism); Lane, 1976 (political); Lane, 1981 (power); Oppenheim, 1961 (freedom); Vedung, 1976 (comparative method); Zannoni, 1978 (elite).

41. Graham, 1971: 92.

42. Heeger, 1975: 15. Heeger's analysis of synonyms reminds us of the technique used by Zannoni, 1978 in his paper on the concept of elite.

43. Heeger, 1975: 38.

44. Heeger, 1975: 34ff.

45. Heeger, 1975: 21ff., 25ff., 37ff.

46. Heeger, 1975: 40.

47. See Heeger, 1975: 63.

48. See Sartori, 1981: 15. Note the spelling "inten*s*ionalist," not "inten*t*ionalist." Some people use the expressions "connotative" and "denotative" definitions.

49. The definition and the following example are adapted from my own work on evaluations of the Swedish energy conservation program, Vedung, 1982.

50. Hempel, 1952: 39ff; Sartori, 1981: 6ff., 15ff.

51. See Hempel, 1952: 6ff. and Oppenheim, 1975: 290.

52. Heeger, 1975: 17f.

53. This is discussed in Sartori, 1970: 1040ff.

54. See, for example, Sartori et al., 1975: 32ff., *passim* and Sartori, 1976: 58ff.

55. Sartori, 1970: 1042 ("omnis determinatio est negatio").

56. Beardsley, 1975: 222; Ehninger, 1974: 45.

57. See, for example, Carney and Scheer, 1974: 3.

58. See Ehninger, 1974: 14f.

59. See Ehninger, 1974: 15f.

60. See, for example, Vedung, 1977: 41ff.

Chapter 3

1. This general view of interpretation is taken from Andrén et al., 1978: 16f.

2. Naess, 1966: 28.

3. Naess, 1966: 28ff. However, Naess also introduces a definition of the expression "interpretation of terms."

4. Strömholm, 1976: 75ff.; Peczenik, 1974: 69ff.; Evers,1970: 44ff.

5. Holsti, 1969: 12f.

6. Nohrstedt, 1982.

7. Strömholm, 1976: 79; Peczenik, 1974: 99.

8. Quoted with minor changes from Popper, 1962a: 246. Cf. Popper, 1962a: 293.

9. Popper, 1961: 3.

10. Scriven, 1976: 71f.

11. Scriven, 1976: 72.

12. The basis for this argument is taken from an excellent, but unpublished essay by Westholm, 1980.

13. This example is drawn from my study, Vedung, 1981, so far mimeographed. For another example, drawn from Hessler, 1956, see Vedung, 1977: 87ff.

14. Evers, 1970: 49. See also Strömholm, 1976: 75ff. and Peczenick, 1974: 109.

15. Galtung and Naess, 1968: 23ff.

16. Galtung and Naess, 1968: 23ff.

17. Galtung and Naess, 1968: 24.

18. See, for example, Strömholm, 1976: 25.

19. Naess, 1966: 31f.

20. Naess, 1966: 38ff. We may note in passing that clarification exhibits similarities with operationalization.

21. Rawls, 1971: 60.

22. Rawls, 1971: 66ff., 73ff., 83.

Chapter 4

1. Carney and Scheer, 1974: 3ff.; Copi, 1972: 5ff.

2. Fredriksson, 1969: 67f.

3. Tingsten, 1966c: 163, 111f., 131, 99, 186f.

4. Tingsten, 1966c: 70f., 186. For another example, see Popper, 1962b: 40f.

5. Bok, 1978: 16.

6. "A Ford, Not a Lincoln" has since been used by R. Reeves as the title of a book very critical of the president. Empson, 1947 offers many examples of literary usage of ambiguities.

7. U.S. Senate, 1975: 260-279.

8. U.S. Senate, 1975: 11f., 278.

9. U.S. Senate, 1975: 52f., 264f., 279. See also 109ff., 117f., 148f.

10. U.S. Senate, 1975: 260-279.

11. Both of these arrangements are found in Kahane, 1976: 101f.

12. Mueller, 1973: 30ff.

13. *Keesing's Contemporary Archives.*

14. Tingsten, 1966b: 39. See also Tingsten, 1966a: 30ff., 112ff., 166ff.

15. This line of reasoning is adapted primarily from Sissela Bok's treatise on *Lying: Moral Choice in Public and Private Life,* 1978: 32f.

16. I first ran across the idea of meta-conflicts in a small paper by the theologian Anders Jeffner, 1970, who talks about controversial relationships between the position of the analyst and the position in the material. See also Heeger, 1975: 67.

17. Weldon,, 1953: 11ff., 18.

18. Weldon, 1953: 11f., 17ff.

19. Weldon, 1953: 19.

20. Popper, 1962b: 13f. Cf. Weldon, 1953: 19, 28, 87ff., 101ff., 117ff. We have, of course, disregarded reportative definitions here.

21. Popper, 1962b: 15f.

22. Popper, 1962b: 9. For other examples of meta-semantic critique, see MacIntyre, 1970: 96f. and Oppenheim, 1968: 125ff.

Chapter 5

1. Naess, 1966: 108ff.
2. Our examples are taken from Milic, 1979: 188ff.
3. Lidforss, 1965: 72f.
4. For surveys, see Fischer, 1970: 282ff.; Copi, 1972: 72ff.; Carney and Scheer, 1974: 21ff.; Fearnside, 1959: 5ff.
5. According to a report in *Svenska Dagbladet,* October 9, 1976.
6. *Svenska Dagbladet,* October 10 and 18, 1976.
7. Cf. Andrén et al., 1978: 64ff.
8. As in many other passages, Mannheim's position is not very clear. Based on what he writes in Mannheim, 1968: 56f., 70ff., 76, 104, 239ff., 244, 253ff., 262ff., 274, we can reconstruct this interpretation. It should be emphasized, however, that there are other statements in the book that can be interpreted in entirely different ways. Sometimes he does not seem to mean anything more advanced than that ideology can only be understood if one knows and understands its genesis (pp. 2, 241; this notion is treated at the end of this section). At times he even seems to adopt a position closely related to the one on which my further critique of epistemological relativism is based, i.e., the Rickert-Weber doctrine that the validity of the results of social science can be established apart from how they originated. Cf. Merton, 1968: 559f. Mannheim's collection of essays is actually so difficult to interpret that the reader who wants to understand the nuances of his position should read Mannheim's own presentation.
9. Runciman, 1963: 162ff.; Hermerén, 1972: 175f.; Naess et al., 1956: 205; Hartung, 1952: 31ff.
10. Black, 1949: 91ff.; Rapoport, 1954: 11.
11. The distinction between awareness and the accounting of this awareness is put to interesting use in Bergström, 1972: 36ff.
12. In the literature of political theory, positions critical of Mannheim have been advanced by, among others, Sabine, 1939: 9f.; Levine, 1963: 10f.; Naess et al., 1956: 208; Björklund, 1976: 20f., 40ff. The most detailed critique is still A. von Schelting's influential work on Max Weber's philosophy of science, 1934; 94ff. See also von Schelting's review of *Ideology and Utopia,* 1936: 664ff. Other works are Popper, 1962b: 212ff.; Nagel, 1961: 498ff.; Merton, 1968: 556ff.; Runciman, 1963: 166ff. Also consult Carlsnaes, 1981: 206ff. Among those who seem to defend Mannheim's position, note Mills, 1940: 316ff. and Lavine, 1942: 342ff.
13. Mannheim, 1968: 2 (my italics); cf. 241. The same notion recurs in Stark, 1958: 9. Stark's book carries the telling title *An Essay in the Deeper Understanding of the History of Ideas.*

Chapter 6

1. On inferences, see for example Carney and Scheer, 1974: 3ff.; Copi, 1972: 5ff., 17ff.; Fredriksson, 1969: 13ff.
2. See, for example, Flew, 1977: 12ff.
3. Brody, 1973: 74.
4. Brody, 1973: 74f.
5. Brody, 1973: 76.
6. Copi, 1972: 33f.
7. Toulmin, 1958: 146ff. For overviews of propositional calculus, see Blumberg, 1967; 14ff. and Kemeny, Snell, and Thompson, 1966: 5ff. For alternative methods that utilize "truth trees" or "natural deduction," see Blumberg, 1976: 165ff., 179ff.

8. Copi, 1972: 155ff., 309ff.

9. Sabine and Thorson, 1973: 79.

10. MacIntyre, 1970: 87.

11. Quoted from Tingsten, 1936: 173.

12. Raiffa, 1968: 75f. See also Barry, 1965: 3ff. and Levine, 1963: 14ff.

13. Arrow, 1973: 281ff. See also Murakami, 1968: 82ff.; Riker and Ordeshook, 1973: 78ff.; Frey, 1978: 68ff. Also see Myrdal, 1958: 86f. on viewpoints on birth control in principle and in private.

14. Olson, 1965: 64ff., 86ff., 98ff., 125ff. For a similar line of reasoning, see Downs, 1957: 244ff.

15. Keesing's, October 27, 1978.

16. MacIntyre, 1970: 85ff.

17. MacIntyre, 1970: 87f.

18. MacIntyre, 1970: 89.

Chapter 7

1. See, for example, Beardsley, 1975: 7ff.; Brody, 1973: 53ff.; or Hospers, 1981: 78ff.

2. See, for example, Popper, 1968: 14-15, 18, as well as Chapter 5.

3. See, for example, Lakatos, 1970: 95ff.

4. Larsson, 1970: 12f. Cf. Ruin, 1968: 34; Algotsson, 1975; 24ff.

5. Black, 1952: 281ff. The example is constructed based on Lafferty, 1971: 20ff.

6. Barry, 1970: 48ff. For a couple of other examples, see Holmström, 1972: 53ff., 81ff.

7. It would be more adequate to speak of three groups of theories. Other theories of truth—e.g., the verifiability theory, the performative theory, and the theory of logical superfluity—have no immediate relevance for rational assessment and so will be passed over. For more on this, see White, 1970: 91ff and Brody, 1973: 57ff.

8. White, 1970: 102ff. We will carefully bypass the issue of what comprises the relation between fact and proposition. For arguments on this, see White, 1970: 105ff. and Brody, 1973: 62f. See also Bergström, 1972: 92; Gregor, 1971: 44, 53; Popper, 1972: 44f.; Popper, 1974; 223ff; and Tarski, 1949: 52ff.

9. Hospers, 1981: 115f. and Brody, 1973: 62.

10. Pap, 1949: 372f.

11. White, 1970: 124. See also Ezorsky, 1967: 427ff.

12. White, 1970: 125; Ezorsky, 1967: 428.

13. White, 1970: 125ff.; Ezorsky, 1967: 428ff.; Brody, 1973: 58f.

14. White, 1967: 130.

15. Hospers, 1981: 116f.; Pap, 1949: 356f.

16. White, 1967: 130ff.; White, 1970: 109ff.; Brody, 1973: 59; Hospers, 1981: 117.

17. MacIntyre, 1970: 14f. Cf. Popper, 1962b: 41 (Hegel's theory of truth).

18. Tingsten, 1966c: 36.

19. Tingsten, 1936: 69ff.

Chapter 8

1. For introductions to ethical problems, see Frankena, 1973 and Hospers, 1981: 566ff.

2. For a short exposition, see Dahrendorf, 1968: 1ff.

3. Lindblad, 1981: 158; Westerståhl, 1970: 9.

4. Hägerström, 1966: 55, 57. Hägerström's ethical theory is much more complex than indicated here. For a more thorough account, see Petersson, 1973: 72ff., 126ff.

5. Weldon, 1953: 13ff., 43, 97ff.

6. von Mises, 1927.

7. These distinctions are used by Moritz, 1968: 8f. Cf. Hermerén, 1972: 184f.

8. The figure is adapted from Moritz, 1968: 93.

9. There are, in fact, several different forms of naturalism. Consult the short but excellent accounts in Hospers, 1981: 568ff. and Frankena, 1973: 97ff. See also Oppenheim, 1968: 20ff., 93ff.; Hudson, 1970: 65ff.; and Nielsen, 1967: 127ff.

10. There are also several types of nonnaturalism. For an overview see Hospers, 1981: 572ff. and Frankena, 1973: 102ff. See also Oppenheim, 1968: 23f., 53ff.; Hudson, 1970: 65ff.; and Nielsen, 1967: 128f.

11. Frankena, 1973: 101. For overviews of the main arguments pro and con naturalism, see literature referred to in footnote 9.

12. Frankena, 1973: 103ff. See also footnote 10.

13. Harrison, 1967: 78ff. See also Moritz, 1968: 45ff. and 52ff.

14. Ayer, 1952: 102ff. For general expositions of noncognitivism see Frankena, 1973; 105ff.; Hospers, 1981: 575ff.; Hudson, 1970: 107ff. See also Moritz, 1968: 79f., 87, 90 and Hedenius, 1963: 16ff.

15. Hudson, 1970: 37ff., 132ff. and Frankena, 1973: 105ff. See also Urmson, 1968: 24ff., 38ff., 62ff., 72ff.

16. Hare, 1964, *passim,* 1963: 16, 23, *passim.* See also Hudson, 1970: 155ff.

17. See, for example, Hudson, 1970: 295.

18. See Gustavsson, 1981b: 217.

19. Brecht, 1959: 121f.

20. The *locus classicus* for this distinction is Stevenson, 1944: 174ff. See also Hempel, 1965: 84f.; Rescher, 1969: 53; Oppenheim, 1968: 10f.; or Hermerén, 1972: 13. Dewey, 1930: Introduction and Pt. I, sec. 2 is critical of this distinction.

21. For general statements, see Hempel, 1965: 84f.; Oppenheim, 1968: 28ff.; and Simon, 1976: 45ff.; 61ff.

22. Hempel, 1965: 85ff. Cf. Myrdal, 1944: 1052 and Hedenius, 1961: 97ff.

23. Hempel, 1965: 93f.

24. Hempel, 1965: 93f. and Oppenheim, 1968: 28ff.

25. Myrdal, 1958: 228 and Myrdal, 1970: 52ff. For a practical example, see Goldmann, 1971: 1f.

26. For valuable comments on this problem, see Dahrendorf, 1968: 6ff. and Nagel, 1961: 485ff.

27. Tingsten, 1966c: 5f. See also Tingsten, 1941: 9ff. For a full expositions of different interpretations of Tingsten's position, see Vedung, 1977: 160ff.

28. Oppenheim, 1968: 36ff.

29. Oppenheim, 1968: 63f. For a few other examples of meta-methodological conflicts with respect to the assessment of value judgments, see Sabine, 1939: 15; Popper, 1962a: 68ff.; and Tingsten, 1966c: 56.

References

Algotsson, Karl-Göran (1975) *Från katekestvång till religionsfrihet: Debatten om religionsundervisningen i skolan under 1900-talet* [From Obligatory Catechism to Religious Freedom: The Debate Over Religious Education in the 1900s]. Stockholm: Raben & Sjögren.

Alston, William P. (1964) *Philosophy of Language*. Englewood Cliffs, NJ: Prentice-Hall.

_____ (1967a) "Emotive meaning," pp. 486-493 in P. Edwards (ed.) *Encyclopedia of Philosophy*, Vol. 2. New York: Macmillan.

_____ (1967b) "Meaning," pp. 223-241 in P. Edwards (ed.) *Encyclopedia of Philosophy*, Vol. 5. New York: Macmillan.

_____ (1967c) "Vagueness," pp. 218-221 in P. Edwards (ed.) *Encyclopedia of Philosophy*, Vol. 8. New York: Macmillan.

Anderson, James E. (1979) *Public Policy-Making*, 2nd ed. New York: Holt, Rinehart & Winston.

Andren, Gunnar, Lars O. Ericsson, Ragnar Ohlsson, and Torbjörn Tännsjö (1978) *Rhetoric and Ideology in Advertising*. Stockholm: Liber.

Arrow, Kenneth J. (1973) "Formal theories of social welfare," pp. 276-284 in P. P. Wiener (ed.) *Dictionary of the History of Ideas*, Vol. 4. New York: Scribner.

Austin, John L. (1975) *How to Do Things with Words*. New York: Oxford University Press.

Avineri, Shlomo (1968) *The Social and Political Thought of Karl Marx*. Cambridge: Cambridge University Press.

Ayer, Alfred J. (1952) *Language, Truth and Logic*. New York: Dover Publications.

Barry, Brian M. (1965) *Political Argument*. New York: Humanities Press.

_____ (1970) *Sociologists, Economists and Democracy*. London: Collier-Macmillan.

Beardsley, Monroe C. (1975) *Thinking Straight: Principles of Reasoning for Readers and Writers*. Englewood Cliffs, NJ: Prentice-Hall.

Bergström, Lars (1972) *Objektivitet: En undersökning av innebörden, möjligheten och önskvärdheten av objektivitet i samhällsvetenskapen* [Objectivity: An Inquiry into the Meaning, Possibility and Desirability of Objectivity in Social Science]. Stockholm: Prisma.

von Beyme, Klaus (1969) *Politische Ideengeschichte: Probleme eines interdisziplinären Forschungsbereiches* [The History of Political Ideas: The Problems of an Interdisciplinary Research Field]. Tübingen: J.C.B. Mohr.

Björklund, Stefan (1976) *Politisk teori* [Political Theory], 4th rev. ed. Stockholm: Bonniers.

Black, Max (1949) *Language and Philosophy: Studies in Method*. Ithaca, NY: Cornell University Press.

_____ (1952) *Critical Thinking: An Introduction to Logic and Scientific Method*. Englewood Cliffs, NJ: Prentice-Hall.

215

─────── (1968) *The Labyrinth of Language*. New York: Praeger.

Blumberg, Albert E. (1967) "Logic, modern," pp. 12-34 in P. Edwards (ed.) *Encyclopedia of Philosophy*, Vol. 5. New York: Macmillan.

─────── (1976) *Logic: A First Course*. New York: Knopf.

Bok, Sissela (1978) *Lying: Moral Choice in Public and Private Life*. New York: Random House.

Brecht, Arnold (1959) *Political Theory: The Foundations of Twentieth Century Political Thought*. Princeton, NJ: Princeton University Press.

Brodbeck, May (1968) "Meaning and action," pp. 58-78 in M. Brodbeck (ed.) *Readings in the Philosophy of the Social Sciences*. New York: Macmillan.

Brody, Baruch A. (1973) *Logic: Theoretical and Applied*. Englewood Cliffs, NJ: Prentice-Hall.

Brown, R. (1963) *Explanation in Social Science*. London: Routledge & Kegan Paul.

Bunge, Mario (1967) *Scientific Research: The Search for System*. Berlin: Springer.

Carlsnaes, Walter (1981) *The Concept of Ideology and Political Analysis: A Critical Examination of Its Usage By Marx, Lenin, and Mannheim*. Westport, CT: Greenwood Press.

Carney, James D. and Richard K. Scheer (1974) *Fundamentals of Logic*, 2nd ed. London: Collier Macmillan.

Cohen, Morris R. and Ernest Nagel (1934) *An Introduction to Logic and Scientific Method*. New York: Harcourt, Brace & Co.

Conway, M. Margaret and Frank B. Feigert (1972) *Political Analysis: An Introduction*. Boston: Allyn & Bacon.

Copi, Irving M. (1972) *Introduction to Logic*, 4th ed. New York: Macmillan.

Dahrendorf, Ralf (1968) *Essays in the Theory of Society*. Stanford, CA: Stanford University Press.

Davidson, Donald (1963) "Actions, reasons, and causes." *Journal of Philosophy*, 685-700.

─────── (1980) *Essays on Actions and Events*. Oxford: Clarendon Press.

Deutsch, Karl W. (1966) *Nationalism and Social Communication: An Inquiry into the Foundation of Nationality*, 2nd ed. Cambridge, MA: MIT Press.

Dewey, John (1930) *Human Nature and Conduct: An Introduction to Social Psychology*. New York:

Donnellan, Keith S. (1967) "Reasons and causes," pp. 85-88 in P. Edwards (ed.) *Encyclopedia of Philosophy*, Vol. 7. New York: Macmillan.

Downs, Anthony (1957) *An Economic Theory of Democracy*. New York: Harper & Row.

Dray, William (1957) *Laws and Explanation in History*. Oxford: Oxford University Press.

Easton, David (1953) *The Political System: An Inquiry into the State of Political Science*. New York: Knopf.

Ehninger, Douglas (1974) *Influence, Belief, and Argument: An Introduction to Responsible Persuasion*. Glenview, IL: Scott, Foresman.

Elster, Jon (1978) *Logic and Society: Contradictions and Possible Worlds*. Chichester: John Wiley.

Empson, W. (1974) *Seven Types of Ambiguity*, rev. ed. London: Chatto & Windus.

Evers, Jan (1974) *Att analysera argument* [Analyzing Arguments]. Lund: Gleerups.

Ezorsky, Gertrude (1967) "Pragmatic theory of truth," pp. 427-430 in P. Edwards (ed.) *Encyclopedia of Philosophy*, Vol. 6. New York: Macmillan.

Fearnside, W. Ward and William B. Holther (1959) *Fallacy: The Counterfeit of Argument*. Englewood Cliffs, NJ: Prentice-Hall.

Fischer, David Hackett (1970) *Historians' Fallacies: Toward a Logic of Historical Thought*. New York: Harper & Row.

Flew, Anthony (1977) *Thinking Straight*. Buffalo, NY: Prometheus Books.

Føllesdal, Dagfinn and Lars Walløe (1977) *Argumentasjonsteori og vitenskapsfilosofi* [Theory of Argumentation and Philosophy of Science]. Oslo: Universitetsforlaget.

Frankena, William K. (1973) *Ethics*. Englewood Cliffs, NJ: Prentice-Hall.

Fredriksson, Gunnar (1969) *Det politiska språket* [Political Language], 4th ed. Staffanstorp: Cavefors.

Frey, Bruno (1978) *Modern Political Economy*. Oxford: Martin Robertson.

Galtung, Johan (1969) *Theory and Methods of Social Research*, rev. ed. Oslo: Universitetsforlaget.

_____ and Arne Naess (1968) *Gandhis politiske etikk* [Gandhi's Political Ethics], 2nd ed. Oslo: Pax.

Geach, Peter Thomas (1976) *Reason and Argument*. Oxford: Basil Blackwell.

George, Alexander L. (1959) *Propaganda Analysis: A Study of Inferences Made from Nazi Propaganda in World War II*. Evanston, IL: Row, Peterson.

Goffman, Erving (1959) *The Presentation of Self in Everyday Life*. Garden City, NY: Doubleday.

Goldmann, Kjell (1971) *International Norms and War Between States: Three Studies in International Politics*. Stockholm: Läromedelsförlagen.

Goodin, Robert (1980) *Manipulatory Politics*. New Haven, CT: Yale University Press.

Graber, Doris A. (1976) *Verbal Behavior and Politics*. Urbana: University of Illinois Press.

Graham, George J. (1971) *Methodological Foundations for Political Analysis*. Waltham, MA: Xerox College Publishing.

Gregor, A. James (1971) *An Introduction to Metapolitics: A Brief Inquiry into the Conceptual Language of Political Science*. New York: Free Press.

Grip, Gunvall (1979) *Innehållslig och funktionellt: En granskning av Vedungs idéanalytiska infallsvinklar* ["Content-oriented and function-oriented: an assessment of Vedung's approaches to political messages"]. Department of Political Science, Uppsala University, Uppsala, Sweden. (mimeo)

Gustavsson, Sverker (1971) *Debatten om forskningen och samhället: En studie i några teoretiska inlägg under 1900-talet* [The Debate on Research and Society: A Study of Some Contributions in the Twentieth Century]. Stockholm: Almqvist & Wiksell.

_____ (1981a) "Where research policy erred," pp. 45-58 in Björn Wittrock and Peter R. Baehr (eds.) *Policy Analysis and Policy Innovation: Patterns Problems and Potentials*. London: Sage Publications.

_____ (1981b) "Three basic questions in political inquiry." *Scandinavian Political Studies* 4: 209-219.

Hadenius, Axel (1979) *Från ämne till problem: Om konsten att fixera sin forskningsuppgift* [From topic to problem: on the art of determining research designs]. Department of Political Science, Uppsala University, Uppsala, Sweden. (mimeo)

_____ (1981) *Spelet om skatten: Rationalistisk analys av politiskt beslutsfattande* [The Tax Game: Rationalist Analysis of Political Decision Making]. Stockholm: Norstedts.

Hägerström, Axel (1966) *Socialfilosofiska uppsatser* [Essays in Social Philosophy]. Stockholm: Orion/Bonniers.

Hancock, M. Donald (1972) *Sweden: The Politics of Postindustrial Change*. Hinsdale, IL: Dryden Press.

Hansson, Svante [ed.] (1969) *Moderna ideologier* [Modern Ideologies]. Stockholm: Wahlström & Widstrand.

Hare R. M. (1963) *Freedom and Reason*. London: Oxford University Press.

_____ (1964) *The Language of Morals*. London: Oxford University Press.

Harrison, Jonathan (1967) "Ethical subjectivism," pp. 78-81 in P. Edwards (ed.) *Encyclopedia of Philosophy* Vol. 3. New York: Macmillan.

Harsanyi, John C. (1976) *Essays on Ethics, Social Behavior, and Scientific Explanation.* Dordrecht, Holland: D. Reidel.

Hartnack, Justus (1967) "Performative utterances," pp. 90-92 in P. Edwards (ed.) *Encyclopedia of Philosophy,* Vol. 6. New York: Macmillan.

Hartung, Frank E. (1952) "Problems of the sociology of knowledge." *Philosophy of Science* 19: 17-32.

Hedenius, Ingemar (1967) *Liv och nytta* [Life and Utility]. Stockholm: Bonniers.

————(1963) *Om rätt och moral* [On Rights and Morals], 2nd ed. Stockholm: Wahlström & Widstrand.

Heeger, Robert (1975) *Ideologie und Macht: Eine Analyse von Antonio Gramscis Quaderni* [Ideology and Power: An Analysis of Antonio Gramsci's Quaderni]. Stockholm: Almqvist & Wiksell International.

Hempel, Carl G. (1952) *Fundamentals of Concept Formation in Empirical Science: International Encyclopedia of Unified Science,* II, 7. Chicago: University of Chicago Press.

————(1965) *Aspects of Scientific Explanation and Other Essays in the Philosophy of Science.* New York: Free Press.

Hermerén, Göran (1972) *Värdering och objektivitet* [Valuation and Objectivity]. Lund, Sweden: Studentlitteratur.

Hessler, Carl Arvid (1956) *Stat och religion i upplysningstidens Sverige* [State and Religion During the Swedish Enlightenment]. Stockholm: Almqvist & Wiksell.

Holmström, Barry (1972) *Koreakriget i svensk debatt* [Swedish Controversy on the Korean War, English summary]. Stockholm: Rabén & Sjögren.

Holsti, Ole R. (1969) *Content Analysis for the Social Sciences and Humanities.* Reading, MA: Addison-Wesley.

Hospers, John (1981) *An Introduction to Philosophical Analysis,* rev. ed. London: Routledge & Kegan Paul.

Hudson, W. D. (1970) *Modern Moral Philosophy.* Garden City, NY: Anchor Books.

Jeffner, Anders (1970) "Några problem vid livsåskådningsanalys" ["Some problems in the analysis of philosophies of life"]. *Svensk teologisk kvartalstidskrift* 46: 49-57.

Johansson, Leif (1980) *Kärnkraftsomröstningen i kommunerna* [The Nuclear Power Referendum in Municipalities]. Lund, Sweden: Studentlitteratur.

Kahane, Howard (1976) *Logic and Contemporary Rhetoric: The Use of Reason in Everyday Life,* 2nd. ed. Belmont, CA: Wadsworth.

Kemeny, John G., J. Laurie Snell, and Gerald L. Thompson (1966) *Introduction to Finite Mathematics.* 2nd ed. Englewood, Cliffs, NJ: Prentice-Hall.

Krippendorff, Klaus (1980) *Content Analysis: An Introduction to Its Methodology.* Beverly Hills, CA: Sage Publications.

Lafferty, William (1971) *Economic Development and the Response of Labor in Scandinavia.* Oslo: Universitetsforlaget.

Lakatos, Imre (1970) "Falsification and the methodology of scientific research programmes," pp. 91-196 in I. Lakatos and A. Musgrave (eds.) Criticism and the Growth of Knowledge. Cambridge: Cambridge University Press.

Lane, Jan-Erik (1976) "On the use of the word 'political,' " pp. 217-244 in Brian Barry (ed.) *Power and Political Theory: Some European Perspectives.* London: John Wiley.

————(1981) "Semantic analysis of the concept of power," in G. Sartori (ed.) *Social Science Concepts: A Systematic Analysis.* (mimeo)

Larsson, Reidar (1970) *Theories of Revolution: From Marx to the Russian Revolution.* Stockholm: Almqvist & Wiksell.

Lave, Charles A. and James G. March (1975) *An Introduction to Models in the Social Sciences.* New York: Harper & Row.

Lavine, Thelma Z. (1942) "Sociological analysis of cognitive forms." *Journal of Philosophy* 39: 342-356.

Levine, Robert A. (1963) *The Arms Debate*. Cambridge, MA: Harvard University Press.

Lewin, Leif and Evert Vedung [eds.] (1980) *Politics as Rational Action: Essays in Public Choice and Policy Analysis*. Dordrecht, Holland: D. Reidel.

Lidforss, Bengt (1965) "Harald Hjärne," pp. 71-75 in A. Alsterdal and O. Sandell (eds.)*Bengt Lidforss i urval* [Selected Writings of Bengt Lidforss]. Stockholm: Wahlström & Widstrand.

Lindblad, Ingemar (1981) *Om den politiska vetenskapens grunder* [On the Foundations of Political Science], 3rd. ed. Stockholm: Almqvist & Wiksell.

Lindblom, Charles E. (1968) *The Policy-Making Process*. Englewood Cliffs, NJ: Prentice-Hall.

Luce, R. Duncan and Howard Raiffa (1957) *Games and Decisions: Introduction and Critical Survey*. New York: John Wiley.

Lundquist, Lennart (1972) *Means and Goals of Political Decentralization*. Lund, Sweden: Studentlitteratur.

Lyons, John (1977) *Semantics*, Vol. 1. Cambridge: Cambridge University Press.

MacIntyre, Alasdair C. (1970) *Herbert Marcuse: An Exposition and a Polemic*. New York: Viking.

Mannheim, Karl (1968) *Ideology and Utopia: An Introduction to the Sociology of Knowledge*. New York: Harcourt, Brace & World.

Meehan, Eugene J. (1967) *Contemporary Political Thought: A Critical Study*. Homewood, IL: Dorsey.

Melden, A. I. (1961) *Free Action*. London: Routledge & Kegan Paul.

Merton, Robert K. (1967) *On Theoretical Sociology: Five Essays, Old and New*. New York: Free Press.

——————— (1968) *Social Theory and Social Structure*. New York: Free Press.

Midgaard, Knut (1980a) "On the significance of language and a richer concept of rationality," pp. 83-97 in L. Lewin and E. Vedung (eds.) *Politics as Rational Action: Essays in Public Choice and Policy Analysis*. Dordrecht, Holland: D. Reidel.

——————— (1980b) "Det rationella politiska samtalet" [Rational Political Discourse]. *Statsvetenskaplig Tidskrift*, 136-139.

——————— Halvor Stenstadvold, and Arild Underdal (1973) "An approach to political interlocutions." *Scandinavian Political Studies* 8: 9-36.

Milic, Louis T. (1979) "Grilling the pols: Q & A at the debates," pp. 187-208 in S. Kraus (ed.) *The Great Debates: Carter vs. Ford, 1976*. Bloomington: Indiana University Press.

Mills, C. Wright (1940) "Methodological consequences of the sociology of knowledge." *American Journal of Sociology* 46: 316-330.

Mises, Ludwig von (1927) Liberalismus [Liberalism]. Jena: Fischer.

Moon, J. Donald (1975) "The logic of political inquiry: a synthesis of opposed perspectives," pp. 131-228 in Fred I. Greenstein and Nelson W. Polsby (eds.) *Handbook of Political Science*, Vol. 1. Reading, MA: Addison-Wesley.

Moritz, Manfred (1968) *Inledning i värdeteori: Värdesatsteori och värdeontologi* [An Introduction to Value Theory: The Theory of Value Statements and Value Ontology], 2nd ed. Lund, Sweden: Studentlitteratur.

Mueller, Claus (1973) *The Politics of Communication: A Study in the Political Sociology of Language, Socialization, and Legitimation*. New York: Oxford University Press.

Murakami Y. (1968) *Logic and Social Choice*. London: Routledge & Kegan Paul.

Myrdal, Gunnar (1944) *An American Dilemma; The Negro Problem and Modern Democracy*. New York: Harper & Bros.

———— (1958) *Value in Social Theory: A Selection of Essays on Methodology.* London: Routledge & Kegan Paul.

———— (1970) *Objectivity in Social Research.* London: Duckworth.

Naess, Arne (1966) *Communication and Argument.* London: Allen & Unwin.

———— (1968) *Demokratisk styreform: en presiserings-meny* [The Democratic Form of Government: A Menu of Clarifications]. Oslo: Universitetsforlaget.

———— Jens A. Christophersen, and Kjeld Kvalø (1956) *Democracy, Ideology and Objectivity: Studies in the Semantics and Cognitive Analysis of Ideological Controversy.* Oslo: Oslo University Press.

Nagel, Ernest (1961) *The Structure of Science: Problems in the Logic of Scientific Explanation.* London: Routledge & Kegan Paul.

Nielsen, Kai (1967) "Ethics, problems of," pp. 117-134 in P. Edwards (ed.) *Encyclopedia of Philosophy,* Vol. 3. New York: Macmillan.

Nohrstedt, Stig Arne (1982) *News from Nigeria.* Uppsala, Sweden: Scandinavian Institute for African Studies. (mimeo)

Nordenfelt, Lennart (1974) *Explanation of Human Actions.* Uppsala, Sweden: Philosophical Society and the Department of Philosophy, Uppsala University.

Nozick, Robert (1974) *Anarchy, State, and Utopia.* New York: Basic Books.

Ogden, C. K. and I. A. Richards (1923) *The Meaning of Meaning: A Study of the Influence of Language upon Thought and of the Science of Symbolism.* London: Paul, Trench, Trubner.

Olson, Mancur, Jr. (1965) *The Logic of Collective Action: Public Goods and the Theory of Groups.* Cambridge, MA: Harvard University Press.

Oppenheim, Felix E. (1961) *Dimensions of Freedom: An Analysis.* New York: St. Martin's Press.

———— (1968) *Moral Principles in Political Philosophy.* New York: Random House.

———— (1975) "The language of political inquiry: problems of clarification," pp. 283-335 in F. I. Greenstein and N. E. Polsby (eds.) *Handbook of Political Science,* Vol. 1. Reading, MA: Addison-Wesley.

———— (1981) *Political Concepts: a Reconstruction.* Oxford: Basil Blackwell.

Pap, Arthur (1949) *Elements of Analytic Philosophy.* New York: Macmillan.

Peczenik, Adam (1974) *Juridikens metodproblem: Rättskällelära och lagtolkning* [The Methodology Problem in Jurisprudence: The Study of Legal Sources and the Interpretation of Laws]. Stockholm: Almqvist & Wiksell.

Petersson, B. (1973) *Axel Hägerströms värdeteori* [Axel Hägerström's Theory of Philosophy]. Uppsala, Sweden: Department of Philosophy, Uppsala University.

Plamenatz, John P. (1954) *German Marxism and Russian Communism.* London: Longman.

Popper, Karl R. (1961) *The Poverty of Historicism,* 2nd ed. London: Routledge & Kegan Paul.

———— (1962a) *The Open Society and Its Enemies. I. The Spell of Plato,* 4th ed. London: Routledge & Kegan Paul.

———— (1962b) *The Open Society and Its Enemies, II. The High Tide of Prophecy: Hegel, Marx, and the Aftermath,* 4th ed. London: Routledge & Kegan Paul.

———— (1968) *The Logic of Scientific Discovery,* 3rd ed. London: Hutchinson.

———— (1972) *Objective Knowledge: An Evolutionary Approach.* Oxford: Clarendon.

———— (1974) *Conjectures and Refutations: The Growth of Scientific Knowledge,* 5th ed. London: Routledge & Kegan Paul.

Quade, Edward S. (1975) *Analysis for Public Decisions.* New York: Elsevier North-Holland.

Raiffa, Howard (1968) *Decision Analysis: Introductory Lectures on Choices under Uncertainty.* Reading, MA: Addison-Wesley.

Rapoport, Anatol (1954) "What is semantics?" pp. 3-18 in S. I. Hayakawa (ed.) *Language, Meaning and Maturity.* New York: Harper & Bros.

_____(1964) *Strategy and Conscience*. New York: Schocken.

_____ (1980) "Various meanings of 'rational political decisions,' " pp. 39-59 in L. Lewin and E. Vedung (eds.) *Politics as Rational Action: Essays in Public Choice and Policy Analysis*. Dordrecht, Holland: D. Reidel.

Rawls, John (1971) *A Theory of Justice*. Cambridge, MA: Harvard University Press.

Reeves, Richard (1975) *A Ford, not a Lincoln*. New York: Harcourt, Brace, Jovanovich.

Rescher, Nicholas (1969) *Introduction to Value Theory*. Englewood Cliffs, NJ: Prentice-Hall.

_____ (1970) *Scientific Explanation*. New York: Free Press.

Riggs, Fred W. (1970) "The comparison of whole political systems," pp. 73-121 in R. T. Holt and J. E. Turner (eds.) *The Methodology of Comparative Research*. New York: Free Press.

Riker, William H. and Peter C. Ordeshook (1973) *An introduction to Positive Political Theory*. Englewood Cliffs, NJ: Prentice-Hall.

Rosengren, Karl Erik [ed.] (1981) *Advances in Content Analysis*. Beverly Hills, CA: Sage Publications.

Ruin, Olof (1968) *Mellan samlingsregering och tvåpartisystem: Den svenska regeringsfrågan 1945-1960* [Between the Unity Government and the Two-Party System: The Swedish Government Question from 1945 to 1960]. Stockholm: Bonniers.

Runciman, W. G. (1963) *Social Science and Political Theory*. Cambridge: Cambridge University Press.

Russell, Bertrand (1921) *The Analysis of Mind*. London: Allen & Unwin.

Sabine, George H. (1939) "What is a political theory?" *Journal of Politics* 1: 1-16.

_____ and Thomas Thorson (1973) *A History of Political Theory*, 4th ed. Hinsdale, IL: Dryden Press.

Sartori, Giovanni (1970) "Concept misformation in comparative politics." *American Political Science Review* 64: 1035-1053.

_____ (1976) *Parties and Party Systems: A Framework for Analysis*, Vol. 1. Cambridge: Cambridge University Press.

_____ (1981) "Guidelines for concept analysis," in G. Sartori (ed.) *Social Science Concepts, A Systematic Analysis*. (mimeo).

_____ Fred W. Riggs and Henry Teune (1975) *The Tower of Babel: On the Definition and Analysis of Concepts in the Social Sciences*. Pittsburgh: International Studies Association.

von Schelting, Alexander (1934) *Max Webers Wissenschaftslehre: Das logische Problem der historischen Kulturerkenntnis: Die Grenzen der Soziologie des Wissens* [Max Weber's Philosophy of Science: The Logical Problem of the Historical Perception of Culture: The Limits of the Sociology of Knowledge]. Tübingen, Germany: Mohr.

_____ (1936) "Review of K. Mannheim, Ideologie und Utopie." *American Sociological Review* 1: 664-674.

Scriven, Michael (1976) *Reasoning*. New York: McGraw-Hill.

Simon, Herbert A. (1976) *Administrative Behavior: A Study of Decision-Making Processes in Administrative Organization*, 3rd ed. New York: Free Press.

SIPRI [Stockholm International Peace Research Institute] (1979) *Nuclear Energy and Nuclear Weapon Proliferation*. London: Taylor & Francis.

Stark, Werner (1958) *The Sociology of Knowledge: An Essay in the Deeper Understanding of the History of Ideas*. London: Routledge & Kegan Paul.

Stevenson, Charles L. (1944) *Ethics and Language*. New Haven, CT: Yale University Press.

Stinchcombe, Arthur L. (1968) *Constructing Social Theories*. New York: Harcourt, Brace & World.

Stokey, Edith and Richard Zeckhauser (1978) *A Primer for Policy Analysis*. New York: W. W. Norton.

Strauss, Leo (1962) *Natural Right and History*. Chicago: University of Chicago Press.

Strömholm, Stig (1976) *Allmän rättslära: En första introduktion* [General Legal Theory: A First Introduction], 3rd ed. Stockholm: Norstedts.

Tarski, Alfred (1949) "The semantic conception of truth," pp. 52-85 in H. Feigl and W. Sellars (eds.) *Readings in Philosophical Analysis*. New York: Appleton-Century-Crofts.

Taylor, Charles (1964) *Explanation of Behaviour*. London: Routledge & Kegan Paul.

Thouless, Robert H. (1974) *Straight and Crooked Thinking*. London: Pan Books.

Tingsten, Herbert (1936) *Den nationella diktaturen: Nazismens och fascismens idéer* [National Dictatorship: The Ideas of Nazism and Fascism]. Stockholm: Bonniers.

——————— (1941) *Idékritik* [Theoretical Criticism]. Stockholm: Bonniers.

——————— (1966a) *Från idéer till idyll: Den lyckliga demokratien* [From Ideas to Idyll: Fortunate Democracy]. Stockholm: Norstedts.

——————— (1966b) *Strid kring idyllen* [The Conflict Over the Idyll]. Stockholm: Norstedts.

——————— (1966c) *De konservativa idéerna* [Conservative Ideas]. Stockholm: Aldus/ Bonniers.

Toulmin, Stephen E. (1958) *The Uses of Argument*. Cambridge: Cambridge University Press.

Toulmin, Stephen, Richard Rieke, and Allan Janik (1979) *An Introduction to Reasoning*. New York: Macmillan.

Ullman, Stephen (1962) *Semantics: An Introduction to the Science of Meaning*. New York: Barnes: Barnes & Noble.

U.S. Senate (1975) "Alleged Assassination Plots Involving Foreign Leaders: An Interim Report of the Select Committee to Study Govrnmental Operations With Respect to Intelligence Activities." Senate Report No. 94-465, November 20.

Urmson, J. O. (1967) "Austin, John Langshaw," pp. 211-215 in P. Edwards (ed.) *Encyclopedia of Philosophy*, Vol. 1. New York: Macmillan.

——————— (1968) *The Emotive Theory of Ethics*. London: Hutchinson.

Vedung, Evert (1971) *Unionsdebatten 1905: En jämförelse mellan argumenteringen i Sverige och Norge*, [The Dissolution of the Union in 1905: A Comparison of Swedish and Norwegian Arguments, English summary]. Stockholm: Almqvist & Wiksell.

——————— (1976) "The comparative method and its neighbours," pp. 199-216 in B. Barry (ed.) *Power and Political Theory: Some European Perspectives*. London: John Wiley.

——————— (1977) *Det rationella politiska samtalet: Hur politiska budskap tolkas, ordnas och prövas*, [Rational Political Discourse: Interpreting, Ordering and Assessing Political Messages]. Stockholm: Bonniers.

——————— (1981) *Vad föreskriver lagen om kommunal energiplanering?* ["What does the municipal energy planning act prescribe?"]. Department of Government, University of Uppsala, Sweden. (mimeo)

——————— (1982) Energipolitiska utvärderingar 1973-1981 [Energy Policy Evaluations]. Stockholm: Energy Research and Development Commission.

Webster's New Collegiate Dictionary (1975) Springfield, MA: Merriam-Webster.

Weldon, T. D. (1953) *The Vocabulary of Politics*. Baltimore: Penguin.

Westerståhl, Jörgen (1970) *Att studera politik: En introduktion* [Studying Politics: An Introduction]. Stockholm: Tiden.

Westholm, Anders (1980) *Den innehållsliga idéanalysens funktion och den funktionella idéanalysens innehåll: En metaspråklig idéanalys* ["The function of content-oriented analysis and the content of function-oriented analysis: a meta-linguistic analysis"]. Department of Government, Uppsala University, Sweden. (mimeo)

White, Alan R. (1967) "Coherence theory of truth," pp. 130-133 in P. Edwards (ed.) *Encyclopedia of Philosophy*, Vol. 2. New York: Macmillan.

——————— (1970) *Truth*. Garden City, NY: Doubleday.

White, Morton (1965) *Foundations of Historical Knowledge*. New York: Harper & Row.

Wiener, Philip P. (1961) "Some problems and methods in the history of ideas." *Journal of the History of Ideas* 22: 531-548.

Wieslander, Hans [ed.] (1970) *De politiska partiernas program* [The Programmes of the Political Parties], 3rd ed. Stockholm: Prisma.

Wittgenstein, Ludwig (1967) *Philosophical Investigations,* 3rd ed. Oxford: Blackwell & Mott.

von Wright, Georg Henrik (1971) *Explanation and Understanding*. London: Routledge & Kegan Paul.

————— (1976) "Replies," pp. 371-413 in J. Manninen and R. Tuomela (eds.) *Essays on Explanation and Understanding: Studies in the Foundations of Humanities and Social Sciences*. Dordrecht, Holland: D. Reidel.

Zannoni, Paolo (1978) "The concept of elite." *European Journal of Political Research* 6: 1-30.

Name Index

Subject Index

About the Author

Evert Vedung is Associate Professor in the Department of Government, Uppsala University, Sweden. His publications include studies of the policy intentions of Swedish and Norwegian politicians during the dissolution of the union between the two countries in 1905, of the decision-making process in Swedish nuclear energy policy, and of evaluations of the Swedish energy conservation program. He has coedited *Politics as Rational Action* and published several articles on the comparative method.